Acknowledgements:

My wife, Fran, & my boys: Dusty, Luke, & Henry
My professors: Richard Terrill & Roger Sheffer
My pastors: Scott Maxwell, Bill Bohline & Derek Rust
My readers: Sharon Nelson & Jeff Giles
My partners: Bloomington police officers past & present,
the best of the best

*This book is dedicated to the prospect of justice and to
police officers everywhere who, as guardians,
risk everything to make that prospect possible.*

Contents

Preface

Like the driver who cranes his neck as he passes an accident scene, the human psyche seems to possess an unwholesome morbid curiosity for human carnage. Police officers are believed to have a bank of these carnage-type war stories that they can share at a moment's notice, but these aren't the stories most cops want to tell. There is a price to pay for every call an officer responds to that tears away at his belief system or makes him question why things happen as they do. Contrary to the oft-quoted remedy of becoming numb over time, these calls exact a tangible toll on an officer's spirit.

Of course, cops are loath to admit they suffer from anything they experience on the job, and until they're seated in a circle of steel folding chairs, chain-smoking with twenty serious-looking, fidgety strangers, they will probably remain stoic.

My wife always felt slighted when she learned, long after the fact, that I had been involved in some sensational incident that I had either not shared with her at all or had minimized to the point of insignificance. My philosophy was: Leave it at the office.

Like every career cop, I've witnessed enough death and misery to last several lifetimes, and have been forced to answer some weighty questions: What is the meaning of life? How can people do this to one another? Where is God in all this? How am I supposed to keep my pants up with all this crap on my belt?

Like a gambler betting on a better tomorrow, many of the younger officers find solace in allowing these serious questions to stew. But they don't go away, and usually don't fit in so well with the silly stories.

We've heard the stories of the burglar who left his wallet and ID on the victim's counter or the robber who shot himself in the leg as he hastened his getaway. While these amuse, they don't tell the human side of either the burglar or the cop who responded. These, for the most part, are not my stories.

Unlike the informal telling of an anecdote, the writing process forced me to delve deeper into the meaning of these events and the effects the events had on the characters involved. This scrutiny often uncovered some idiosyncratic flaws in the actor's character (usually mine) that might have been conveniently left out of a casual retelling. Painful as it is at times, I have included these.

While several of these essays include some sanity-saving silliness, most of them examine the human side of not just gawking at the human carnage but of wading into it up to our chins. For all the stories we laugh about over beers, there are a hundred more we don't mention. These, for the most part, are those stories.

Author's Note:

Many of these stories involve some element of tragedy, and for every tragedy there are family and friends whose grief has a collateral effect, like dominoes falling in a row. My intent in writing these essays was neither to trivialize nor to re-victimize the actors presented in these essays, but to allow readers some insight into their experience and the experience of the officers attending them. I have changed the names both of officers and victims to protect their privacy.

When possible I used recorded transcripts to document witness, victim, and suspect statements used in these essays. When transcripts were unavailable I documented these statements to the best of my ability from memory.

The Unholy Grail

At sixteen I had no idea or concern about what I might be when I grew up. Aside from the teen-aged fantasies of filling in for James Bond, the thought of being a police officer had never crossed my mind. Like most sixteen-year-olds, I was into chicks, sports, cars, and movies—in that order. While movies were a distant fourth to chicks, the idea of *midnight* movies was up there with splitting the atom and space exploration. A midnight movie had a mysterious allure that added to the aura of excitement, anticipation, and most importantly, like all movies, there was popcorn.

My mother probably would have considered a midnight movie as trouble-waiting-to-happen if I'd have thought of it myself. But when my honor-student friend Mike called to invite me, and offered to provide the wheels—that was different. Even with Mike driving, I knew my mother would wait up and worry until I returned home.

My friend Mike was somewhat of an enigma. He had National Honor Society status, having earned straight As

4

throughout his scholastic career, without ever bringing a book home. I despised that. He was president of our junior class at Robbinsdale Senior High, a member of the swimming team and the yearbook club, and he played the guitar quite well.

He planned on either taking over his father's funeral director business, being a rock star, or becoming an attorney. He was also a major pothead. With long, thick, coal-black hair combed to the side and turned just over a thick black unibrow, he had all the makings of a hippie, a nihilist, or some kind of bohemian intellectual tattoo artist.

Mike was also instrumental in setting me up with my first paying job, as a Christmas tree trimmer, when I was fifteen. We worked on tree farms in Wisconsin trimming the various evergreens for about three dollars an hour. During our twelve-hour day we were allowed only a half hour for lunch and two fifteen minute rest and water breaks. I was so exhausted by lunchtime, I could hardly raise the shears to clip the upper branches of the pines. Mike's next-door neighbor was our employer, and though he had no official ties to the Nazi party he was well versed in their practices. I remember him telling us not to worry about those *annoying* lightning bolts as we held our shears to the darkly marbled, thundering sky, trimming off that top branch at a forty-five degree angle. I have no idea how many acres of trees we trimmed or even how many farms we worked. We came home completely spent, and covered head-to-toe with wood ticks. We did this for several weekends. I probably made a couple hundred bucks and thought I'd done all right.

When Mike called our house asking if I could join him for the midnight showing of *Monty Python's Holy Grail,* my mom had to consider it for a moment. While Mike was an honor student, I'd been struggling to earn a B average to qualify for the reduced car insurance rate. I was also on the swimming team, and for all she knew, I was a pretty straight shooter. While Mike continued to say, "Well?...Well?..." into the earpiece, my mom finally consented, with the caveat that I'd get up the next morning and clean that pig's-sty room of mine rather than sleeping in till noon, which was my preferred M.O.

Mike's father lent him the Chrysler Cordoba and Mike maneuvered it in jerky increments into a parking space at the Brookdale Theater in Brooklyn Center. The marquis flashed, "Monty Python, Midnight Showing!" We popped a couple of beers and Mike demonstrated his uncanny proficiency at rolling a joint on the first try without sending the greenery all over the car and ending up with a flimsy, scrunched-up road-kill-looking cigarette. In addition to his skills with rolling paper, Mike could take a toke off a joint without coughing like he'd just walked out of a fully engulfed house fire. I could not inhale any kind of cigarette without hacking like a lifelong coal miner. It hardly made the whole smoking experience worthwhile, but like the young men who enlist in the army because they think they'll look tough in the camouflage, something other than logic was guiding my thought process.

With a slight buzz, and red slits for eyes, we bought our movie tickets. Like tourists checking out the sights, we meandered our way past the Brooklyn Center police officer moonlighting as theater security. Through the darkness and the crowd of mostly teens and college kids, we found our seats on the left side of the theater closer to the front. The movie started to jeers and cheers, and Mike and I soon realized we were not the only ones who had sampled the libations prior to settling in for the flick. There was one guy, however—I'll call him "the Guzzler"—who was louder and more obnoxious than anyone else. I don't know if he was making an effort to achieve that honor or if the chemicals in his system were aiding him in that endeavor. Whatever the case, he was starting to get on every-one's nerves. He sat two rows behind us, and shortly after the movie started we could hear him opening beers. After tipping back the bottle a few times, he began to belch loudly with added effort to enhance volume, distance, and tonality. He laughed after each belch as if no one but him understood the humor of this physically cathartic experience.

The Python Troop kept the crowd laughing, but folks in our row were starting to turn around to glare at the Guzzler. I finally craned my head around to give him the stink-eye, only to find him staring back at me with a confident expression of contempt. I realized, as did most of the rubberneckers from our row, that we would not be causing any trouble for our belching friend. He wore a red flannel lumberjack shirt and looked the part, easily weighing more than two hundred and fifty pounds, with long red hair descending over mountainous shoulders. His legs were stretched straight out like oaken timbers over the back of one of the few empty seats where his mud-caked boots hung freely. I quickly averted my eyes away from him and on to the projection room as if I had some aesthetic concern with the sharpness of the picture or the tonality of the audio system rather than the loud-mouthed A-hole seated behind me. As if the loudness, belching, and laughing weren't enough, when he finished a beer, he rolled the bottle down the sloping cement floor through the seats. I wondered how he'd managed to sneak *bottled* beer into the theater.

About the time Eric Idle had the crowd in stitches singing "Brave Sir Robin," our beer-guzzling friend rolled his fourth beer down the floor and laughed as it bounced like a pin-ball off chair legs and people's feet, clattering its way to the front. I chanced another look-see and was surprised to spy the lone police officer making his way down the carpeted aisle toward our seats. He stopped directly beside the Guzzler's row and motioned with his finger for the Guzzler to follow him. The Guzzler played stupid, which did not appear to be a stretch, as he continued staring at the screen, laughing in both the right parts and during others in which he alone saw the humor. The officer bent down and dragged what was left of the Guzzler's twelve-pack into the aisle. He then motioned again for the man to follow him and told him that he was being ejected. Finally the Guzzler turned to the cop and snarled, "Beat it, rent-a-cop, I'm not going anywhere."

With that the officer leaned over the two people between him and the Guzzler and grabbed his flannel shirt. The Guzzler pulled against the cop's grip but the cop managed to hang on. Some of the crowd started taunting the officer at this time, calling him a pig and telling him, "Get lost," and, "Down in front," since he was obstructing their view. Nobody near the Guzzler had any complaints about him being ejected, but no one was going to stick up for the cop. He was on his own. There were people in the crowd who would probably come to the Guzzler's aid if forced to take sides. I'd lost interest in the comedy on the screen as my attention was now drawn entirely to the drama unfolding behind me. The volume of the movie seemed to grow faint, almost silent as the movements of the two combatants accelerated. I adjusted myself in my seat, as everyone around me did, to get a better view.

I noticed that the officer had all the accouterments of a regular street cop strung onto his belt, but he had none of them in hand. A tug-of-war broke out with the Guzzler's shirtsleeve, and like an irritated grizzly, the Guzzler started to fume and growl. Some of the crowd started to stand up on their seats for a better view, and the jeers toward the cop became progressively louder and more derisive.

Finally the Guzzler stood up, towering above the average-built cop, and pulled his sleeve viciously back, releasing it from the cop's grip. He grunted with the effort and then swung fiercely at the officer's head. The cop managed to avoid the haymaker and pulled the man out into the aisle to the taunts of nearly the entire crowd. The Guzzler punched the cop with an ineffectual jab as the unflappable cop wound up and tagged the Guzzler with a roundhouse punch that snapped the man's head back like a speed bag and cracked his cheekbone with such volume that it quieted the crowd as the Guzzler landed flat on his back. A felled sequoia, the Guzzler was down for the count.

The cop wasted no time as he grabbed the collar of the motionless man's shirt, and pulled him up the aisle toward the concessions counter. The taunting was reduced to sporadic, cowardly jeers, spoken in muted tones so they could not be traced. The cop was now a bona fide badass. While everyone else sat down, I continued to watch him until he'd pulled the man out of the theater and into the concessions area. There was a chance the Guzzler might regain consciousness and resume fighting. I wondered what would have happened had the Guzzler beaten up the cop. The cop, after all, had among other things, a shiny black .357 Smith and Wesson revolver, up for grabs to the victor. That weapon in the hands of the Guzzler could have made for an interesting night at the movies.

Mike finally yanked on my T-shirt and I sat down, but throughout the rest of the movie I couldn't stop thinking about that altercation and the audacity of the cop to take on the Guzzler, one on one, with no back up and without using his tools of the trade.

My "Use of Force" instructor at Police Skills Training (the equivalent of the Police Academy) would later tell our cadet class never to walk into a probable violent situation without adequate backup. He reminded us that no matter what the odds, no matter the size of our opponent(s) or the weapons they possessed, we had to *win*. It wasn't just the fact that your life and that of your partner's was at stake, but, rather, the entire criminal justice tradition. Through life experience, and its subsequent moral lessons, most people adhere to the proposition that if you fight with the police you *will* get your butt kicked and subsequently be thrown in jail. Imagine if that perception changed to, "If you fight with the cops you'll most likely beat them up, take their guns, and laugh about it with your buddies while you continue your crime spree with your new weapons." That doesn't work for most of us.

Mike couldn't stop talking about the movie as we walked out of the theater and headed for the Chrysler. I couldn't stop thinking about the fight. I knew police officers didn't make a lot of money, and I figured this one was probably working this gig to earn a bit more, or maybe just enough. It seemed like a tough way to make a couple extra bucks. As far as his decision to confront the Guzzler alone—perhaps he'd just had enough, or maybe he didn't care if he got hurt. Whatever the case, his action struck me as both extremely foolish and incredibly brave—braver than any of the hokey stuff I'd seen on TV. I wondered if all cops were like this, or if this one was just a little "off"—maybe too much time alone with Clint Eastwood's *Dirty Harry*.

Everyone at the movie surely mentioned the fight on their way home that night, and probably talked about it with their friends the following day. They all may have had a different take on the cop and the Guzzler. Those seated farthest from the altercation might have thought the cop was picking on him simply because he was a *longhair*. People near the Guzzler knew he was not only drunk, but also a loud, rude, obnoxious slob. None would have confronted him, however, because he had that arrogant, bully quality of being untouchable. This comfortable self-assurance allowed bullies like him to be insulated from smaller, more prudent types. The comfort, safety, and quality of the moviegoers' experience depended on that lone officer. He had equalized the situation and, in so doing, unwittingly influenced my career direction.

For some unknown reason that only high-schoolers could possibly understand, Mike and I stopped hanging out after our junior year. One contributing factor was the inpatient drug treatment of a mutual friend who hung out with us from time to time. We both felt the ominous undertones of his prognosis. I still liked Mike. We greeted one another in the school hallways and practiced together daily with the swim team, but we no longer socialized.

Like a letter I'd been meaning to write, I allowed our friendship to fade and lost track of Mike after high school. Last I heard, and not surprisingly, he was a successful attorney in Arizona. I don't think the events at the theater had the same impact on him, though I know he enjoyed the movie since we saw it together again later that same year. For me it was like seeing it for the first time.

"...Brave, brave Sir Robin, bravely turned and ran away..."

Discontent of Winter

Donny got out of his car only twice, first to auger a hole in the ice and sink his line, and finally to retrieve it at quitting time. I don't recall either of us ever getting a bite, much less landing a fish. The remainder of the ice fishing experience was accomplished from inside his rusty 1974 Chevy Impala, whose windows pinched our protruding fishing rods between the window and its frame. The car's engine and heater remained running for the entire time we spent on the lake, unless the sun was shining through clear blue skies or the day was uncharacteristically warm. The only thing cold in the car was the beer in the backseat cooler, usually a case of Grain Belt bottles, next to which curled my sleeping white German Shepherd.

With speech communications degree in hand, I marched out into the world and found in short order that my services as a degreed communications "expert" were not in as high of demand as I'd hoped. I had a couple of interviews with high-profile companies like Hewlett Packard and General Mills, but they were looking for that special someone who, as it turned out, was someone more special than me.

So with the pile of rejections growing deeper by the day, I threw my hat into the real estate field and started night-schooling my way toward a license. Since I'd finished college and quit my convenient night job as security guard at Graco, I basked in a newfound freedom during the daytime hours. My lifelong friend, Donny, who'd recently graduated from the University of Minnesota with a degree in political science, was also experiencing this new lease on life. He also lacked both the burden of employment and the ambition to rush out and find a job. Pragmatic-minded outsiders might have described this freedom we shared as more of an introduction to sloth, a general malaise or, simply, self-inflicted unemployment. To make his winter days more tolerable, or maybe just to allow for a change of scenery from his couch to something else, Donny decided to take up ice fishing.

There was little pressure for either of us to work a menial job for sustenance since we had both moved back with our parents, whose houses were situated one house apart on the same street. Except for our sojourn during college, we had lived in these houses all our lives.

Part of Donny's motivation for his new hobby came from his mother, Eve, who had encouraged him to take a job with his father, Frank, an insurance salesman. But Donny had no interest in sales at that juncture. Like me, he wanted a job with a little more excitement, something a little sexier than insurance. Neither of us knew what that might be but, for the time being, it didn't really matter. After all, we'd just graduated from a prestigious university after years of arduous study and self-sacrifice.

Donny's mother was getting tired of his steadfast presence on the couch in front of the TV. She attempted to derail his television asphyxia by making him suffer through her daytime soap opera, *General Hospital*. She would come to understand the true extent of this backfire when Donny became a more dedicated viewer than she was.

When I started ice fishing with him, I soon realized that, regardless of the circumstances, quitting time was 1:30 p.m. so that he'd have enough time to put away the fishing gear (throw everything in the trunk of the Impala) and head home for the 2:00 p.m. start. Having witnessed his almost manic devotion to the show, I watched it with him a couple times to see if I too could be brought under its spell, but found I was mercifully immune. Though I'd almost rather have stuck needles under my fingernails than watch the soap, I respected his intrepid devotion nonetheless.

During our daily ice fishing junkets I noticed that Donny had become deeply enmeshed in some unique rituals. He fished at only one lake, Twin Lake, which was not known for good ice fishing or for its scenic value. Situated just off the intersection of Hwy 100 and Hwy 52, it was most widely used for summer water-skiing. The roads have been reconfigured since our ice fishing days and I doubt that cars are even allowed on the lake anymore. But even in those days, there were rarely any other cars on the lake when we fished.

By the time the bottled Grain Belt had stretched our bladders to capacity, Donny was usually beckoned home by the soap opera. Otherwise, we stepped approximately one foot from the Impala and relieved ourselves on one of its rear tires. On the bitter cold days the question, "To pee or not to pee?" became the primary factor for deciding whether or not we stayed.

This was my first experience with drinking in the late morning. At first I passed, thinking this practice could become habit-forming; I thought spending the prime of my life getting buzzed before noon was probably something I should avoid.

As the days on the lake started to pass, one beer became two, two beers became three, etc., etc. We got to the point where we were feeling no pain by quitting time, and a nap was nearly mandatory upon our return home. Donny's true mettle and dedication to the soap were tested daily as he battled this overwhelming temptation to sleep as he suffered through the whirlwind of emotion inspired by the soap.

Needless to say, our parents were less than impressed with our less than stellar attempts to gain employment. Donny's mother started suggesting rather poignantly that he consider alcohol rehab, while my parents suggested I start paying rent. Both of these suggestions were met with shrugs of indifference, but eventually I started paying a token pittance for my keep, while Donny managed to dodge the twelve-step descent to unwanted, premature sobriety.

My real estate licensing classes came to a close and I managed to pass the test, thus making myself available for employment with a real estate company. Among other things, I learned that a real estate agent was called a realtor (real'-tor). This has to be the most mispronounced job title of all time. Nearly everyone refers to realtors as *real-a-tors,* most likely derived from the word real-e-state. I looked at a couple lawn signs and decided to call a company I'd never heard of, Real Estate Plus, which specialized in relocating business execs.

This company was well managed and the owner-trainers had good intentions and great expectations for my future as a full-time agent, but this was not to be my destiny. The real estate market was at an all-time low as the interest rate blossomed to an all-time high of 18.5 percent and higher. The most important words in the real estate market at that time became *assumable mortgage.*

So I dressed up in a suit every day for about two months and went to work until I realized that although I had a job and an office to arrive at and return home from everyday, there was one thing missing from my Fred Flintstone bliss—I had not made one cent.

Though I wasn't prepared to rejoin Donny's ice fishing junket in the Impala, I needed a paying gig. My degree in speech communications was not going to be a big asset in my job search. There were few employers in the Help Wanted ads seeking a no experience, fresh out of college, pimple-faced Speech Communications graduate with an ill-fitting JC Penney suit. Then it struck me; I had a minor in law. I could be a lawyer! No. Law school was geared more for people who actually thrived on the Socratic method of teaching and were willing to study—a lot. Okay, so law school was out. I could be a cop! Cop school had to be easier than law school and probably involved far less study and mental anguish. It might even be fun! It always looked like fun on TV. They never sat at desks all day and did nothing like I was doing now, and even if they did, I bet they got paid for it. I assumed there would be substantial competition for police job openings since the only education required was a two-year Associates of Arts degree in Law Enforcement. For once I would be overqualified. Things were suddenly looking up.

From my nearly immaculate desk at Real Estate Plus, I made a call to the U of M employment counselor, explained my transcript, lack of skills, and ambition, and asked her what steps I needed to take in order to become a licensed law enforcement officer in the State of Minnesota. I assumed there were standards for such things. I was a bit dismayed by the list of requisite preparatory classes and such that were needed. After all, I was a graduate of an esteemed university and had a full four years of advanced learning under my belt rather than the measly two-year minimum.

The employment counselor stifled her natural enthusiasm and reverence at my lofty qualifications and argued that, although I had indeed earned this minor in law, I hadn't really followed the proper coursework to be certified for the Police Skills Law Enforcement Program. I begged. She paused, hemmed and hawed a bit, and finally allowed that if I could get my advisor to sign off on it, I would be good to go.

My advisor scratched his signature across the form, like he was signing the ninety-ninth document on a real estate closing, and acted genuinely surprised at my sincerely grateful, vigorous handshake. After a no-tears thank you and goodbye to the real estate world, I was on my way.

I reported to the Police Skills Class at Minneapolis Community College for the fourteen-week program, which consisted of classroom instruction, physical training and self defense, practical exercises, shooting proficiency, and emergency driving. There were about twenty, twenty-something-year-old students in my group, with four young women and one Hispanic male making up the only minorities. (These would be the only members of our class to be recruited by police agencies prior to the conclusion of our program.)

I knew no one in the group, but latched on quickly to the two other smart-asses, Terry Peters and Tim Kleinhenz. Terry wasted no time telling me that he would be a third generation cop. He said his great grandfather was gunned down in his prime by the Ma Barker Gang. Terry's father, George Peters, was appointed by the President of the United States as the acting Minnesota area Federal Marshal. Tim had already done some part-time work for the Orono Police Department. We were a motley crew at best and appeared to have no chance of ever wearing a uniform, yet there we were.

While one of our first instructors attempted to get our attention by clearing his throat and finally resorting to the old stand-by, "Okay then, why don't we get started," Peters continued to talk and laugh loudly. He was the only student talking when I noticed the annoyed teacher as he scanned the assigned seating chart and connected the name with the voice. Speaking loudly to get his attention, he asked Peters if he was related to the much-esteemed Marshal Peters, to which Terry straightened himself in his chair and, beaming with pride, answered, "Yep, that's my dad."

The instructor replied, "That's nice," then shouted, "Would you mind shutting the fuck up so I can get started?"

Terry's eyes widened before retreating into their sockets. "Yes, sir. Um, I mean no, sir."

I turned back and couldn't stifle a smirk as Terry collected himself enough to give me a surreptitiously placed middle-finger salutation.

Most of our instructors were police officers or detectives, moonlighting as teachers to earn an extra buck. Their subjects were presented dryly, but usually embellished with a plethora of interesting war stories. When the war stories started to flow, some of the instructors fell prey to the fond reminiscing of their glory days and, once under the spell, they spiraled down, leap-frogging from one story to the next. There would never be a complaint from the students. We were mesmerized by the criminalist who solved the boat death with one fiber found in the propeller, or the medical examiner who was stumped by an apparent natural death until he noticed the discolored fingernails on the deceased and found that the old lady had fed her old man a teaspoon of sweet-tasting rat poison every morning with his orange juice. This was great stuff, and the cops who made these breakthroughs didn't mind imparting their genius—even if the solving was mostly fortuitous.

I wasn't that concerned with the PT (physical training) since I'd been weight training, running, and swimming throughout high school and college. With only one hour each day reserved for PT and Self Defense I knew there was little they could throw at me that would resemble the five-hours-per-day swimming practices I endured throughout high school and my first year of college. Peters and I usually partnered up for the self-defense tactics, "brother-in-lawing" one another on lazy days, but sticking it to each other when under the instructor's watchful eyes. Peters outweighed me by forty pounds and could throw me around like an inflatable dummy. However, in sticking with the adage—"The bigger they are..."—"Payback's a bitch," became the daily catch phrase as painful moans echoed throughout the expansive gymnasium.

Included in the PT was use of force techniques—restraints, punches, kicks, handcuffing, gun retention, nightsticks, etc. These self defense tactics seemed impractical for the most part, and our instructors harped on us to make these moves second nature, or the fights we found ourselves in would quickly deteriorate into ground combat—wrestling. Indeed, this warning was prophetic.

My first instance of mixing it up in a true self-defense situation came only months into my police career when I responded to a call of an in-progress domestic assault. My partner, Ray, arrived at the suspect apartment shortly after I did. The two of us listened outside the door for sounds of a struggle. Hearing only some grumbled arguing between two young men, Ray knocked on the door. A young male opened the door and studied us with raised eyebrows. "Yeah?"

"We were called here to check out a possible disturbance," Ray said.

"Well the only disturbance here is you," the young man replied, as he started to close the door.

Ray blocked the door with his foot and explained politely, "Whenever we're called to these we're required to make sure everyone's okay."

"Everyone's fine. Goodbye," and he pushed against the door Ray was holding.

Sensing this call was going south, I used my portable radio to request a routine backup. Ray and I pushed back on the door in unison and flung the young man onto his living room floor. We invited ourselves in.

"Get the fuck out of my place," he said, springing back to his feet.

Another young man appeared in the living room and rushed toward our position at the door. "Who invited you two into our place?"

"One of your neighbors called," I said.

He rolled his eyes. "You wouldn't be here if we weren't gay."

His partner's comment seemed to further infuriate the first man, who would have preferred to keep their sexual orientation private. "Shut up Mark!" Then he shouted at us, "Get out of our apartment!"

"Just let us do our job, and we'll leave," Ray said. "Is it just the two of you here?"

"You can leave now," the man said, and pushed Ray's chest.

Ray grabbed the man's arm, and the fight was on. Strangely enough, Ray and this young man separated briefly and put up their dukes as if they were going to slug it out, Marquess of Queensbury rules. I noticed that the man who squared off with Ray was wearing glasses, and the thought flashed through my mind, *How can you slug a guy in the face who's wearing glasses?* Before a punch was thrown, the other young man, Mark, charged at me in a tackling move, and the two of us crashed to the floor. All the kicks and punches, blocks and restraints we'd learned were not coming to mind as we rolled around on the floor rabbit-punching one another.

Both Ray and I were slightly larger than our adversaries, and I could tell early on that I could physically dominate my combatant. Rather than wrestling him into a neck restraint, as I should have, I found myself tumbling over furniture like a character in a John Wayne western, glass items crashing all around us. Like a knot you accidentally tie and it holds, I finally wrestled him into some improvised restraint and found myself lying on top of him next to Ray, who was also lying atop his foe. The four of us lay panting, as though we'd just tumbled to the ground after finishing a marathon. I felt ridiculous, but I was too exhausted to move. I radioed that we were "code four," meaning we no longer needed assistance, and from our positions of power we cuffed our arrestees and started walking them out to our squads.

Firearms training was new to me, having never even seen a real handgun close up in my life. The first days on the range were marked with some nervous fidgeting as I surveyed the human silhouettes downrange; thankful they were unarmed, immobile, and—paper. I would have a small but distinct advantage over these, my first adversaries. Range safety was stressed by the instructors for obvious reasons, and we were threatened with expulsion should we violate any of the range rules. First and foremost was to treat all weapons as though they were loaded and to point all muzzles down-range.

Ironically, I find that when I'm ignorant and apprehensive about a serious matter, my mind tends to wander rather than keying in to the important points. And it wasn't that the range officers were trying to trick us; they shouted over and over again that when we moved with the Remington 870 pump shotgun we were to carry it at port arms. This was demonstrated more than once by the instructors who held the long gun diagonally across their torso with the muzzle pointed up. One hand grasped the butt stock, the other held firmly to the ribbed wooden pump on the underside of the barrel. Of course when I stepped to the firing line and was ordered to advance with the shotgun, I placed the muzzle down like a hunter carries his rifle, so if the gun accidentally discharged, the pellets would be fired into the dirt rather than the chin of the cadet standing beside me. My first step was punctuated by the screaming range officer's admonition, "Goddammit, you—," pausing as he read the name on my shirt—"Greelis, you fucking idiot! What did I just say? Port arms. Port arms! I don't give a rat's ass how you carry that shotgun when you're walking through the fields with your faggot Uncle Elmer, but when you're on this police range you will carry it PORT ARMS! You got that?"

"Yes, sir," I said, holding the shotgun like a marching soldier and praying, *Feet don't fail me now,* since my knees seemed to be moving to some unheard jig. As he screamed at me, he jerked the shotgun away from me and then slammed it back into my chest to punctuate his point. This seemed like a breach of long-gun safety, but I decided to keep that to myself. I felt like I was as good as done at this point, and I hadn't yet fired a single round.

I tried to gain my composure as I stood at the firing line, knowing that one more failure at the range would probably constitute the end of my career in law enforcement. I took stock of the moment and asked myself what I was doing. Did I really belong here? These people were serious. I could be back on the lake, buzzed by noon in the Impala. I regretted my ignorance of guns and hunting, since most of the male cadets were hunters and could walk through this familiarization with their eyes closed. After hearing the instructors talk about primer explosions, gaseous exchanges, case extractions, and forceful recoil, I started to develop beginner-shooter's apprehension. We didn't expend more than twenty rounds that afternoon and I managed to get through the day without further incident. But this range experience humbled me.

Ironically, in my second year as a street officer, I tried out for a coveted opening on the SWAT team and, after succeeding in try-outs, was offered a position on the team. The shooting practice we received was just what the doctor ordered. I found that with continued practice, I was developing into an above-average shooter, which was a major improvement for me. We had a contest on a SWAT range-day where a life-sized (paper) bad guy held a hostage in front of him, exposing only about an inch or two of his own forehead as target. We were instructed to draw and fire two rounds at the suspect, as quickly as possible, from a standing position about ten feet away. I watched as the veterans on the team drew and fired their model 66, .38 caliber revolvers at the tiny target presented by the caricature bad guy. Though some of the rounds missed the bad guy, no one shot the hostage.

Craig and I were the only members left to shoot and he offered me the next try. I deferred since I was the new guy, and Craig stepped to the firing line. Craig was a soft-spoken Vietnam vet who carried the same model 39 Smith and Wesson 9mm semi auto on the street that he'd packed while in the service. The wooden-handled grips had notches carved in them all the way down the handle, from days when he and his squad mates traded lives with the enemy, day by day. When given the signal, Craig drew and fired two rounds with such speed that the space between the shots could hardly be detected. His rounds landed about a centimeter apart in the middle of the bad guy's forehead.

The guys on the team smiled sympathetically at me, knowing my reputation as a fledgling shooter. I knew that I had no chance to beat Craig's score by drawing, aiming, and squeezing the trigger as I'd been trained. I usually took longer to draw and bring the weapon up to eye level than the entire sequence had taken for Craig. I decided to just go for it. I would simply draw as quickly as I could and, once the gun was out in front of me, I would let go with both shots, allowing chance to decide the fate of the crook and the hostage, since ability was moot. That was the idea of the exercise anyway—point and shoot.

There had been no holes shot in the hostage and the holes Craig had surgically placed in the crook were covered up with black tape so there could be no question of whose holes were whose. At the signal I drew and fired like a western dueler, in one motion without aiming. Like Craig's, the reports from my shots seemed to ring as one. I stared at the target expecting the hostage to be wearing the deadly see-through tattoos of my recklessly ambitious attempt, but instead I found my rounds to be almost directly over Craig's. The team leader glanced from his stopwatch to the target and back to his stopwatch. He shook his head in disbelief. "Two point three-eight," he smiled. "You beat him by two-tenths of a second."

My reputation and self-confidence received a wholly undeserved boost that day since, while Craig's shooting was based on skill or possibly even reflex, mine was simply dumb luck. But I would take it, and in weaker moments even consider the possibility of skill having played some small part in my trick shooting of the day.

To be eligible for licensing as a peace officer in the State of Minnesota I had to earn passing grades on the final tests for PT, self-defense, emergency driving, first aid, and gunfire. Specific skills aside, the most difficult aspect of the final testing would be the practical tests. Cadets were required to perform car stops, using proper positioning and procedure. We had to handle domestic disturbances and, finally, had to deal with a belligerent drunk (role player) who was not averse to fighting with police.

As recruits we lacked the confidence earned only with experience, so the trainers allowed some latitude on these practical exams. We probably all failed these tests and would fail them repeatedly as police officers until we experienced some minimal degree of on-the-job success. If nothing else, the tests were eye-openers for what to expect, since these scenarios would be repeated many times over the span of our probationary year as a sworn officer.

Officers chose different tactics in dealing with obstinate drunks and fighters, based on their skills and physical confidence. A *presence* developed along with this confidence that was indescribable, yet readily discernable, both by fellow officers and the people we dealt with. Contrasted with simple command presence, it constituted not only an *appearance,* but also true unflappable self-assurance, whether dealing with a oppositional child or an angry drunk professional wrestler. Any officer, whether a 250-pound chiseled male or a 100-pound petite female, could possess it, though some never would regardless of time on the job, physical prowess, or exposure to serious calls.

With humility acting as sculptor, the first chunk of my ego was chiseled off when I faltered at the range and, though the written tests would not challenge me greatly, there would be other stumbling blocks to trip me up on my road to graduation. Even then, the real tests wouldn't begin until I was forced to make decisions and judgments under pressure on the street.

Communications was one aspect of training that could be taken only so far in a classroom setting, but one that would be crucial to one's success, safety, and even survival as a police officer. Notwithstanding my degree, my introverted personality was challenged early on to expand well beyond its comfort zone. My usual practice of using eye contact as a last resort, a protected resource of sorts, would not work in this profession. When an officer gave an order or told someone they were under arrest, that officer needed to look his arrestee directly in the eye and make him a true believer.

As graduation started to feel more like a distinct possibility I had one more unforeseen challenge. With all the PT, self-defense, and rolling around on mats (and without even having been kicked in the balls), I'd felt some discomfort in my testicles and found a pea-sized tumor to be the cause. Doctors suggested the possibility of cancer and, since testicular cancer usually struck the young with great speed and insidiousness, the doctor suggested the lump be removed ASAP and checked for cancer.

With the threat of cancer looming over me, I requested to test out of the physical trials prior to surgery since my doctor anticipated a lengthy, painful recovery. The Skills program director complied, and I was allowed to complete the early tests for PT and self-defense.

My surgeon explained that he would make a five-inch incision into my lower abdomen. He would extract the suspect testicle from my scrotum and lift it, still attached, through the opening in my abdomen, where the lump would then be biopsied and tested while I lay unconscious under the effects of general anesthesia. My testicle would lay waiting on my stomach, naively acquiescing like a lamb to the slaughter. Should the tests show cancer, the testicle would be removed; if not, it would be tucked back into its sack, resuming its familiar tandem status.

At twenty-two I was frightened by the possibility of the words *cancerous tumor* documenting an outcome on a doctor's report with my name on it, especially when juxtaposed with the word *testicular.* And what if the surgery proved the tumor to be malignant? Unflattering nicknames such as Lefty came to mind. I inquired as to whether or not the doctor would be inserting a prosthetic nut in place of the one removed should things go south on the operating table. He said he hadn't thought of it. Well, he was in his fifties, most likely married for twenty years and growing more hair on his dusty balls than his head, but I still thought a certain balance and proportion would be important to a single bon vivant—which I definitely wasn't. After a heavily weighted pause for consideration, he said he would insert such a device should I request it—which I assumed I just had.

Through the grace of God I was found to be cancer-free. I wouldn't need the extra marble after all, and my balls were allowed to celebrate their first reunion on the operating table at North Memorial Hospital. I carried around an inflatable dough- nut that I sat on for the final two weeks of classroom instruction.

I'd entered the program on a lark, thinking the vocation to be some facile pursuit I could fall back on until times or luck changed and some significant opportunity presented itself. The young men training alongside me, however, were dead serious about this job and already showed pride in their early accom- plishments. This was their career-to-be. Even my smart-ass brethren, Peters and Kleinhenz, were bearing down and attempting to walk the walk. As my training progressed, I began to realize that being a police officer was much more complicated than I'd thought. My idea of some mope in a blue uniform, dragging around a full-size car with a radio, lights, and siren, was not holding water. I knew I wasn't quite there yet with the rest of the class, as far as taking pride in the voca- tion and showing some dedication and loyalty to it.

I was miles from conducting myself as an officer when I received notice that I'd completed the Skills Program, having passed all the required segments of training. I was now eligible to take the State POST Board Licensing Test, and be hired.

What I still didn't know, and wouldn't learn until well into my probationary period as a police officer, was that attitude, more than anything else, would define us as officers. My attitude upon entering the Skills Program had been one of casual indifference. With my degree in hand, I carried within me an air of cockiness that may not have been visible to anyone, but was still present—until I stepped onto the range. Once hired as a cop I met officers who had never set foot in a college, but were both smarter and better cops than I would ever be.

It became readily obvious to me during my probationary period that certain officers had given up on *serving* their community. They were there to collect their paycheck *only* and wanted no obstacles impeding the most direct course from their in-box to the bank. They felt disenfranchised and shit-on for whatever reason, by the city, the department, their spouse, or by life in general—and were not offering any magnanimity.

This malaise was easy to fall into and nearly every officer stumbled into it sometime in his career. Once it was brought to the offending officer's attention—usually by a sensitive, caring partner screaming in his ear to get his shit together—most could crawl out, brush themselves off, and charge headlong back into the fray.

When faced with this attitudinal struggle, it was always helpful for me to think back on how I felt when presented with my badge—#130. There was an indescribable awe that went along with holding that simple shiny artifact in my hand, knowing my number was the last in a long series of numbers scratched onto badges and given out to others who had offered their lives to maintain the history and legacy of justice. If cornered and forced to reply, most cops would concede that, corny as it might seem, they held an inexplicable reverence for their badge.

Though the wearers are greatly outnumbered at times, these numbered badges placed side by side comprised a considerable force. Outsiders might think the assigning of a number to be impersonal or mechanical, but that was furthest from the truth. That number was a ticket for which there was no price—unattainable except for those who agreed to stand watch night after night, down range from the firing line—a blue line separating civilization from anarchy.

I knew that although I had passed all the tests and possessed the badge to flash, I hadn't really earned the right to wear it yet. My road to honoring that commitment would be a long and tenuous one. Strangely, I still wasn't convinced I belonged with these gung-ho devotees. Everyone else seemed so sure. A part of me was still back on the lake drinking beer with Donny, in the Impala.

This wasn't real estate; this was law and order. Instead of the leather briefcase I brought to the office at Real Estate Plus, I would be conducting business from a squad car, wearing body armor around my chest and a gun on my belt. I stood at the crossroads with badge in hand, unsure if I should forge ahead, but unwilling to quit.

The smart-ass club was broken up at graduation. Peters was hired on with Ramsey County, and Kleinhenz put on the navy blue uniform of the Brooklyn Park PD. I had a short stint with the Hennepin County Sheriff's Office before I was hired by the Bloomington PD, having visited the city a handful of times as a guest at Twins games and Met Center concerts.

Excited to show Donny my new badge, I ran one house over and interrupted his soap opera. He'd secured an evening job at the Liquor Depot downtown, so his afternoons were still free.

He held the badge in his hand, briefly considering its heft and shine before handing it back to me and returning his attention to the soap. "Nice," he said flatly. "Now all you need is a Magnum PI (his definition of a semi-automatic pistol) and you'll be set."

In addition to his grasp of daytime TV, Donny was now considered by some to be of legendary status in the eclectic world of ice fishing, but it was obvious that he knew even less about guns than I.

Wild Blue Yonder

I didn't know any real police officers as a child, and only had a passing interest in the profession when I applied to the Police Skills program (what was once called the Academy) in 1980. Like most children, I had a distorted view of police officers, direct from Hollywood. From *The Rookies* to *Starsky and Hutch*, these cops were bigger than life and, in some ineffable way, set apart and untouchable. That they could possess any ordinary traits or *normal* habits and emotions was completely foreign and irrelevant to me. I never imagined a uniformed police officer being out of uniform, hanging around in a dirty T-shirt, talking over the fence to his neighbor about flowers, or dogs, or the single chick that had just moved in across the street.

Our Police Skills instructors told us that dogwatch (2300 hours to 0700 hours) was the only shift *real* cops worked. It was the shift for real police work like breaking up barroom brawls and arresting drunks as they engaged their vehicle's "autopilot" to get them back home. If the drunks managed to pass through our gauntlet, we intervened later at their homes, when

31

their angry right hooks tattooed the frowning faces of their insensitive wives. The instructors added, only slightly face-tiously, that without booze we'd all be out of a job. Of my twenty-five classmates, only ten would ever work in law-enforce-ment. Twenty years later, I've lost contact with all but three.

After a six-month introduction to law enforcement, via my abbreviated deputy sheriff's job with Hennepin County, I was hired by the City of Bloomington in 1982 as a police offi-cer. Three other rookies were hired along with me. Toby Jensen was seven years my elder at thirty-one and had started his career as a street cop in Alameda County, California. He had moved from Minnesota to California where he'd earned some valuable work experience, fathered two children, and gotten divorced. (The divorce part was an-all-too familiar pattern in law enforcement.) Now, having moved back to his home state, he was starting over. Jim Hampton and Rick Laveau were in their early twenties, homegrown and completely green—like me. We met one another for the first time at the police depart-ment, where Training Sergeant Hank Sweet introduced us and started our orientation process.

Sergeant Sweet told us his dream of one day becoming a police chief. He assured us that his goal was attainable for him and could be for us as well if we made long-term goals and fol-lowed through with them. He was smooth, suave, articulate, and wore a great deal of hair spray on his well-coiffed salt and pepper pseudo-ex-marine hairstyle. He had a powerful presence that, on the one hand, was somewhat intimidating but, on the other, relaxed you with his slightly off-color, cliché, police speech, mannerisms, and attempts at humor. He was Dirty Harry in the suburbs.

While Sweet shared some personal war stories with us between orientation topics, an older uniformed administrator with a ubiquitous grin, light gray hair, and eyes to match, entered the office and introduced himself as Captain Barrington. He commenced to drawing an accident-scene scenario on the blackboard and explained it. "So you're on patrol in your police cruiser, stopped at a red light. The traffic light turns green for you, and you proceed into the intersection only to be T-boned by a car that ran the red light and collided with your squad." He stopped and looked into each of our faces. "Was this accident preventable on your part?"

Having not entirely evolved past my rebellious University of Minnesota leftist stage, I broke the room's cautious silence. "No, the accident was not preventable. There's no way the officer could have known that car would blow the light and collide with him."

Barrington looked around for dissenting opinions and, receiving none, replied, "On the contrary, the accident was preventable. Before proceeding into the intersection, the officer should have paused to see if oncoming traffic was slowing as they approached, to gauge whether or not they would come to a complete stop."

"But you can't sit there in a busy intersection when you have the green light just waiting for approaching cars to see if they're going to stop," I countered. "You'd be a menace."

Barrington studied me as he might a steaming pile of dog-doo in his path, and then unconsciously reformed his grin. "When you have an accident in a city vehicle there will be an investigation to determine whether or not the accident was preventable. Just a tip—nearly all accidents are preventable. Having a preventable accident can lead to disciplinary action." He looked at me and smiled. "Any questions?"

This time I had the good sense to keep my mouth shut. His smile dissolved as he continued to stare at me. "Thank you, and welcome to the Bloomington Police Department." He turned abruptly from our group and left the training room.

"Oooo-kay," Sweet said, breaking the group's guarded silence. He looked at his watch, probably noting the time and date so he could give an accurate account of my abbreviated tenure with the Bloomington PD. Then with his trademark cop-talk, he said, "Let's blow this pop stand."

Prior to leaving for the range, Sweet issued us our shiny new stainless steel Smith and Wesson, model 66, .38 caliber revolvers. I looked at this weapon in awe as I cradled it in my hands like a priceless artifact. My own shiny six-shooter. Wiping the drool from our chins, we strapped our pistols onto our previously impotent gun-belts because, after all, what was a gun-belt without a gun? We felt the weight of our weapons on our hips, but only in pounds. Toby was probably the only one among us who truly understood the apocalyptic possibilities associated with our new hardware. A twenty-four-year-old of average (at best) maturity with a pistol strapped legally to his leg was an almost unconscionable thing, and yet there I was. I can't speak for every rookie, but that spinning the pistol around one's finger and then asking the bandito in the mirror à la DeNiro's *Taxi Driver*, "Are you talking to me?"—probably happened.

We all qualified at the range that day with Toby exhibiting far greater handgun proficiency than the rest of us. I figured his experience counted for something, and I held out hope that maybe in time I too would become a decent marksman.

Sweet dropped us off at the Police Department later that day, and we didn't see him much after that. He was promoted to Lieutenant and assigned to Professional Standards, which was the euphemism our department used for Internal Affairs. This proved to be an ironic transfer since a subsequent investigation of a local bookie would expose Sweet as one of many gamblers implicated in the sting. He was disciplined with some sort of slap on the wrist, and then, like all office-related gossip, it reached its saturation point, dried up, and was forgotten. Sweet chose to retire early a couple of years later. Rumor had it, he returned to driving cab, a profession he reminisced about as a cop with a certain degree of nostalgia. He was arrested by our department a couple of years later on sports gambling and bookmaking charges. I sought out his mug shot and was struck by how severely he'd aged from the sharp-dressed training sergeant with the Hollywood cop-talk and the shiny hair.

The new training sergeant did not have near the amount of thick shiny hair or the apparent joie de vivre of his predecessor—but after clicking his heels together for ten years in Bloomington, he would actually become Chief of Police somewhere in Kansas. Sergeant Chip Gunther was an intelligent, pasty-faced, tooth-sucking, pedantic type who considered those of higher rank as possible stepping-stones, and those of lower rank simply as stones to be stepped on.

I believe that my first shift as a uniformed police officer was as surreal an experience as my birth, and I was equally prepared for it. My uniform, fresh off the shelf, served only to make the event more of a masquerade. Though I wore a badge, I had no idea what I was doing or what was expected of me. I knew that my classroom prep would be of little value to my work on the street. Coming from suburbia and living a fairly straight life, I was very naive. I'd had only one encounter with a police officer prior to my being hired as one, and that was when I jumped the fence at the Minnesota State Fair in an attempt to defer the admission fee to other more deserving pursuits inside. A horse-patrol officer noticed my leap and thundered toward me. The earth shook and I was enveloped in a cloud of dust—from which emerged a giant uniformed officer on an enormous chestnut steed. I considered myself lucky to have maintained bladder control as the horse stopped on a dime just short of stomping me into pulp. The officer kindly walked me to the front gate where I gladly paid the admission fee. If he'd treated me differently—who knows?

We met our field training officers (FTOs) on our first real shift and sat with them in the roll-call room. My FTO was Jason T. Havelman. I later shortened his name to "JT" and it stuck. JT was at that time and remains today an enigma. No one has quite figured him out, and I believe he likes it that way.

I was unsure of him from the start, and I would later learn he was equally skeptical of me. Police officers in general comprise the most cynical group of our species, and JT was no exception. He looked me up and down without expression but then, like Bluto of *Animal House* (or Spock of *Star Trek*), raised one eyebrow in bemused consideration. Aside from the lifted eyebrow, his face remained deadpan. (I later learned that the raised eyebrow thing was a joke meant to lighten the tension.) I checked him out in my peripheral vision and found his uniform and general appearance to be "strack"—military slang for impeccable.

I was beginning to realize that although police departments were considered "para-military," there was a strong residual culture among police officers that mirrored many military practices, and those with military experience were favored. As I got to know the seventy-some officers in the patrol division, I learned which officers had military service. Of the officers who had fought in Vietnam, I found that no generalizations could be made of them. Some wore their service time on their sleeve, reflecting their military experience in everything they did, from their haircut to the military lexicon that paralleled police work. Others never mentioned their service time and offered no indication of ever having served overseas.

JT's role as FTO, mentor, evaluator and friend was tested early in our relationship. Still too immature to use even an speck of sound judgment, I went to a drive-in movie in town with a friend while only several weeks into my FTO period. This friend was a habitual pot smoker, and when he handed off a well-rounded joint to me, I allowed judgment to escape from the crack-opened window of my truck as I took a hit off it. Once the cab of my tiny Mazda pick-up truck was completely saturated with smoke, a slam on the driver's side window brought me out of my MJ-induced, munchie-chomping delirium. Through the smoke I could clearly make out the deep lines of disappointment etched in the stone face of a uniformed cop—JT. Though we shared the same schedule, he'd picked up the extra shift and was working in the area of the drive-in. He had recognized my pick-up and had come over to say hello.

I hesitated to roll down the window, knowing that any doubt he might have about the consistency of the billowing smoke in my truck would be eliminated once I opened it. His disappointment and my discomfort seemed to deepen with each second I procrastinated until I could stall no longer. Having no other option, I rolled the window down slowly and deliberately. With each revolution of the knob I released not only the smoke, but also my immaturity and myriad deficiencies. His expression remained the same as the smoke curled into and over his face. He said little and did not mention the obvious. I introduced my friend as my reddened eyes both betrayed me and tacitly asked forgiveness.

After returning from the drive-in that night, I lay in bed considering what I was doing, what the masquerade meant, and when it would end. I realized that my choice to end it might have been taken from me that night. I was not police material. I doubted that I possessed the requisite qualities of resolve, dedication and, most importantly, integrity, to enforce the law. After all, I had convincingly demonstrated what a fraud and hypocrite I was to be wearing the uniform. I decided before I fell off to sleep that if given the chance I would amend the damage I'd done. Though I had tarnished my badge indelibly, I would attempt to scale it back as best I could, and walk the walk of my FTO and those like him—whatever the sacrifice. To my surprise, I felt the same way when I awoke the next morning.

Strangely enough, there were no disciplinary consequences for my egregious misconduct. Had JT chosen to inform the ever-vigilant Training Sergeant Gunther, I certainly would have been handed my walking papers. As it was, JT never brought it up. Not wanting to press the issue, or my luck, too soon, I cushioned my curiosity for a comfortable fifteen years before I asked him why he hadn't reported me. He said he saw something in me that gave him hope, and he left it at that.

Though I survived the ax, my partner Rick Laveau wasn't so lucky. Sergeant Gunther found my recruit partner's attitude problem to be unredeemable and fired him while he was still an expendable probationary employee. (Gunther would have had to show cause for the termination after Rick completed his one-year probationary period.) Rick called me at home the night he was fired and, with a conscious and decipherable attempt to will his voice from cracking, told me he'd been let go. I couldn't believe it. Rick seemed to me to be destined for greatness, much more so than the three of us hired with him. He was a very sharp, witty, and seemingly natural police officer. It became common knowledge soon after his departure that he'd been asked to resign due to attitude problems. I considered my devil-may-care attitude at the drive-in and thanked God and fortuity (and JT in this instance) for showing up when I needed them—as they would in perpetuity for my entire career. As if Leveau's leaving wasn't disappointing enough, Jim Hampton followed his friend off to the West Coast where both were hired as police recruits in a much larger police department.

Both quickly distinguished themselves as exemplary officers. As of this writing, Rick is commander of his department's Intelligence Division, while Jim transferred to the city's Fire Department, where he works as an arson investigator.

I soon became indoctrinated in the many police traditions, one of which was the police lexicon. The product of a four-year liberal arts education, I was a bit miffed to learn that the word *fuck* was traditionally included in nearly every phrase uttered by an officer when out of public earshot. Many times when one did not know exactly what to say while in a group of cops one could simply say, "Fuck!" with conviction or whatever tonality seemed appropriate, and one stood a very good chance of being *right.* I found after a period of time that I needed to consciously delete this obscenity from family time and all non-police functions in order to maintain the facade of civility.

JT, however, rarely used profanity and never took the Lord's name in vain. I tried to follow his example in this and other respects. He was very organized. While other officers lugged pursuit cases (large, hard plastic briefcases) filled with blank reports, state statutes, policy manuals, and sundry other police paraphernalia to and from their squads, JT brought only his stainless-steel clipboard and his flashlight. He was one of the last "hat-men." The traditional police garrison hat was not required headwear in our department. Only a handful of tradition-minded old-timers wore them. This was one practice I chose not to emulate.

As we stood for inspection at our first dogwatch roll call, the street sergeant checked our uniforms for proper fit and cleanliness, and checked the shine on our boots. After the reading of roll-call notes we were dismissed to the street. My employment with the city started in March and I gladly welcomed the cool night air the outdoors offered. Walking through the garage door that led to the squads gave me a peaceful confirmation as to why I had sought out this vocation. I would not be stuck in a dungeon of an office, prisoner to desk and phone, at least not until I became a detective. Rather I'd be moving along with the ebb and flow of life outdoors, commingling with the other creatures of the night. I later learned that my police radio replaced the phone as my ball and chain, and that the ebb and flow of the night was as capricious as a Minnesota winter.

JT demonstrated how to check out the squad prior to start of shift, including the operation of emergency lights and siren. Unlike most recruits, I had never seen the inside of a squad car, except for the ones we'd practiced in during the Skills Program. I should have asked my questions then, but chose instead to wait until I was seated in the squad's passenger seat beside JT. I looked out the squad's windshield, and as I examined the glass I allowed curiosity to dissolve my conscious restraint as stupid rookie questions began to flow too quickly from thought to voice. "Good thing these squads have bulletproof glass cause we'd really be vulnerable without it." JT didn't know me yet, and was unsure whether or not I was joking. Unfortunately, I was serious and, after a short pause and the single lifted eyebrow, he figured this out. He told me in his unique monotone that the squads had only standard windshield glass. He pointed out a hole in the windshield of the squad parked beside ours. He said the hole was caused by a sniper, shooting at the oncoming squad. The bullet passed between Officer Klinehoffer and his FTO as they occupied the front seats. I must have looked completely bewildered. After all, this wasn't LA or Chicago. This was Bloomington, home of the Twins, the Vikings, and the North Stars. *Snipers?*

JT now understood the true extent of how green his rookie was. He must have suppressed a pained sigh of exasperation, since I didn't hear it. I decided that maybe it was a good idea to hold back on questions for a while because, contrary to the popular maxim, there really is such thing as stupid questions and I was quickly becoming a master of them.

After a quick lesson in how to load and unload the squad's Remington 870 pump shotgun and its proper *squad-ready* condition, we were prepared to hit the streets.

From the passenger seat in JT's squad, I looked around at the cars that shared the night and the streets with us, and noticed that nearly everyone stared at us. The teen drivers slowed down, glanced and then looked away as I returned their glance. Children stared, and continued to stare, and many times waved, until we parted ways. Adult women attempted not to be caught looking, but adult men varied eye contact according to age, socio-economic class (many times evidenced by the make and model of car they occupied), ethnicity, and whether or not they'd just committed a crime or some lesser moving violation. Depending on which group they belonged to, they might completely ignore us or challenge us to a stare-down.

The other thing I noticed was the continuous gibberish of the "10-code" on the police radio. I thought at the time that even if I had an inkling of what the canned voices were talking about, I still wouldn't understand the radio because the quality and clarity of the sound was incomprehensible. It didn't sound that bad on *Adam 12*. It had been at least ten minutes since my last stupid question, so I casually threw caution to the wind. "Can you actually understand what they're saying?"

Again, I received JT's raised eyebrow, followed by the weighted pause, and then the answer, "Yeah. You just need to listen carefully, and you'll start to pick it up."

Of course he was right, but I was beginning to doubt my ability to perform even the most basic functions. How could I act on what was broadcast if I couldn't understand what was said?

Being a lover of all things cliché, I was overjoyed to see that our first stop that night was the local Winchell's Doughnut Shop. At first I thought JT was teasing me when we pulled into the lot, but then I noticed two other squads empty out and enter the establishment.

Prior to becoming a police officer, I had never been given anything free simply because of who I was or what I wore, so having Vince the Doughnut Prince, as I would come to know him, hand me a greasy doughnut from his greasy bare hand over the greasy counter, and simply smile back at me, was more than I could handle. First of all, Vince was probably about sixteen years old and, from first appearances, one could guess that personal hygiene was not a priority. His long, oily, sandy-blonde hair hung in adhesive clumps from the dirty paper baker's cap he was forced to wear. His teeth, of which there were few, resembled what I imagined bat's teeth must look like, pointed and darkly translucent. Secondly, I could not make peace with just taking the doughnut from him without at least *acting* like I was going to pay for it so I stuck my hand in my pocket to get some change. Vince looked at JT and said, "New guy or what?...Fuuuck."

"First night," JT replied.

Vince laughed, "Fuuuck, duuude, just take it."

Finally, I didn't even want a doughnut. I couldn't remember the last time I had eaten a doughnut prior to that night. Now I grimace considering the number of doughnuts I consumed during those first three years on dogwatch. The Doughnut Prince and I became late-night warrior brothers, partnered in our varied nocturnal shifts, keeping one another awake, sharing our thoughts on concerts we'd seen and our favorite bands—many times overlapping.

At the start of my police career I was in the best physical shape of my life. I'd been involved in sports, weight training, running, and swimming for years prior to being hired. I had watched my diet and had disciplined myself to avoid foods like candy bars, chips, and, of course, doughnuts. This first night, I thought, I would conform to my peers and allow myself a doughnut.

Two or three months later, while under the tutelage of a substitute FTO, I stopped a car for speeding and advised the driver that I would be issuing him a citation. In a rare instance of attempted bribery, this very obese driver in a cheap plaid sport coat held his money clip, bulging with ones, in front of his face, and asked if there was ANYTHING he could do to change my mind. Working the doughnut cliché one step further, I asked him with a straight face if he had a glazed doughnut with him. He looked at me, weighing my sincerity, and then from his position in the driver's seat, he scanned the interior of his car as though he might have carelessly discarded one in the backseat earlier that morning. Coming up empty handed, he turned back to me, crestfallen. I advised him against using the money-clip ploy in the future and issued him his well-deserved citation.

Weeks later I was finally positioned in the driver's seat. JT sat beside me as my passenger, holding tightly to the squad's dash in mock terror. We got our first call of the night: *Disturbance at White Castle.* Disturbances at White Castle meant only one thing—drunks fighting—since few customers visited the Castle sober after bar closing. Not that you can't eat a slider sober, they just seemed to taste better with a buzz on—at least that's what I'd heard. People tended to fight more at White Castle than any other fast-food place. Why? It could have been the toxic mixture of chemicals in the clientele's' blood, or maybe it was the toxic mound of onions commingling with the pooled grease atop the sliders. Finally, it could have simply been tradition.

Two other squads were dispatched to the fight, one of which was the street sergeant, Gary Milton. Sgt. Milton was an ex-Marine. He was stereotypical in some ways and unique in others. One could describe his personality as *passionate* about his work, or *intense*. Others might use more abrasive adjectives, but I'll just say that, in addition to the above, his fuse was short and easily lit.

When we arrived, the two combatants were wearing out. The actual throwing of punches had ceased due to over-exertion and fatigue—the fatigue due almost entirely to their extreme intoxication. One of the combatants was ready to walk away and willingly complied when JT suggested they both do just that. The other combatant, however, a thirty-something longhair with a scraggly brown beard became braver in our presence, and started calling the other man a pussy and such for walking away. My part in this, as in most of my early calls, was to stand in the background trying (but failing) not to look like the FNG, and attempting to stay out of the way of the real police who were actually standing in harm's way.

Using force on someone other than my big brother, Bob— who typically cleaned my clock when we clowned around— was very foreign to me. As the bearded man started toward the retreating man, JT, along with Sgt. Milton, grabbed him by his arms. They advised him to settle down and leave the area or be arrested for DC (disorderly conduct). With only the alcohol raging through his system to guide him, he turned to Sgt. Milton and told him to fuck off. Sgt. Milton, who was blond, blue-eyed, and of pale complexion, overheated almost instantly, became of purple complexion, and started screaming. As the three of them scuffled, I found myself standing behind the group of skirmishers like a mannequin with real, but glazed-over, eyes. Through the confusion, tussling, and jousting for position, Sgt Milton managed to restrain the man with his nightstick by squishing it under the man's chin and against his throat. Both the long-hair and Milton wore nearly identical purple faces with nearly the same intensity in their eyes. Milton looked at me and shouted, "Don't just stand there, Steve, cuff him up!"

Steve? Cuffs, cuffs, cuffs—that would be handcuffs! Mine I hoped were enveloped in the appropriate leather container on my handy-dandy utility belt. Having temporarily lost my mind, I searched my belt both visually and physically until I found them wedged somewhere between my flashlight and my pepper spray.

Milton interrupted my thankful prayer to God that I hadn't left them in my locker, shouting, "Hurry the fuck up, Steve, or ah, Gree—ah—." Of course he didn't know my name yet, I was one of the new guys.

Handcuffs in hand, I shakily attempted to hand them to Milton, who of course already had his hands full. His eyes narrowed as he considered my incompetence, stupidity and general worthlessness. JT said calmly, "Go ahead, Richard, cuff him up."

I positioned myself behind the choking, gasping, kicking, cursing man, all eyes on me, since the fight would be as good as over once the suspect's hands were restrained behind his back.

"Hurry up!" Milton shouted again.

Of course I had been taught how to properly handcuff a resisting suspect, and I was fairly confident in my abilities to apply them. I grabbed onto a wrist and started to push the cuffs against it, but then suddenly, without warning, the ceiling of the Castle fell in on me along with the moon, the stars, and all the planets as I realized I had put my cuffs away locked. I could not open them without keying them open, and the cuff key I'd been issued was God knows where. I stood there attempting to pull them apart, staring at them like *they* rather than *me* were flawed. "They're locked," I croaked.

"God-dammit!" Milton spat. "Somebody get this guy cuffed."

The cuffs were quickly becoming a moot issue since the arrestee appeared to be nearly dead or at least unconscious from Milton's incorrect application of the nightstick to the man's throat. Officer Warner, who had come to assist, smiled at my proclivity for mayhem, and produced his handcuffs from his belt. He handed them to me and I placed them slowly and clumsily, one at a time over the man's thick, sweaty wrists—incorrectly of course, with the keyholes pointed the wrong direction, but their purpose and mission fulfilled. As JT and Milton relaxed their grips on the man, he collapsed to the floor. Sgt. Milton gave me a look of contempt and something just less than that to JT who was somehow, ipso-facto semi-responsible for my performance or lack thereof.

Once Milton left, JT congratulated me on the smooth handling of our first arrest. I assumed Milton would be in the chief's office later that morning suggesting I be tarred, feathered and fired. (He later made that request, sans the tar and feather, to the patrol commander.) JT assured me that some time in the history of the Bloomington Police, there had probably been another rookie who was almost as bumbling as me. He just couldn't think of one at the time.

Shortly after I started, the rookies had a contest (one of many) to see who could tow the most expensive car from a "Handicapped Parking Only" zone. There were Corvettes, Lexuses, Porches, and BMWs, but late one July summer morning I spied the quintessential car in the Handicap Zone at the Granada Royale Hotel. A cherry, 1970-something Rolls Royce. This car cost more than my house. It probably cost more than the real estate owned by the entire dogwatch platoon. As the tow truck backed up to the Rolls, I watched like a little boy preparing to purchase the complement of Boardwalk and possess the greatest monopoly of all. In time, the writing of parking tickets, or any ticket for that matter, would become more of a monotonous chore and provided little gratification.

Towing a pricey car was minor compared with the true power we wielded. I couldn't believe the enormity of power and discretion I had. At twenty-four years old I was arresting men my father's age for beating up their wives. I was raised to respect my elders, not to "talk back" and never to be contrary or impudent. I quickly learned that I needed to disregard those lessons of etiquette at times, however contradictory that seemed. This was true culture shock for me. I had never raised my voice to an elder, much less used force on one. I had in my hands the power to take away a person's right to drive, to end his career, his marriage, his relationship with his children, his freedom, and ultimately his life—and I wasn't even a Nazi.

Another culture shock for me was fighting. Luckily, most of our combatants were drunks who weren't very good fighters when sober much less while balancing on rubber legs. For some reason, experienced fighters—boxers and martial arts types— were seldom interested in mixing it up with cops. My detective partner, Ted, said that every rookie cop should have as a job prerequisite some experience in bar fighting—as he did. Like many of the young cops, I had the asset of years of weight training, which made me appear stronger than most of our adversaries. The appearance of strength, coupled with the uniform and belted accouterments, was usually enough. The times when we actually had to fight, I found that we were rolling on the ground wrestling, rather than facing off for fisticuffs like in the movies, and it really wasn't that bad. The ratio of cops to combatants was usually in our favor, and the fact that we were sober, and they weren't, made a telling difference.

Some of the older cops had their own ways. They understood they could no longer stand toe-to-toe with the twenty-year-olds, and so compensated with other tactics. Jim

Mitchner, "Mitch," who was not in the least bit ornery or can-
tankerous when treated *properly*, was nearing retirement when
I finished my one-year probation. I backed him up on a car stop
at night when a well-dressed young driver in a black BMW told
him summarily to "fuck off." Disrespect toward police officers
is a daily occurrence these days and considered a minor irri-
tant, but in the not-so-distant past, uniformed officers expected
at minimum a semblance of respect. His sensibilities thwarted,
Mitch swung his flashlight down on the yuppie's thigh with
enough force to make his femur ring like a tuning fork. There
was no fight. The driver was in too much pain to exit his vehicle and, even if he could, he probably assumed (correctly) that
if he attempted any confrontation, the humorless cop with the
flashlight would render him toothless. So the throbbing pain
coupled with the probability of costly dental work kept him
painfully but passively glued to the BMW's fine Corinthian
leather seat. The incident was over, and this yappy yuppie would
be limping to and from his BMW for a week or so. Time enough
to contemplate the error of his judgment. Luckily for Mitch, he
retired just prior to our society becoming overly litigious, whereupon officers started getting sued for enforcing what they considered to be their minimum thresholds of respect.

   I met my Waterloo at a party-call about four years into my
career. These calls were summer-night weekend staples, when
about fifty cars lined the adjoining streets and beer cans and
bottles littered the curb around the party house. Once the beer
started to flow, the "guests" grew impatient and chose the neighbor's shrubs over the long line to use the restroom. The neighbors, having just fortified their shrubberies with some product
that promised to guard against everything but human urine,
started to call the police, lighting up the dispatcher's lines.

   In this instance, as in most large party calls, two officers
approached the front door of the party-house to advise the

homeowner (usually the absent homeowner's teenage son) to end the party and send their guests home—immediately. The teenage boy who answered the door in this case slammed it shut upon seeing the blue uniforms. Needless to say, this reaction at the door was a bad sign. We waited outside the house for more squads to arrive since there appeared to be more than a hundred partiers. As we waited, we stood in groups and talked in hushed tones. As I chatted with a group of three other officers, a bottle smashed through a window from inside of the house and flew straight into my face, shattering as it struck my left eye. Just as paper covers rock, rock crushes scissors, and scissors cuts paper—beer bottle breaks face. My hand rose reflexively to cup my eye, and was instantly coated with a warm rush of blood that poured down my face and disappeared into the navy blue abyss of my uniform and the night.

The reactions of the officers around me conveyed the seriousness of my injury. My eye shut reflexively on contact and I wondered if it was still intact in its socket. There was an ambulance on the scene and one of my compatriots escorted me to the rig. The street sergeant, Brad Farhaven, looked at me, then to the awaiting troops, and shouted, "Okay, we're going in!"

I heard unifying whispered warrior chants from the newly inspired group, as the officers prepared to go in the house. Our largest officer, Lonnie Carson, stood at least six-and-a-half feet tall and weighed more than 350 pounds. With twelve spirited officers behind him, he crashed through the locked entrance door swinging his flashlight like a medieval knight wielding a broadsword. Shortly after this emotionally charged frontal assault, I was joined in the ambulance by fellow officer, Kevin Thompson, whose scalp was opened by a lightening blow surgically delivered by a giant of a man, at least six-and-a-half-feet tall, weighing more than 350 pounds, wielding a flashlight.

With side-by-side beds in the Fairview Southdale emergency room, Doctor Justice closed Thompson's scalp, and then deftly sewed my face back together. We watched one another and tried not to wince—for the other guy's sake—as the doctor pulled his needle and thread. Trooper Anna Tucker held our hands as Doctor Justice, in typical emergency room style, worked quickly and aggressively. Notwithstanding the doctor's name, I wondered aloud whether he'd been issued any citations recently as he scrubbed my lacerated face with what felt to be reckless abandon. When he finished, I had three sets of sutures surrounding my left eye, but I could still see. My scars would heal completely, making the deep gashes almost imperceptible. Justice had prevailed, as the good doctor truly had magic hands.

The medicals we responded to were often emotionally taxing. So many of the victims seemed at the threshold of death's doorstep or recently tipped over it. Providing CPR to unresponsive non-breathing victims was a fairly common occurrence—bringing them back from there was by far the exception. Humor at these scenes, however inappropriate it seemed to the outsider, was the key to maintaining one's sanity.

Shortly after my one-year probationary period, my buddy, Bishop (Bish) and I were called to an apparent DOA of a ninety-year-old woman. When we got to the residence, the ever-present family members were in the early stages of the grieving process. They pointed to the room where their deceased loved one had been discovered. Bish and I tiptoed through the stuffy living room as muffled cries and sporadic sniffles broke the silence like the first snaps of popcorn in a pan.

We entered the room, which was nothing more than a stuffy, converted closet, and found the old woman seated on the room's only chair at her sewing machine. She was very old indeed, and dressed the part with her gray and brown hair woven up tightly into a matronly bun, her chin resting on her chest. Bish, who had recently settled his first divorce, whispered, "She's too old for me anyway."

With little to do other than wait for the medical examiner I performed a perfunctory check for a pulse on her wrist. The carotid artery was the preferred indicator, but I didn't really think it mattered at this juncture. After holding my index and middle fingers over the notch on the underside of her wrist for about five seconds I pulled my hand away in shock as I felt a very thready, weak, but unmistakable—pulse. I looked at the old woman who was a dead ringer for a dead gomer, and then at Bish who said with a smirk, "Don't fuck with me."

"You try it," I said defensively.

Bish's eyes widened as he too felt the beats. "Fuck me!" he whispered.

I got up to grab my oxygen.

"Hold up a minute," Bish said.

"You're the boss," I said, facetiously acknowledging his slight seniority.

We hadn't asked the family whether or not the old woman had a DNR (Do Not Resuscitate) order, since the question seemed moot at the time. Now we needed to know. If there was no DNR order we were mandated to drag her off her chair onto the floor and start CPR. Properly applied chest compressions typically broke the brittle ribs of the elderly at the breastbone. You could feel them break with the pressure of your compressions, and sometimes even hear them fracture. This woman was so close to death that the act of pulling her off the chair onto the floor and then proceeding to bounce our weight off her chest would have killed her for sure. Still, that was protocol.

I dragged my oxygen kit next to the old woman's chair and opened it up. I extracted the positive pressure valve and mask from the kit in slow motion. Before removing her from her seat on the chair, we sat for a minute in silence, considering our solemn vow to serve and protect, as we waited for the old woman to die. I thought her caretakers must have had some practice in determining whether she was dead or alive since she probably appeared dead every time she napped— which was probably quite often. I held her limp, lukewarm hand in mine and continued to monitor her barely discernable pulse as she sat perfectly still, circling the drain.

A tentative knock on the door startled us as one of the living room mourners asked us if everything was okay. Bish, whose forehead was now beaded with sweat, lifted his hands baffled, then turned toward the door, "Yup, everything's fine. Be out in a minute."

As we turned back to the old woman we could see her color drain from her face, her blood having surrendered to gravity's sovereign inevitability. The faint beats from her failing heart that had pulsed moments ago ceased to register against my fingertips. I checked her carotid artery, but like a timer that had reached zero, the metronomic beats had come to rest. Even without the confirmation of her pulse, we could see she had just died, her paleness having turned an ashen gray. We both breathed a sigh of relief. I returned her still-warm hand to her lap where her other hand rested on her rumpled navy blue dress. I sat across the sewing machine from her and envisioned her soul's departure, hoping my final exit would be so peaceful. Bish left the room to check the progress of the M.E.

Sometime during my second or third year on the street I decided I enjoyed the brotherhood among officers, and the quixotic aspect of the job, well enough to play it out till the end—which meant until I was fifty or so and could collect my pension. That translated to about twenty-six years as a cop.

This decision wasn't made as a result of tally sheets listing the pros and cons of the job, or any other logical consideration. Rather, the decision to stay was more like the progression of gears on a big rig as it lumbered down an incline on a back road at midnight, the determined trucker shifting into overdrive wanting only to deliver his load and get back home.

Losing at Chicken

I noticed the following morning, with little satisfaction or pride, that my name and picture were on the front page of the Minneapolis *Star-Tribune*. Of course my presence in the photo was merely incidental to the story. I hadn't even seen a photographer in the area of the wreck or spoken to a reporter. My partner and I were forever memorialized standing by the crumpled rollover, oblivious to the camera and too tired to mask our complete exhaustion.

The dogwatch shift, 2300 to 0700 hours, had an almost narcotic effect of sapping one's strength minute by minute, so that when the end of shift arrived and the quittin'-time bell rang, you were completely spent. Of course that's when the call came out: *10-52 (accident with injuries)* southbound 35W between the 94th Street and 98th Street exit ramps.

My partner, Toby, and I were at the gas pumps, refueling our squads for our day-watch reliefs when we heard the call go out. We looked at one another with that, "why don't we just shoot ourselves and make it easy" look, knowing we would be assigned the call since we were least senior on the shift. Sure enough, the dispatcher called out our squad numbers, and we responded, screaming out of the lot with lights, sirens, and the necessary adrenaline rush to keep us conscious.

We arrived at the 94th Street entrance ramp to the freeway and found it already closed to traffic by a State Patrol Squad. We squeezed past him and pulled up behind several Bloomington squads positioned behind the rollover, with their wig-wags still blinking. There was another car facing the wrong way about a hundred feet south of the rollover with the front end smashed, bulldog-nosed-flat to the windshield.

I took in the scene and grabbed the oxygen from my squad's trunk while Toby grabbed his medical kit. We walk-jogged or maybe just stumbled to the car, lying on its top, its wheels skyward. The rollover was a blue-gray sixties-vintage Ford Galaxie 500, not without rust but still solid. The engine made clinking sounds, and faint smoke rose from its bowels. Different engine fluids followed gravity's directional pull from the tanks they had occupied to the overturned hood and finally onto the pavement and into the ditch. I could smell the ubiquitous presence of antifreeze, redolent of most head-on crashes.

I glanced at the windshield and stopped in my tracks, dumfounded. I was taken back by its complete saturation in red. If someone had taken a full can of burgundy paint and launched it against the interior glass they could not have covered it more thoroughly. Though I'd responded to many car accidents in my first year as a cop, this was my first true high-speed head-on cruncher, and my first fatality. Toby's voice interrupted my trance as he directed me to the other side of the Ford. The woman whose life blood was lost to the windshield lay in a crumpled fetal ball between her overturned car and the ditch. In addition to her grotesquely deformed head and facial injuries, she had several compound fractures. The ivory protrusion of her ulna through the skin of her forearm hypnotized me momentarily as the gears of my mind turned in slow motion.

Two other officers and a pair of medics had beaten us to the scene and were performing CPR on this woman. Their attempts to save her were, of course, futile from the start, but then futility seemed the norm on medical emergencies. We had to try. I was losing a bet with another dogwatcher that I could save one person I attempted to resuscitate on our four-month shift period. I was seven and zero, so far, and felt like the Grim Reaper when I arrived at a serious medical. Officers on medicals with me feigned sympathy for my victims as though their fate was sealed upon my arrival.

Satisfied that this woman was covered, Toby nodded for me to follow him to the other car involved in the crash, a two-door Chevy Nova. Officer Smalley, a fifteen-year vet, stood leaning in toward the driver. I approached Smalley and asked if he needed anything. He smiled and advised me to "check it out," nodding to the interior of the Nova. I noticed the driver to be a woman in her thirties. She stared straight ahead and panted, repeating the word "hee" with each breath. She was in shock, but appeared uninjured, having her seatbelt fastened even still. I looked down at her hands, which shook spastically near her thighs. I then noticed the skin and musculature just above her knees, curled back to the bone and shaved about five or six inches toward her thigh. Both knees had nearly symmetrical injuries from being pushed upon impact under the dashboard below the steering wheel.

I attempted to get her attention and ask her if she needed anything, but got no acknowledgement from her. Officer Smalley laughed, and asked me if I was serious.

"She's fuckin' mental—AWOL from some group-home in Burnsville."

I didn't reply. I wasn't sure yet how I felt about this woman. The direction of her car and the lack of skid marks behind her vehicle represented strong evidentiary responsibility for the accident, if it was in fact an accident. I turned to Toby, who raised his eyebrows and threw his hands out to his sides.

"I'll get a blanket," he said, as he walked back toward his car.

Though Toby started with me as a rookie in our city, he had about ten years experience in Alameda County, California, as a sheriff's deputy. He had seen it all before, but tended to hold his opinions to himself unless asked. He had a logical, straightforward philosophy of police work: Do the job in as little time as possible, with the least amount of physical exertion as possible, and report your actions as concisely as possible. He wasn't lazy, just logical and frugal. At thirty years old he was seven years my senior, and it showed in his judgment and job knowledge.

Officer Smalley shook his head, disgusted that Toby would supply comfort to this "victim." He glared down his nose and headed back to his squad. I leaned back into the window and examined the woman's face. I told her that Toby had gone to get her a blanket and that the medics would be assisting her soon. She continued to breathe, "hee-hee-hee-hee...," and stared straight ahead.

Her line of sight traveled straight out from her car, which was positioned fairly straight, facing the wrong way, in the far left southbound lane. With her peripheral vision, she could have seen the overturned car one hundred feet northwest of her—spirit willing. I watched her eyes closely. They were frozen in their trance-like stare. Her expression was one of intensity, not of any particular emotion, just severe. Her face was flush, her eyes wide but unfocused, her mouth pulled back tight in a frown barely moving with the panted exchange of air. Her panting mimicked a woman in labor, the rise and fall of her chest barely perceptible.

Toby interrupted my study as he handed me a thick gray woolen blanket. I tucked it around her torso and under her chin. I stepped back from the car and turned around facing south, where she had come from.

I tried to imagine both women's final images and thoughts prior to the crash. Someone with a protractor, measuring tape, and some mathematical formulas would figure out the speeds of the cars at time of impact by measuring skid marks, adulterations of pavement, debris, and vehicle damage. But most likely, both women saw the other approaching and had a couple seconds to think if not react to the inevitable crash.

Whatever action (or inaction) they took was either too slow or not dramatic enough since the vehicles appeared to have met precisely head-on. I got the feeling that the only thought experienced by the woman in the Galaxie was that of shock and terror as she froze with fear. Perhaps she simply slammed on the brakes, causing her vehicle to continue straight ahead in a lengthy skid prior to impact. Either way, I figured there was very little time to consider her life, family, relationships, or any kind of flashback of life's highlights. Probably just enough time for an "Oh my God!" before *lights out*.

As for the offending driver, her thoughts were more of a mystery. Did she plan on this suicidal course of action, or was it an accident, or the product of a disturbed mind? After all, her vehicle had produced no skid marks. If it was not an accident then she was directing the events and waiting for them to unfold as they did. Waiting, in effect, for an unwitting partner in her self-directed suicide. I wondered if one could be so set on a certain course of action that there would be no second thoughts as you accelerated into an oncoming car. Wouldn't it be normal or even reflexive to take your foot off the gas pedal or take evasive measures? One would have to possess the resolve of unquestioned certainty to continue to accelerate. Her fastened seat belt did not fit this scenario.

Toby and I haggardly changed out of our uniforms before we stumbled out of the police department into the adjacent parking lot. Too tired to fall back on cliché adages of what a shame it was and what should become of the mental driver, we walked into the parking lot in silence. We exchanged wearied head-nods and collapsed into our personal cars. We then turned our respective radios up to max volume and headed out for our respective homes.

Whether it was my state of complete exhaustion or my new-found defensive driving techniques that kept me under the posted speed limit for the first time in my life, I was not sure. I had never seen so much damage to a human body. I knew that without the shot of adrenaline I'd received when the call went out, I'd probably be falling asleep at the wheel and in danger of crossing the double yellows. Drivers on their hurried way to work glared at me as they accelerated past me. I could see one of the men mouth the word "idiot" and it reminded me of a George Carlin routine, in which all drivers were categorized as either "idiots" or "maniacs" based on their speed. Like a Grandma on a Sunday drive, hands at 2:00 and 10:00 o'clock, I continued on to my parents' house, where I'd been living while I saved for a down payment for a house of my own.

It was 0900 hours when I entered the kitchen—an hour and a half late in my mother's calculating worried mind. Being an accomplished natural worrier, my mother struggled to accept my chosen profession, which only served to immerse her further in paranoia. She knew something had caused my late return since I always arrived home directly after my shift, dead tired before making a beeline for the solace and solitude of my basement bedroom.

I sat down across from my mother on a kitchen stool and using my elbows as fulcrum I formed a chin rest with my cupped hands.

"What happened?" she asked, trying to just sound inquisitive.

"Got a call right at the end of shift," I mumbled between my hands. "Bad car accident."

She brought her hand to her mouth. "Oh, goodness." She was glad her son had not been in danger, but now needed the details. "What happened?"

"Some crazy lady drove a suicide mission wrong way on 35W. She ran into another woman on her way to work and guess who lost at chicken?"

"That's a terrible way to talk," she said. "You mean one of them died?"

I lay my head down on my arm that rested on the table, the adrenaline finally filtering its way out of my system. "The woman on her way to work died and—"

"Oh, that's terrible. Was it—bad?" she asked.

I spoke into my arm, flippantly. "Yeah, it was bad. They were on the freeway driving freeway speeds. What do you think?"

"Well, what did you do?" she asked.

"Nothing, I just—nothing." I lifted the anchor that was my head off the table and slid off the stool. "I gotta go to bed. I'll see you later."

"Okay," her voice pleaded sympathy. "Goodnight."

I crawled into bed followed by my white German Shepherd, who slept on my feet. I felt so completely exhausted, too tired to sleep. Pictures of the scene invaded my thoughts, stubbornly refusing to vacate. The scene progressed like a slide show: the wreckage of the crashed cars, the painted windshield, the woman's head, and her deformed broken jaw that framed her slack-jawed lifeless expression. Her compound fractures and the contrast manifested between skin, bone, tissue, and blood. The other woman's trance-like expression, her exposed knee-bones and musculature—her panting chant.

My dog was asleep. Her rhythmic breathing, frighteningly similar to the mental woman's panting, startled me back to the moment. I took a long breath, frustrated by my dog's facile entry to slumber as I struggled to relax. I thought of the relaxation exercises my rhetoric professor had taken us through. We first relaxed from the tips of our toes and continued to our eyebrows. Then we pictured a calm, quiet, serene scene that we were familiar with. We made our minds devoid of all other thoughts as we stared more deeply into the scene we pictured.

I attempted this technique, but unwanted, unauthorized scenes of violent soundless crashes and their resultant human carnage now visited all of my peaceful scenes.

My dog now snored. Though it hadn't worked for me, the relaxation exercise had somehow worked its way through me, and by osmosis filtered into her tiny, pea-sized brain. I tapped her gently with my foot until she stopped snoring. I opened my eyes and stared at the white-tiled ceiling. I said a prayer for the dead woman's family, and turned over.

Sleepwalkers

Thankfully for us old-timers, seniority and tradition will probably always play a part in patrol officers' shift picks. When I started working for the Police Department in 1982 our group of four rookies were told we would probably be forced to work dogwatch, the 2300 to 0700 hours shift for three to four years, before we would have the opportunity to join the mid-watch, 1500-2300 hours, and then probably five to seven years until a day-watch, 0700-1500 hours, might open up for us. We were ambivalent about this prediction since we had been told that most of the *real* police work happened on dogwatch anyway, that the mid-watch was mostly traffic enforcement and accident reports, and that day-watch was for pussies and old-timers planning out their retirement. Of course at the time, we didn't fully understand the toll dogwatch took on our lives.

There were advantages to working nights, though as I consider them now, they seem almost insignificant. At minimum, the summer evenings were cooler and the roads less congested. Stopping at semaphore traffic lights became optional after 0200 hours since the headlights of oncoming traffic telegraphed their approach from a great distance.

I found high ground during thunderstorms and sat back like a guest at a drive-in movie, watching the panoramic lightning shows that *normal* people slept through. Each night the shape of the moon was measured against that of the previous night, and an acknowledgement of another shimmering performance was given the stars. These celestial bodies provided most of the ambient light we had to work with; surprisingly, it was usually enough. Streetlights and the remnant light from late-night strip malls came into play to a much lesser extent.

I tried to leave one of my squad windows partially open during the shift to get a feel for the night. This nocturnal essence changed seasonally, and almost daily in the summers, with new weeds and flowers and their accompanying pollen, the newly mowed lawns and stagnant humidity. The brightness varied like an incremental, remote-controlled lightbulb, with the brightest nights seeming to coincide with the most cloudless, scentless, brisk winter evenings. The darkest nights were those accompanied by summer thunderstorms whose scent bore an ineffable redolence of seminal freshness.

With the bright winters came a bleakness and a crisp familiarity to the nights, whose biting cold wavered only slightly with the risen sun. Our uniform allowances afforded us the opportunity to buy an assortment of winter coats, wool sweaters, and insulated Gortex boots that kept us as warm and as comfortable as we could get, crammed into a Ford Crown Vic for eight hours.

The first nights back after days off were difficult adjustments. We worked a seven-days-on, three-days-off, seven-days-on, four-days-off, schedule. The few days off were barely long enough to reacquaint us with our families, not to mention a normal sleep pattern. The first night back burdened us with mental and physical fatigue as we worked through what would have been our next night of sleep. This cyclical adjustment provided for a constant, fluid source of bitching.

A couple of the guys said they continued their dogwatch sleep pattern into their days off. They stayed up all night and slept from 0800 hours to 1500 hours or so. Some put cardboard cutouts in their windows to get their rooms properly darkened, while others wore eye masks and earplugs. If their wives were stay-at-home moms, or had jobs that allowed them to sleep in occasionally, a conjugal opportunity arose. Divorce was common. The absurdity of this situation forced most officers to adjust their days off to those of their family.

There was a constant nagging feeling of incongruence as I drove my squad past all the darkened houses. My body reminded me with weighted eyelids that I too should have been sleeping, but I was working. Lovers spooned in funky blissful slumber as the winter winds blew curled troughs of snow across the flat, vacant streets. The nocturnal mammals, mostly raccoons and deer, ignored us for the most part, coming and going to and from their homes in the Minnesota River Valley that surrounded the south and eastern borders of the city. As far as they were concerned, we usually filled in for the Grim Reaper. After being struck and immobilized by a car, the next and last thing they'd see was one of us leveling a shotgun at them. *Greetings from the police department—Boom!*

Everything toward the end of the shift had a soporific effect, from the sun rising, blinding our already beleaguered eyes, to the annoying alacrity of the morning disc jockeys. Everything tempted us toward the overdue comfort of our beds. As the sun rose and traffic picked up, I felt the light-headedness of exhaustion, and though the commuters sipped from their coffee mugs in an attempt to wake up, I allowed for my wearied body to begin its process of shutting down. Some of the guys could drink coffee up until the end of their shift, drive home, jump in bed, and pass out. The caffeine wouldn't allow me that light-switch sleep capacity, so I stayed away from it after midnight.

Not only could I not drink coffee before sleep, I couldn't just drive home after a shift and jump directly into bed. I needed to unwind. Jogging a couple miles or reading a good book would have been suitable avenues for this wind down, except I felt too wrung out for such inspired ventures. Instead, I'd switch on the tube, grab a beer, and watch some *Donahue*. His guests seemed like they'd just walked off my shift and onto his show. Alcoholics, domestic abusers and their victims, child abusers and their victims, drug abusers, pregnant teens and their mothers, etc., etc. And Phil seemed so concerned. He had that furrowed brow when the atrocity was laid out for all to consider. Then he'd ask them why they didn't just—do whatever the obvious fix was to remedy the problem. This question caused his guests to slowly tear up and finally capitulate in a sobbing catharsis how this particular weakness was the result of some other abuse they'd experienced as a child. Phil would then shake his head and throw out his hands in mock empathy, exasperation, and wonderment. But we knew Phil could take it. We saw through his TV pain, and knew that with Marlo Thomas waiting for him at their LA mansion, he'd endure the atrocities he'd been forced to confront, and somehow abide with the inevitable sadness his guests were forced to live out —day after day after miserable day. This was good sleeping material and, after about a half hour of Phil, I was halfway to dreamland.

Some of my fellow howlers recorded all the cop shows and watched them as their preamble to naptime. The shift seemed about equally split on the cop show mentality. Once I became a cop I had no desire ever to watch a cop show again, and in all honesty I've never seen a segment of *Homicide, NYPD, Third Shift*, or the host of others I've heard mentioned by cops who discussed these series like they were discussing a personal experience. I still enjoyed taking in a good cop flick at the theater, like *Seven*, but I quickly realized that reality took a back seat to action. I also enjoyed reading good crime stories, fiction and nonfiction, like Wambaugh wrote, but the days of cheering on Starsky and Hutch had ended. Police work just wasn't that exhilarating or glamorous, nor was it such a one-sided victory. People got hurt on both sides, and it was very rarely glorious, but there was camaraderie.

Historians, like the Vietnam vets I've spoken to, contend that most soldiers who fought that war didn't end up fighting for honor, glory, God, or country, as many had initially sought out to do. After all the protests and flag burnings and hurled insults and goobers, the soldiers ended up fighting for one another. Their diving on a grenade was motivated by a sense of undying, unselfish loyalty and friendship. That's the same mentality of a well-gelled shift of cops, and the dogwatch cops tended to jell better than the others—mainly because they experienced more danger and weirdness together. When you heard the unmistakable change in the timbre of your partner's voice as he requested backup at his location, you knew he needed help right now, and you put your foot all the way down on the gas.

As dogwatchers, we were outsiders, both departmentally and publicly. There was a stigma attached to a person who would sacrifice his or her personal life to push a squad around in the dark and encounter the trauma of life firsthand. We were ostracized by our non-cop friends, who thought we were nuts for working this shift. These friendships, once gone, were difficult to restore, and few of us were interested in maintaining them at the cost of providing the entertainment via anecdotes about the strangest shit we'd encountered our last working weekend. Even among the other cops, the dogwatch was separate, mostly made up of the new guys with a sprinkling of veteran officers who still enjoyed mixing it up a little.

These veteran dogwatchers were usually a tad eccentric; having the opportunity to pick other shifts they chose instead to remain with the dogwatch on a semi-permanent basis. Officer Charles Brown was one such officer, working only dogwatch for years at a time. He spoke Joe Friday monotone and wrote his near-perfect reports as though they were computer generated. Though he possessed a heart of gold, he saw the world through glasses that separated police and their ilk from everyone else, and didn't much care to associate with the everyone-else crowd. Police work was his life—dogwatch. Rocky earned his nickname as a longtime dogwatch sergeant, difficult to sway once he'd made up his mind. A tough, stubborn ex-Marine, who would stand toe-to-toe with anyone. Whether or not his confidence was a facade, his eyes reflected only the stubborn self-assurance of someone who would not be intimidated. Then there was Big Tim and Little Tim. The larger of the two was a retirement-aged, small-town-minded cop in a city that had outgrown him. His small-townness endeared him to the older citizens who remembered the city as he did, when it was open farmland. Little Tim was smaller than his larger namesake, but at 6' 4", 250 pounds, his name was still a bit of a contradiction. He spoke of too much exposure to Agent Orange in Vietnam, and he struggled with Hodgkin's disease. His mind slipped away from him in the darkness of the shift, and he was forced to resign. These veterans, and others, set an example for the rookies—not always the right one—but with experience as their guide.

This ass-backward lifestyle of a dogwatcher allowed for more humor on the job and wilder parties. The extreme intensity of the shift was matched by an equally extreme unwinding—or maybe unraveling—at our after-shift parties. I never imagined partying at 0700 hours, but it was really the only possible time while working that shift. I had a Long Island Tea Party on a hot summer morning after dogwatch that drew the entire shift of about fifteen officers. I bought one half gallon each of rum, vodka, and whiskey and tipped them into the cocktail mixture. At about 1000 hours the punch bowl was empty and my German Shepherd was tripping through the house wearing someone's uniform shirt. My Great Dane was retrieving wooden kitchen utensils from my neighbors' yards as intoxicated police officers fired them off my back step as far as they could. I awoke at 1200 hours to a retirement-age cop standing beside my waterbed, making waves with his arms, in an attempt to make me seasick.

My girlfriend at the time, later to become my first ex-wife, rushed home in a panic after I'd called her at about 1230 hours. She said I was speaking only in French and had an element of urgency in my voice. I had no memory of calling her, but my freshman French teacher, who prognosticated that I would never speak his native tongue, would have been proud.

Later that same night, this motley group of partiers assembled for dogwatch with hangovers unparalleled. The sergeant giving roll call prayed for a slow night, as the malodorous breath of the platoon mimicked a busy day's intake at detox. My friend Officer Bishop pulled over a car early in the shift for repeatedly driving over the yellow line. He suspected DWI or at minimum DWHUA (driving with head up ass) and so ordered the driver out to put him through the battery of field sobriety tests. He thought he'd skip the more complicated tests like the ABCs and the standing on one foot, since he knew his hangover precluded any convoluted demonstrations or exertions, physical or mental. He decided instead to go right to the "walk the straight line" test. We had all demonstrated these tests to hundreds of drunks and so were quite confident in our own ability to perform them. After all, if a sober, uniformed police officer could not demonstrate these supposedly simple tests, how could a normal everyday citizen be expected to perform them?

Bish first explained the test, directing the subject to walk a straight line, in heel to toe manner for ten steps, then pivot, turn around, and walk back to him in the identical pattern. Following the verbal directions was, of course, part of the test. With the intrepid temerity of a dedicated police officer nursing a throbbing hangover, Bish told the man he would demonstrate exactly how he wanted him to perform this test.

In order to make the test appear simple, most cops relaxed their hands at their thighs rather than holding them straight out to the side like a tight-rope walker, since that made the test appear not only difficult but almost dangerous. Bish started to walk, attempting with a certain nonchalant élan to keep his hands at his sides, but quickly threw them straight out as he found that he was not only unable to walk the straight line without the stabilizing effect of his outstretched arms, he could barely walk at all. He staggered across the pavement with his head pounding a discordant rhythm as he nearly fell with each pained step. The driver looked at him in beguiled wonderment as Bish stared down at his feet, prayerfully willing them into proper alignment. Just when he sensed a ray of hope for completing the demo without puking or falling down, he walked into a *No Left Turn* street sign that took a pretty good gash out of his forehead. The driver rushed forward and asked if he was all right. Bish, whose head was now hungover, dizzy, and throbbing, as it bled freely down the side of his face, told the driver he was just fine and advised him to get back in his car and continue on his way.

The street sergeant did not allow any sick time that night since he'd heard about the party, but the radio stayed mercifully quiet after Bish's near-death experience with the nefarious road sign.

Hotels and convenience stores became our late-night sanctuaries. The night clerks in these establishments became the nocturnal siblings with whom we developed symbiotic relationships. Most of the all-night convenience stores offered cops free coffee and fountain drinks. Any kind of freebie offered to cops guaranteed a contingent of them congregating at that location. I'm not saying cops are cheap, just really, really frugal. After all, everyone likes a freebie. Squad cars, parked outside the establishment, ensured the safety of the clerk, so everyone was happy.

I remember driving eastbound down 98th Street approaching France Avenue where the four-lane road declined gradually as it wound gently back and forth past the dark majestic oaks that surrounded Normandale College. It was 0300 hours and I was making a conscious attempt to battle the considerable weights on my eyelids. As they started to close I physically forced them open, using my thumb and index fingers as pincers. We knew these "main drag" streets so well we could *nearly* pilot our squads down them in our sleep. As my squad's tires jolted against the curb I awoke, startled and alarmed that I'd actually fallen asleep at the wheel. I reflexively slammed on the brakes and, after a few deep breaths, came to the realization that I could not stave off the overwhelming forces of slumber playing tug of war with my consciousness. I needed to pull over to gather some steam. After gathering my composure, I drove 20 mph to the Pik-Quik at 90th and Penn with the radio blaring heavy metal. I stumbled into the store and thumbed through a couple magazines as Terri, the night clerk, told me about her younger years growing up in Iowa. Very few topics involving Iowa can be described as riveting and this was no exception, but I left the store a half hour later with new purpose in my step—it was now time for my lunch (breakfast really) break.

Breaking the shift into palatable increments was SOP for most dogwatchers: answer some calls, run some traffic, visit the hotel or convenience store of your choice, and then repeat until breakfast break. At 0400 hours, after my break, I sometimes met with Minnesota State Trooper Anna Tucker and we ran radar together from a church parking lot on 98th Street. This combined multi-jurisdictional traffic enforcement taskforce approach consisted of us positioning our squads side by side, so we could monitor one another's radios and alert the *resting* officer when he/she was dispatched to a call. This was a contingency for emergency drowsiness only and was rarely used. Usually we would just park and chat. Our radars were technically running, but there was only sporadic traffic, and our attitudes and energy levels were such that our effort was something less than diligent. Driving down a speeder at that point could be downright dangerous, not to mention futile, irrelevant, and inane.

Most relationships between young dogwatch cops and their wives, girlfriends, and significant others were challenged by the crazy hours that limited contact, and also by the changes the darkness of the shift brought on, and its sometimes devastating effect on their loved one. I took part in a motorcycle chase that ended when the young rider slid off the road and crashed his bike into the Clark's Submarine Sandwich shop. His leg broke on impact with the mostly brick building, his femur protruding from his thigh like the ivory tusk of an elephant, as he writhed in the pre-shock agony of frayed nerve endings. Later that morning, I stood dumbly reticent, avoiding eye contact like a child before the school principal, as my fiancée asked if anything interesting had happened on the shift.

There was an ambivalence felt by most officers that kept them on this shift, but with a price. Behind the loyalty, brotherhood, and pure comedy that could never be replicated by any other profession, we walked in the shadow of constant darkness.

For too many dogwatchers, so much time on this shift seemed to beg for an overly cynical, hastily burned-out officer who ultimately ran for the exit marked *early retirement*. There were no Disney endings to any of the stories played out on the shift. The domestic assaulters were arrested and conditionally released—forbidden to see their victim spouses until after court, which could be months away. Rollie, the crippled, chronic drunk continued to spot us as he limped through the liquor store lot and give us his familiar greeting, either by hand signal or verbally, delivered with due passion, "Fug-eyu, pigch!" The drunk drivers were released to a responsible adult after they'd sobered up the following morning. The assault victims lay on hospital beds in the ER, their stitches starting to itch and ache as the booze and the *real* anesthetic wore off. The children who'd been beaten or sexually abused by their "loved ones" were placed in shelters until the investigation was completed. The used-up ticket books were replaced with new ones, and the squad cars were gassed up for the next shift.

Julie Andrews would not turn circles in the verdant, sun-nourished bosom of the Alps and grow intoxicated with "the sound of music." There would be no young love blossoming "on the street where you lived," and no young orphaned pauper boys would be united with their rich, loving great-uncles. There was only bad news, earthy manure shovelsful. Each night brought more of it, a busy night bombarded the young officers with it, while slower nights provided only a glimpse, a drizzle to remind the young officers of the downpour they could expect the following night—and the night after that. Swimming against this current of misery could be so taxing, that when the young rookie officer's blissfully ignorant in-laws asked him how he liked his new job, he hesitated in solemn assessment before he replied simply, "It's okay, I guess."

Creepy Crawlers

My hand-held radio interrupted my daydream as I stood behind the counter at Winchell's Doughnut shop, looking hard at a maple-covered bear claw, considering saturated fat and mortality. The dispatcher was sending me to transport a hooker who'd been arrested by undercovers in a prostitution sting at a local hotel. Knowing next to nothing about prostitution, I allowed what meager confidence I had to dissipate as a dash of anxiety started brewing an unhealthy concoction in my gut.

An SIU (Special Investigations Unit) detective I'd never met answered my knock on the hotel door and greeted me with a roll of his eyes, signaling either his apology for getting me involved, his exhaustion or boredom, or more likely still, his low opinion of the woman seated in handcuffs on the bed. I responded with a head-nod signaling that whatever he meant, I was right there with him.

She was probably about my age, wearing a dark print dress and spiked heels. Though she was not crying now, her Tammy Faye Bakker eyes revealed that she had been before I arrived, but even on her best day she would not have been described as particularly attractive. She was anorexic thin with short, slept-on brown hair and scraggly quarter-inch wispy gray hairs growing from her chin. Other than the streaking wet mascara, she appeared to wear no makeup on her blemished skeletal face. The vice detectives working the detail that night described her as a typical *crack-whore*.

She did not fuss when I exchanged my handcuffs for the detective's, only asked that I apply them a little looser. The arresting detective assured me that his report was forthcoming and asked me if I would be so kind as to book her at the PD. Though I'd only booked a few arrestees since I'd been on my own, I was fairly comfortable with the process.

I walked her out of the hotel to the stares and questioning glances of hotel guests milling about the hallways and foyer. They knew what she'd been arrested for by looking at her, and were now considering whether they should delete a couple of the stars from the description of the hotel, which happened to be one of the city's finest. Since modern prostitution is accomplished by phoning call-out services, the quality of the hotel is often irrelevant. There is usually an alternate door to enter or an attached bar that circumvents security, making it next to impossible to weed out all the call-out prostitutes.

While transporting my prisoner to the Police Department her self pity turned outward to anger, and she started a barrage of questions that were really more affirmations coming to her as time and hostility filtered the cocaine from her system.

"That guy can't do that!" she offered self-righteously from the back seat.

"What?"

"He can't do that. He's a cop isn't he?"

I didn't really want to get in the middle of anything here, and other than knowing that the detective was in fact a cop, I was afraid I was probably the wrong person to give her legal advice. "You mean the guy that arrested you?"

She nodded her head.

"Yeah, he's a cop."

"Well, he can't just—," she trailed off, shaking her head.

"Hey, I don't really know what happened, but he can arrest you if you offer him sex for money."

"No shit," she said sarcastically. "But he's supposed to just arrest me after I tell him how much it—my services—cost, right?"

"Yeah, I guess."

"That prick made me swallow before he arrested me," she said indignantly.

At this point I acted like I was really concentrating on my driving or the song on the radio or anything else, since I had no idea what to say next. I thought she was probably right and that I would probably end up in court having to repeat her accusation.

"He can't come in my mouth and then arrest me! I know he can't do that. He either has to arrest me for offering, or pay for services rendered, but he can't do both. Shit, I had to blow him. I didn't get paid, and now I'm on my way to jail for doing it. That ain't right." She looked at me for support.

"You know," I started, "you and him are probably the only ones who really know what happened in there. I'm sure there's an explanation for what happened."

"Yeah, he wanted to get off is the explanation. Who do you think the judge is going to believe, him or me?"

Once at the office, I took her picture and fingerprinted her. She was dirty and she had bad body odor like she hadn't bathed for weeks; her breath was equally malodorous. I ran her criminal history and saw that she'd had two priors for prostitution and another misdemeanor conviction for theft. She was right about whom the judge was going to believe.

As I filled out her booking sheet she told me she was 5' 5", 94 pounds. More out of curiosity than concern I commented, "Fighting the crack monkey, eh?"

She turned away from me, possibly embittered by my cavalier presumption of her addiction.

"It's gotta be tough," I said, feigning compassion.

"Is that what the boys say after they come in my mouth?"

I took her shoes and locked her in a cell. I'd inventoried her cash. She had only two hundred dollars and her bail was a thousand, so she would most likely be spending the night.

After closing the cell door I walked into the restroom and urinated. I then washed my hands. Days later I would wish that I had washed my hands before I urinated and then washed them again after—with something really strong. A shower would have been even better.

It was probably only a couple days later that the itching started. Some guys are grabbing their crotch constantly, groping, grabbing, arranging, itching, and rolling their marbles as though they had a mouse in their undies. I'm not one of those guys, but suddenly I couldn't stop itching myself. I really had no idea why my crotch would itch since I had never experienced this. I'd seen an advertisement on TV for a condition similar to athlete's foot called Jock Itch. I decided I would try their product since this must be my affliction.

After several applications I was itching worse than ever. It was all I could do to sit in my squad car and drive without grinding my fingertips into my pubic area to scratch. My wife noticed my newfound near-constant daily grind and remarked that, unless I had become suddenly taken by my own equipment, I should go to the doctor. It seemed like a silly thing to go to the doctor for, but this itching had to stop. I once had itchy hives covering my entire body in large beet-red blotches that stuck out like the landmasses on a topographical world map. My doctor could not give me a reason for the malady, but he was finally able to clear them up completely with a large dose of Prednisone. Maybe this groin itching was the precursor to the hives.

My doctor had me lower my drawers as he began to check my pubic area with a magnifying glass type instrument. It didn't take long before he set the instrument down and looked over his glasses at me like a father might do after catching his young son, nose deep in a smut magazine.

"Are you married?" he asked.

"Yes."

"Is your wife itching as well?"

"No," I replied. "What is it?"

"It's crabs," the doctor said, with a note of disappointment in his voice.

"Crabs!" I said. "That can't be."

"Oh, it's crabs all right," he said, washing his hands with an overly generous amount of liquid antiseptic soap.

"I thought you could only get crabs by having sex with someone who had them."

"Yep, that's right," he said, almost accusingly. "Who else have you had sex with in the last couple weeks?"

"Nobody," I said, a little self-righteously. "No one except my wife."

The doctor raised his eyebrows. "And what about her?"

"What about her what?" I said, defensively.

"Listen," he said, "I'm not making any accusations. I'm just trying to get to the bottom of this. Is there a chance she could have had sexual contact with someone else?"

"Absolutely not," I said, confidently.

"Okay," he said, in singsong disbelief. "But I'll need to see her. It doesn't do any good to treat one of you, if you've both got them."

"She's just down in the mall. I can go get her if you can get to her this morning."

"Just bring her in straightaway, and I'll see her after my next patient."

"Okay," I said, zipping up, and feeling suddenly disgusted with myself. "Thanks, I guess," I mumbled uncomfortably.

My wife was in Walgreen's busily rummaging through greeting cards when I saw her from the store entryway. I started making my way toward her but then slowed down to rehearse what I might say to her. I came to the conclusion that regardless of what I might say to her, my friendly doctor would be quite blunt, so I decided to do the same.

"Honey?" I said, as I sidled up beside her.

She smiled her acknowledgement as she looked up from the birthday card she was holding.

"I love you," I said.

Her expression changed from smile to confusion.

I whispered in her ear. "The doctor says I have crabs."

She emitted that gasping inhalation that one usually reserves for the scary scene in a horror movie. "What?" she said, louder than I would have hoped.

"He wants to look at you now," I said.

She looked me up and down like I might be an alien posing as her husband. "He wants to look at my what?"

"Well, what do you think?" I said, regretting my smart-ass comment as it passed my lips.

"Do you have something you need to tell me?"

I noticed that the woman standing beside her, acting like she was reading birthday cards, was actually following our conversation. I pulled my wife toward the door. "I swear to you, I have nothing to tell you."

"That doesn't really answer my question."

"You know I have not had sex with anyone but you," I said, with as much conviction as I could muster. She looked deep into my eyes like I imagined a fortuneteller might, and then said none too happily, "All right, let's get this over with."

The doctor called me back into his office after he finished my wife's exam. He told me he couldn't find any crabs on her but suggested that we both take the topical medication just to be sure. He struggled to make eye contact with me as he spoke. I knew he didn't believe me, but it seemed pointless to argue with him.

"Do either of you have any questions?" he asked, as my wife got down from the examining table.

My wife broke the silence. "Is there any other way you can get these other than through sex with somebody."

"No," he said. "That's the only way you get them." He went into some more detail about the life and times of the crab, as I thought of nasty ways to make his murder look like an accident, but nothing he said was going to help my wife understand how I—but not her—had contracted crabs.

My wife was quiet on the ride home, as I drove pensively trying to figure out both how I contracted these disgusting insects and how I was going to convince my wife I was telling the truth when the doctor was trying to convince her otherwise. I don't know if I'd have ever figured it out if my wife hadn't asked me innocently, "Have you gotten into anything at work where you could have gotten them?"

The moment she said it I remembered the dirty crack whore I'd booked, and I reminded my wife about her. She remembered me telling her about it after I'd booked her. We were convinced that I acquired the creepy crawlers from her. My wife never really doubted me, and I give her a lot of credit for that. If the crabs had been on the other foot... Several years after this incident cops started wearing rubber gloves to fingerprint all suspects as a matter of routine prophylaxis.

It occurred to me that my dirty little crack-whore friend could probably have proved her case against the overly dedicated, above and beyond the call of duty SIU detective with the big testosterone gland, if his medical records showed a visit to the doctor, or at least the pharmacist, for the topical lotion used to delouse one's groin after contact with a crab-infested prostitute. I had a difficult time imagining any man allowing this woman to touch him, much less perform any kind of intimate contact with him. I figured that if her assertion were true, the SIU detective must have met his Waterloo when he and his wife started itching. Perhaps he borrowed my truthful excuse to explain his itch. I could never have looked in my wife's eyes and convinced her if I'd been lying. I'm surprised she bought it as it was.

(Sing to the tune of "Jimmy Crack Corn")
Dirty crack whore and I don't care,
Dirty crack whore and I don't care,
Dirty Crack whore and I don't care,
My crabs have gone away.

Reveille

This story is a composite of several medical emergencies.

At 0500 hours on a frigid January morning there weren't a lot
of options for rookie patrolmen like John and me. We'd put
the drunks to bed hours ago and checked the businesses in our
respective areas to make sure they were locked up and had no
occupied 10-37s (suspicious occupied vehicles) in their parking lots. You can only drive around in circles so many times
before the anvils on your eyelids triumph and you're jerked
awake as your squad bounces off a curb. The temptation to
capitulate and allow your eyelids to meet is akin to nabbing
that forbidden apple from that special tree in that really nice
garden. You have a choice at that point: find a hiding place and
give in to the dark side, or find another cop and keep one
another awake.

I found John that morning and, luckily for me, he still had
a speck of life left in him. We met in a church parking lot and
positioned our squads as close together as possible without

knocking our side-view mirrors off. We then turned the heat up to max, and rolled our windows halfway down so we could chat. Our driving force at the age of twenty-four, and the stimulant that kept us awake, was, of course, testosterone. Men generally choose one of three or four strategic areas of the female anatomy to obsess about, and John was a self-proclaimed "leg man." I believe from his exhaustive anatomical analysis of the area that the buttocks were included in this obsession as an extension of the legs. It didn't matter to me what he talked about, as long as he talked, since it kept me awake.

He first listed his current amorous candidates, followed by the progress he'd made with each. Of the listed *victims* I knew only one, who worked as a paramedic in the area. Her name was Janet and she was about three years older than John. He was actively stalking her, but had not yet made his move.

While John was a gifted raconteur and I enjoyed his company his saga was having the same effect on me as a bedtime story has on a child. As I started to nod off, his voice inflections signaled some kind of epiphany to the epic he was unfolding. I felt I should have been more attentive, maybe even supportive. After all, he was doing *me* a favor. I'm sure I reciprocated, in weaker moments, with my own "love gone bad" stories of woe, a *tit for tat,* so to speak. I like to think that my stories would have been delivered with merciful brevity and lacking intimate detail but, at twenty-four—I doubt it. As he approached this cathartic moment I was spared the finale when a warning tone on our police radios signaled an emergency call. A man of action, John shrugged off the interruption and turned up his radio.

The dispatcher was sending us on a "possible heart attack" medical. The combined effect of the adrenaline rush from the call and the discordant cacophony of the sirens rendered us wide awake. Our squads screeched out of the parking lot then zipped over an ice patch as we found traction and raced toward the address.

The squad's emergency lights reflected off the hood of my Ford Crown Victoria in the subdued pre-dawn. The sparse early morning traffic pulled over in response to the squads' lights and siren. This deference to the emergency lights and siren was in stark contrast to rush-hour traffic, which typically continued forward like automatons, oblivious to the sirens.

Paramedic partners Janet and Terry received the same call but, coming from another city, were traveling a far greater distance to the victim's residence. It was common for squads to arrive at medical emergencies prior to the ambulance crew.

In an attempt to confirm the address, I shined my spotlight at the house with its front light on. As I did, the door opened and an arm protruded, waving us in. Our actions were all autopilot from this point. We switched the sirens off, turned the lights to wig-wag so the ambulance would find the house, hit the trunk buttons, and exited squads. We each grabbed our oxygen tanks and medical kits from the trunks and headed cautiously up the icy drive to the front door.

Even before I entered the house I knew the layout of this "10-40 rambler." There are hundreds of these houses on the east side of the city, all built in the fifties, all with 1,040 square feet on the main floor, the same ridiculous floor plan that utilized one room as both bedroom and hallway. Depending on the extent of updating, most of these homes had the same color appliances, counter tops, and linoleum floors.

An old woman wearing a long yellow nightgown pushed the storm door open and turned toward the hallway without looking at us. We knew where the master bedroom was, and followed her.

"Hurry," she panted, "he's in here."

She led us into the bedroom, which smelled of night breath, urine, and stale body odor. We'd been on the same call, and smelled the same odors, at least a dozen times in our first year. Her husband lay face down on the bed. I knew he was dead. John knew he was dead, and so did the old woman, but we would play the game to its conclusion. I pushed on the placid tube of his carotid artery to check for a pulse I knew would be absent. His body had retained its normal body temperature from the bedding, which still covered him, and the warmth his wife provided when she slept beside him. A sense of urgency remained since there was no way to gauge how long his heart had been static. I prepared the first oxygen tank as John solicited the victim's vital medical history from the woman.

"When did you notice him like this?" he asked.

"Oh, just a couple minutes ago when I went to the bathroom. He usually—"

"We need to get him on the floor," I said.

"Oh, is he—?" she muffled her words with her hand as she covered her mouth.

"We'll do what we can, ma'am," I said, speaking for the others who were not yet present. I grabbed the old man's shoulders as John grabbed his feet and we dragged him off the side of the bed. He was heavier than a live victim. His "dead weight" tumbled to the floor like a heavy, but clumsy, densely packed canvas bag. I'd left my coat in the squad but John had worn his into the house, which had become warm, stuffy, and malodorous. He quickly jerked it off and threw it in a heap on the floor as the crotch of the old man's light blue cotton pajamas darkened, the jarring drop to the floor having released his bladder. His wife noticed the broadening wet spot and moaned, helplessly embarrassed. I hooked up the positive pressure facemask to the oxygen tank and turned the valve to maximum liter flow.

John knelt down on the opposite side of the old man and winced as his knees settled into the newly formed puddle of warm urine. He readjusted his position in a futile effort to somehow turn back time so his knees would land in a dry spot instead, and his pants would remain unsoiled. He glanced at me with a "thanks a lot, partner" expression and positioned the face mask over the old man. He waited for me to finish a set of five compressions before he ventilated. I could feel the old man's ribs crack as I pressed down on his sternum with the heel of my hand. There was nothing I could do about it. These broken ribs would make for a very painful recovery if we revived him, but that seemed doubtful.

As John pushed the positive pressure ventilation button on the outside of the mask, the oxygen was forced into the victim's mouth, and hopefully followed the normal path to the lungs. Sometimes the forced air over-filled the lungs, with the overflow oxygen entering the stomach. Oftentimes the trachea was blocked so the air went directly into the stomach rather than the lungs. The squads didn't carry the better airway apparatus the medics had, and we often struggled with this dilemma. Inflating the stomach of an unconscious victim with air caused them to vomit nearly every time. This was no exception. As John ventilated the old man, he vomited into the mask with such force that the vomitus shot out the side of the mask into John's face and hair.

The old woman moaned again and turned away from us. John groaned and glared at me wearing an angry, but pathetic "why me?" expression. I truly pitied him and wished he could have been spared these inglorious acts, but I could not, in all honesty, say that I would switch places with him.

The medics, Terry and Janet, entered the bedroom unnoticed, having left their stretcher in the hallway. John wiped vomitus from his face between ventilations. This action was partly reflex and partly a narcissist's attempt to pretty himself for Janet, about whom he had made no secret of having what we called *impure thoughts.* He realized this "vomit face" motif might be a turn-off. He was able to remove most of it from his face, but the speckles on the tips of his short spiked hair remained. Upon seeing him, Janet noticed the new look and appeared to be fighting back a smile, having experienced the same or some variation, as all medics had at some point. She collected the old man's medications from his wife as Terry prepared the hand-held defibulators. He ordered us to stop CPR and move clear of the victim as he sent the electrical current through the victim's static body. The old man's body jerked up, magnified to the paddles as the current rode through his chest.

Terry studied the portable EKG screen. "Nothing. Let's do it again."

Terry lit him up four or five times and we resumed CPR between each failed effort. Janet and the old woman were standing near the doorway, talking, when the first oxygen container ran out. John held the mask away from the old man's mouth and pressed the button, which emitted only a whisper of escaping O_2. "This one's a goner," he loudly exclaimed.

The old woman wailed as she overheard John's *goner* remark, assuming he referred to her husband. Janet gave John a reproachful glare that included the implicit message that there would be no impure extracurriculars for someone so unrefined and lacking in compassion. John looked up innocently, first at Janet, then at Terry and me. By now we were biting our lips as we continued our wasted efforts to revive the old man.

"I mean the oxygen is a goner," he woefully insisted, but the damage was done.

Janet made contact with an E.R. doctor by phone. After hearing the details of our rescue efforts he gave us permission to stop resuscitation. Her next call, the last one, was to the medical examiner, whose investigators would respond to the rambler in their black Chevy Suburban, a harbinger of the last ride the old man would take in a hearse, which would drop him off post-funeral at what JT, my training officer, referred to as "Skeleton Park."

John and the paramedics escorted the old woman out of the bedroom and into the living room where they awaited the M.E. I remained in the bedroom with the dead guy. I studied his condition, with the airway protruding from his mouth, the EKG leads stuck to his torso, the soiled PJs, and the vomit caked to the side of his face. This image made it easy to reconfirm my desire to die in peace, if there was such a thing. Call it unassisted death. I did not want a troupe of young medical professionals playing "hot-box" against God or the devil with my soul. Sure, they could save me now while I'm young and in the game, but when I'm just "waiting for the spade," as my grandpa used to say, let me go. Show me where to sign up for the DNR (do not resuscitate) program.

After the M.E. arrived, we packed up all our death postponement contrivances and headed out. The M.E. decided to release the body to Gills Bros. Funeral Home and agreed to transport the corpse there since Gills was nearby. John made every possible attempt to amend the damage he'd done with Janet, including a feeble endeavor to explain the "goner" misunderstanding, pushing the stretcher out to the rig for her, and expressing, in Janet's presence, his deepest condolences to the old woman. As usual, the disinterested bystanders, Terry and I in this case, could see the futility of it. Just the image of him in his navy-blue polyester uniform pants with the darkened knee spots, and his vomit-sprinkled hair, was too much. Even

without the "goner" comment, we knew Janet had crossed herself off his list of "stalkables."

As he tagged along beside her on the way to the ambulance, her eyes vacillated from the rig to the rising sun, to her
partner's knowing grin, to just about anything but John's sincere hang-dog expression as he played his final card of small
talk. After she locked the stretcher in the rig and slammed the
back doors shut, she climbed into the passenger seat and closed
the door in John's pleading face. She had another cigarette lit
before Terry could log out the call and radio in that they were
now clear.

As the medics drove out of the shadows and into the light
of the virgin sunrise, John held his ground, which moments
before shared the weight of the object of his lust. He turned
toward me now and stood pensively silent.

"You've still got dead-guy puke in your hair, you know?"

"Yeah, I can feel it," he said. "I just don't want to touch it."
He finally vacated the prized shrine of pavement his feet occupied and walked toward his squad. "I need a shower."

"Make it a cold one."

"Ha-ha."

I pulled the squad back out onto the street and glanced
back toward the house to see the old woman peeking out the
window. I knew her grief was immeasurable. I hoped her faith
could sustain her as I fired up the squad's heater and headed in
to the office for a new tank of oxygen.

Special Weapons and Beer

Laying on the grass, behind the cover of a large oak tree, I had time to consider just how badly I had wanted to be here, actively involved in "the big call." I directed the muzzle of my Remington 870 shotgun toward the Blue Chevette, occupied by a disturbed lone male adult, two driveways down. By now the two toddler occupants of the house, whose front yard I lay in, had grown bored with the camouflaged cop laying in their front yard and had stopped pounding on the window, smiling, and waving at me.

The Bloomington, Minnesota, SWAT team became operational in 1983. An opening on the team one year later prompted an interoffice memo inviting officers with three-years-plus experience to apply and try out for the team. Candidates needed to pass a PT test, along with an oral interview and a practical exercise.

In my mind, SWAT was the pinnacle of police training, tactics, and, above all, experience, since the SWAT guys got to handle the big jobs. I wanted to apply for the position so badly, I could picture myself in the green cammies, toting an M-16, and wearing a very rough expression—some combination of confidence and callousness. Such an expression would need to be practiced but I had time. Unfortunately, I was six months shy of the mandatory three-years experience. I told the team leader of my interest and my deficient time on the job, and he remarked that I should put in anyway. He said that by the time all the testing and interviews were finished, I'd be nearing the requisite time. I did put in and, much to my surprise, I was chosen to join the team. I was then scheduled, along with two standing team members, to attend the weeklong FBI-sponsored SWAT School.

The inaugural group of BPD SWATs had already attended the school. They told us to expect some rappelling, shooting, gas deployment, team-building exercises, and plenty of PT (physical training) for the first couple days. This was exciting for me. Man stuff—automatic rifles, rappelling from tall buildings, breaking glass, gusto, angst—a cornucopia of testosterone-fueled events. I was ready to go. The team leader of the FBI SWAT team, Bill Tanenger, was conducting the PT and team building aspects of the program. (Tanenger would go on to retire from the FBI, become the Chief of Police in Champlin, MN, then be appointed director of the DNR by then governor, Jesse Ventura, and, as of this writing, be appointed Federal Marshall of the Minnesota/Dakotas area by President George W. Bush.) Anticipating the PT, I started a regiment of calisthenics, stretching, and short distance runs. I had never been a distance runner, but thought I would at least prepare myself for the expected medium distances. The first day of school, we ran six miles at a county park. Every aspect of PT and the practical exercises was conducted as a team. The team ran only as fast as its slowest member. I was that member. There were probably ten different agencies represented at this school, and no one wanted their team to finish the run in last place, so we all pushed it. Six miles might as well have been a marathon for me. Tanenger noted our exhaustion and promised a mercifully shorter run the following day. I awoke the next morning with huge blisters on both my feet, and the reawakening of my hibernating shin splints.

Our second day of PT started with another run, but we hung on to Tanenger's promise of a shorter run, maybe a couple miles. I had popped my blisters and applied a product called New Skin, which was like a liquid Band-Aid that promised to dry and resist peeling off like its more traditional predecessor. It didn't work. We ran eight miles that day, which marked personal records for both the farthest I had ever run and the greatest number of expletives uttered in one day.

Mercifully, only the first two days of the weeklong training included PT. Our remaining days were directed more toward SWAT-related skills training. I wasn't sure how I'd feel about rappelling. I probably had the same logical fear of heights that most rational people have. If you fall from a great distance and land on a hard surface—like the ground—your body breaks up and splatters much as a watermelon does. This outcome is discouraged in rappelling, and yet, the full color mind-picture of the aftermath of your fall remains vivid as you reluctantly, and with great caution, crawl over the wall and begin your descent.

Our established members who had been through the school warned us that we needed to abide by the Nike slogan and "Just do it." Regardless of fear, lack of skill, fancy equipment, bowel control, etc.—our team needed to go over and down the wall. Apparently, Sgt. Milton, who attended the first school, had opted not to go down the wall, quoting a line from Clint's *Dirty Harry* character as his excuse: "A man's got to know his limitations." Unfortunately, this line didn't really apply since Harry never used it to weasel out of facing up to scary things in his movies. Our team had been humiliated, and it would not happen again.

As we stood poised atop the St. Paul fire tower preparing as a team to descend the wall, I noticed the nervous ticks of my fellow teammates and wondered what my unconscious jitters might look like. Ray raised his chin and then craned his head from side to side as though his collar was too tight, while Jake, a soon-to-be-sergeant, grimaced shortly and then quickly relaxed, like a snake extending and withdrawing its tongue. Though none of us succeeded in camouflaging our apprehension, we all made it down the wall numerous times. As the morning progressed I became fairly comfortable with the sport, and though I would never match Spider Man's antics, I actually came to enjoy it.

In another team-building exercise, we raced relay-style, donning gas masks and M-16s, toward a predetermined deployment site where we traded our M-16s for a sniper rifle and fired at a paper target of a hostage-taker positioned one hundred yards down range. The idea was to shoot a hole in the paper bad-guy's melon while leaving the hostage's paper noggin intact. Of course the hostage's head presented a much greater target since it was placed in front of the bad guy, obscuring most of his head from view. After regaining our breath and firing, we ran back to our original command post and tagged off with the next member of the relay. The exercise demonstrated to us the difficulty of breathing and sighting in a target, while winded and wearing a gas mask.

Our last day of class was reserved for gas deployment, and included instruction in the various kinds of gas, the modes of delivery, the proper scenarios, and the typical effects gas has on human targets. To further demonstrate this final aspect, we were marched into a gas chamber with our masks on. The chamber was then completely saturated with gas and our instructor ordered us to remove our masks. All forms of gas from CN to CS and pepper spray have always affected me dramatically, while others seemed to somehow stave off the more severe reactions. On this particular exercise, I decided to outsmart the instructor and hold my breath until released from the chamber, even though the instructor had cautioned us, "Whatever you do, don't try and hold your breath..."

Having been a swimmer, I was used to holding my breath for up to forty-five seconds and, after all, how long could he keep us in the chamber? Unfortunately, our instructor had some experience with this sort of thing. Though I feigned a pretty good *gassed* victim, with the coughing and my doubled-over wretched appearance, he wasn't buying it. Not even attempting to camouflage his smirk, the instructor waited until I took that suffocatingly large inhalation that was so painful I thought my heart was on fire. From my doubled-over position, through the *real* uncontrolled coughing, the snot and watery eyes, I could barely make out our instructor, his SWAT patch now appearing as a swastika. He was watching me and grinning with some perverse satisfaction as he checked his watch and finally released us from our living hell. As I collapsed outside the chamber, I thought this was what it must feel like for an animal who messes with a skunk and gets, as his reward, a painful shot of stink-juice in the face.

Having experienced the blinding smoke and lack of oxygen of a working house fire, I think gas is more painful. Though carbon monoxide from a fire will actually kill you, gas just makes you wish you were dead. The instructor ordered us to face into the wind, peel open our blood-red, burning eyes, and breathe deeply. This was the best way to counter the effects of the gas, though the remedy seemed akin to putting a Band-Aid on a shrapnel wound. Through his tear-streaked eyes and his gut-wrenching hacking, Jake looked at me and started laughing. Like ropes in the breeze, I had snot ranging from my nostrils to the ground. I'm sure I appeared to Jake like a child who had sneezed but lacked the means and sophistication to blow my nose. Where all the snot came from I didn't know. It seemed the more I blew my nose, the more it seemed to produce. I made a resolution then and there that I would never be on the down-wind receiving end of gas delivery if I could possibly avoid it.

All in all, the school was decent and I came away with an operational understanding somewhere above the infancy stage I'd had before attending the school. I also came away with a grudge for a certain FBI team leader. That grudge took longer to heal than my blisters since I blamed him for both my injured feet and my bruised ego. Of course, the point of his team-building exercise was to demonstrate that when SWAT situations go south, you could count on nothing as absolute, except your partners, your fellow operators. That was the most important lesson of the school, the most important quality of any SWAT team, and in the end I couldn't help but respect him for driving this valid point home.

After the second hour passed behind the oak tree, my concern for cover and concealment became less than zealous, and I just wanted to get up and stretch— have a beer and go home, kiss every member of my family, and watch a basketball game from my comfy recline-a-rocker in my family room. Even the little boy in the living room of the house whose tree I lay behind had fallen asleep on what appeared to be a comfortable leather sofa. In the arsenal of weapons at my disposal, I had at my waist a trusty six-shooter. In my hands I cradled my Remington 870 pump shotgun, and beside me on the grass lay a loaded 37mm gas gun and a small selection of 37mm gas rounds. From my distance, about one hundred feet from the target vehicle, I doubt my round could have penetrated the closed, tempered window glass. If the order was given to deploy gas into the vehicle, I would either have had to move closer to the target or get creative. The lone subject in the handsome rusted Chevette had in his control a .308 hunting rifle powerful enough to kill both him and the neighbor across the street with the same round. We believed he only wanted to kill himself, but one can never be too sure in situations like this.

The SWAT team commander stationed in the command post had strategic control of the situation, and was probably in no big hurry to bring this, our first SWAT operation, to a close. This was one of those scenarios that was really a win-win situation regardless of how it turned out. If the guy shot himself in his car and no one else was injured, you had to consider it a strategic victory for the police, since the armed suspect was kept from harming anyone but himself. While we would all give the dead guy his due moment of grief, if he really wanted to die, no one could stop him. On the other hand, if our able negotiators were successful in talking him out of his violent proposal of death in the form of a really loud, really powerful, and messy self-inflicted gunshot wound, all the better. Our biggest concern was that if he jumped out of his car and aimed his rifle at us, or some other innocent, we would have no other choice than to assist him in his plan of suicide-by-cop.

Stuck behind the tree, I had no idea where the scenario was leading. I knew the negotiators were working with the man in the car since they had rigged up a "throw phone" and delivered it to him. (This incident took place pre-cell phone.) What finally broke the silence on the police radio surprised me.

Officer Rick Klinehoffer, who was working on the street that day, spoke into his car radio, "I'll be heading to the liquor store for a six pack. My ETA back should be about five minutes."

I couldn't imagine that he would be announcing our debriefing beverages over the radio, nor did I believe that a six-pack would be adequate for the entire team of approximately ten officers. The only other option was to give the beer to the man in the car. I'd never heard of such a thing, but I considered for a moment: *what goes in must come out.* Klinehoffer returned with the beer, and from my spot behind the tree I could see team-member Thompson low-crawling toward the blue Chevette where he handed just one of the Budweiser cans through the driver's wing window to the man in the car. Officer Thompson then made a quick retreat for the cover of Klinehoffer's awaiting squad. Of course the only thing better than one beer is two beers and the only thing better than two...and so on. There was a pause after the man's request for his fourth beer. He must have had a very elastic bladder after spending three hours in the car prior to the three beers served to him in his fine Chevette.

We were advised by radio that gas would be deployed shortly, but much to my disappointment, I was told that I would not be responsible for the delivery. I knew there were other team members in better positions to shoot gas into the vehicle, but it seemed anticlimactic for me to have laid here for hours and then to have had no part in the resolution.

I guessed we were not utilizing the plan of waiting for Mother Nature's call to force him out of the car, making an all out bee-line for the bathroom. To make it to the bathroom, he would had to have made a lightening fast exit from the Chevette and then run up his driveway about fifteen feet to the front door, which his wife had been instructed to lock and dead-bolt. All this frenzied movement with the beers sloshing about in his bladder did not bode well for him. Of course the SWAT team would have never allowed him to make it to the door anyway, but this was not to be.

Again, I was surprised as "beer officer" Thompson began his low-crawl, not quite so low as before, to the position by the driver's door where he appeared to open the beer can. Rather than handing it off gently as he had before, he appeared to fling it into the wing window. Only this time the beer can did not contain beer, but rather a canister of very potent CN gas. The canister exploded almost instantly and the car's interior appeared simultaneously saturated with the billowing gas that completely clouded the interior windows. Just as quickly, the Chevette's door was flung open, and the man staggered out—sans rifle—to be tackled hard by an awaiting arrest team. But there was no fight, no resistance, only the mournful, anguished howls of a man in the throws of sinus and eye implosions. The man wet his pants as he rubbed his eyes, which only made it worse, forcing the gas particles into his eyeballs. In a sinus reaction similar to mine, the man's nose poured forth snot that hung from his reddened beak to the ground, and he continued to bellow and moan as the agony lingered. I felt his pain.

Present-day SWAT teams would not applaud the tactics our fledgling team used on this, our inaugural call-out. There were safety lapses and unconventional tactics that could have been disastrous. Our team was stretching its legs.

There were no volunteers that day to transport the man to jail, but our first SWAT mission was scored as a success. No one was injured, permanently anyway, and our team had the enviable record of one for one.

Her First Inquisitor

On patrol at dusk, in the quiet wake of a February blizzard, I was dispatched to a medical emergency on the east side of town. It had snowed all day with an accumulation of more than eight inches. Like ants after the rain, residents emerged from their garages, pushing snow blowers or shovels in an attempt to clear their driveways before dark. They had less than an hour.

The dispatcher advised me only that the victim had suffered an injury to her hand as a result of cleaning her snow blower. I wasn't far from the call and knew I would arrive prior to both my assist and the ambulance.

"Cleaning her snow blower" resonated in my mind through the piercing whine of the squad's siren. Surely this victim wasn't cleaning the rotors while the machine was under power. The list of things never to do ran through my mind:

Don't run while holding a knife or scissors.

Don't point a gun at anything you aren't willing to kill.

Don't drive without your seat belt fastened.

The list went on ad nauseum, but most assuredly included *never touch any machine's moving parts while under power*. I believe it was my seventh grade wood-shop teacher who told our class that the woodworking power tools we would be using were capable of such bloody atrocities that any variation from the safety rules would result in an F for the course, and most likely some disfiguring and very painful injury. I took these rules to heart.

The safety instructions for lawn mowers and snow blowers directed the user to turn off the machine, and disconnect the spark plug, prior to any repair or adjustments to the blades or rotors. This seemed a sensible warning.

I didn't make very good time to the victim's house. I had been on my way to the city garage to have chains secured to my squad's tires when I received the call, but had to make do without. The city snowplows were playing catch-up and the rear-wheel drive Crown Victoria squad cars struggled in any amount of snow or ice.

I finally pulled in front of the residence and saw the suspect snow blower alone in the drive having cleared the first half of its horizontal path. With the power off, the silent machine seemed impotent like an old inoperable implement of war. It sat like a smoking gun, with melted rivulets of snow descending down the glossy red, engine-warmed sheet metal.

The house was custom built on a choice, east-side lot overlooking the Minnesota River Valley. At the time of the incident in 1989, this house was valued somewhere near a half-million dollars. Only the affluent could afford a house on this street, and we had certain expectations of the affluent, perhaps syllogistic in that: If one could aspire to the ranks of the wealthy, one must have a higher skill or intelligence, hence one should not use really stupid judgment.

I gave the machine a wide berth, walking around it as if

the sleeping monster could awaken on its own and blaze a trail toward me, veering from its horizontal restraints, its rotors slashing, grinding, pulling, and finally throwing its mangled prey onto the packed snow banks enveloping the driveway.

It was dusk now and I saw no blood as I walked by the beast, only footprints spaced as a stable normal adult walked, returning to the house. The entrance door stood ajar with only the storm door to separate the interior from the elements. I knocked and announced myself. A woman's desperate voice came back, beckoning me to come in.

I entered, noticed the fine oak stripped floor, and kicked the snow from my jump boots. I walked toward the sound of running water in the kitchen. A slender woman in her early thirties wearing a black ski jacket leaned into the sink with her hand under the faucet's running water. With her free hand she pushed her dark brown hair over her shoulder, revealing a stoic expression on her pale, uncreased face. She looked down into the sink but away from her hand. Through the moving translucent rush of liquid I could see an impressionistic blur of skin flaps on her index, middle, and annular knuckles fluttering under the pressure of the pouring water. The woman turned and made eye contact with me for a moment, then shook her head in disappointment. I tried not to telegraph my judgment but apparently I did not mask it well enough.

"I know," she said. "I can't believe how stupid this was. How stupid I am."

"What happened?"

"It jammed up," she gasped. "I had to clear it out. I was going to stick the shovel handle in, but I didn't want to walk back in the garage. I thought if I just flicked it really fast—-oh, I can't believe I did it. I can't believe—" She started to sob, her head falling deeper toward the sink. Then she stopped almost as she started, took a deep breath, gained her composure, and sniffled.

I took a couple steps toward her in case her shaky condition caused her to lose consciousness. Though it was difficult to see with the faucet rushing, the stumped knuckles did not appear to be bleeding freely. The cold water along with her condition of shock retarded the blood flow.

I needed to ask her where her amputated fingers were but struggled to find the right words. They would need to accompany her to the hospital so the doctors could try to reattach them. The footprints in the snow belied any evidence of a search for the missing digits but perhaps they had become stuck in the rotors.

I placed my hand on her back and asked to see her damaged hand. She moaned shortly as she brought it up from the sink and averted her eyes. I held her wrist, which was cold from the water, and examined the injuries. The three amputations appeared as they had through the water flow, with skin flaps hiding the site of the amputations the way a turtle hides its head within its neck. None of the fingers bled but rather took on the appearance of baby's skin after sitting too long in the tub—pale and pitted. Her pinky had not escaped injury as I'd originally thought. It hung lifelessly by a thread of skin on the outside knuckle.

"Okay," I said.

She returned it to the rushing water where I now noticed the pinky fluttered back and forth with the pressure.

"I'm not going to dress it since the medics are on their way. They'll want to take a look. I do need to find the fingers so the doctors can try to reattach them."

She moaned. "Oh, I can't believe it. I can't believe I did this."

"Do you know where they are?"

She shook her head. "They're out in the driveway somewhere I suppose. I don't know."

I took my handset radio from my belt and called my assist, Officer Bishop, "Bish," who should have been arriving any moment. I advised him to check the area near the snow blower for the truncated fingers. He acknowledged my request with a less than enthusiastic tone. I heard his car door slam as he arrived on the scene moments later.

The ambulance appeared shortly after and the two medics entered and asked the woman to retell the miserable story of how the accident occurred. She reluctantly complied, reiterating how she couldn't believe her own stupidity.

She appeared brave to me, the kind of person who would have somehow survived if a similar accident had occurred in the wilderness. She was not helpless, sorry for herself, nor overcome with sobbing or self-pity, as most accident victims were. These were the fingers of her right hand. To lose them would be a significant loss in her ability to accomplish intricate motor skills like eating, writing, driving, and so on. This disfiguring injury would change her life.

Bish's voice rang out from my belt-set radio. "Found 'em. They're still in her glove. Three of them, right?"

"That's right," I replied.

One of the medics followed me out to the drive as his partner dressed the injury for transport.

Bish was standing in the drive by the ambulance using his index finger and thumb as pincers to hold the offensive glove by the wrist portion. As I approached Bish, he screwed his mouth into a grimace that took the shape of a moving snake. "Thanks, pal," he said.

The medic took the glove and cut the glove-fingers of it off at the base to remove the amputated fingers within. He pushed them out carefully from the tips of the glove into his awaiting rubber-gloved palm, wrapped them loosely in gauze, and placed them delicately in a small cooler.

"Gonna put them on ice?" Bish asked.

"No, don't want to freeze them. That would damage them further like frostbite. Just going to refrigerate them till we get to the hospital. I think we'll take her by 'copter to North. They have the best limb-replacement doctor there, and that's the only place we'll get to fast enough tonight."

The other medic approached the ambulance, escorting the woman to the side entrance with the steps. She climbed in and sat on a bench in the rear. I looked at her through the open rear doors and she caught my glance. I believe my expression was one of sympathy rather than judgment, but regardless of my intentions she could not accept it, and turned away shaking her head.

The medic in the driver's seat radioed their dispatcher, advising that they would be en route to meet the helicopter for a transport to North Memorial Hospital. The other medic waved to us before jumping into the back with the woman and shutting the doors behind him.

Bish and I smiled at the irony of the ambulance traveling "code three" lights and siren activated, fishtailing down the street at about *five miles-per-hour*.

"You son-of-a-bitch," he said. "You comfort the babe victim in the warm mansion while I dig through the snow bank for a bunch of hacked-off fingers."

"I think you got off easy," I said. "What did you think— we were in there discussing her favorite position? She was not happy."

"Yeah, I suppose," he said, turning to his squad. "Where was her old man?"

"She didn't mention him."

Bish smiled his snaky mischievous grin as he opened the door to his squad.

"One tragedy at a time, Bish," I warned, as he waved me off.

I piled into my squad, bringing a good bit of snow with me. I scratched out my Medical Incident Report and radioed in the disposition of the call. Before I pulled into the whiteout I thought of the brutally truncated fingers and was reminded of a recurring dream I had as a child. It was a sword-fight dream involving an unknown faceless bad guy who was a really wicked swordsman. This nefarious nocturnal swashbuckler met me almost nightly and beat me handily at each meeting, ending the fight with a thrust of his sword that entered the small of my back and exited my abdomen. Though this was only a dream, I was brought to consciousness with my back arched and experienced a palpable penetrating pain in my back. I awoke each time I was run through, with not only the feelings of fear and pain, but also of incompetence and ineptitude. I always lost. It almost seemed predestined, and perhaps it was. The only good part about waking was that it probably saved me from ever experiencing the even more painful withdrawal of the blade.

The dream hadn't recurred for more than twenty years, and I might not have ever remembered it if not for the severing of this woman's status quo. Her loss brought back the draped faceless fighter whose abilities I understood were always superior to mine. The outcome I knew, even before I was spun around for the final thrust, since I relived it again and again. Many nights as a child, I went to bed anticipating and perhaps even inviting my nemesis into my dream. His final parry and thrust were automatic, repeated each duel, his confidence connected to his inevitable victory, his invincibility.

It took four or five minutes for that piercing pain in my back to subside. A residue of the pain remained as I considered my chances of ever defeating my foe. Then I slipped off to sleep, my adversary waiting somewhere in the darkness for another duel, another night.

My dream was private, and my body evidenced no outward sign of pain or injury. The woman who reached into her snow blower would be forced by convention to repeat the story to concerned family and friends who asked about her absence from work and her wrapped hand. They would be expected to show sympathy, but her intrepid demeanor would not accept it. She would give to them her self-deprecating account of the event as she did to me, her first inquisitor.

Bull's-eye

The weatherman had forecast this day to be another summer scorcher, 95 and humid. After waking from sporadic, fitful, daytime sleep, I walked out to my roadside mailbox to collect my bills. The sun baked asphalt stunk of tarry petroleum, its scent rising from the melting pavement in distorted waves like gasoline fumes. My bare feet too tender, I grabbed the mail and jumped from the street onto my lawn.

It felt only slightly cooler that night when I reported for duty at 2300 hours. It didn't take long before I felt the soggy perspiration gathered under my vest. As I maneuvered my squad car through the palpable mist, I pushed my vest together from both sides of my chest, forming an open "V" at my neck. I leaned down to the Crown Victoria's air conditioning vent, training it on the opening, and felt the cool rush of artificial air rush over my chest. Our air conditioners remained on *max* for the entire shift. The cool air felt good for the moment, but like an overheated child standing in front of an open refrigerator, relief was temporary.

We were busy this Friday night, mostly going from party to party, advising homeowners they needed to quiet down and bring their guests into the house; have their guests use their toilets instead of the neighbor's shrubs; and have their guests deposit their beer cans in the garbage rather than firing them at the neighbor's evergreens. Our role as police officers was that of party-poopers whom nobody invited. To the underage crowd, we were bad news, the po-po, 5-0, a blue shade of trouble.

Most of the adult homeowners were cooperative. They didn't want problems with their neighbors, or with us. Our police department had a reputation for ending loud gatherings and for citing violators if they failed to heed our warnings to tone their party down or end it.

Typically, two squads were sent to a "party call." Those initial officers scoped out the gathering and made a determination of whether more squads were needed based on: the number of cars that lined the streets adjacent to the party house, the number of guests teeming through the neighbor's yards, the volume of voices and music emanating from the house, and the age of the guests.

Our city of Bloomington, a suburb of Minneapolis, boasted the third-largest population in Minnesota at about one hundred thousand. (Duluth and Rochester have similar populations.) That number was a bit misleading since the daytime population more than doubled that figure with visitors to the Mall of America and the surrounding hotels, which outnumbered both Minneapolis's and St. Paul's hotel industries combined. These transient guests generated police service and kept the dogwatch on its toes until the bar crowd evaporated and the streets cleared.

All that was left for us tonight were the remnants of the parties that had started hours ago and lingered on into the early morning hours. At about 0230 hours, I, along with two other squads, was dispatched to a re-call of a loud party complaint, having warned the homeowner earlier that night to tone it down—*or else*. Re-calls to parties always resulted in the police ending the party and dispersing the guests. There were no third chances. Recalcitrant partiers refusing to leave were arrested.

When we arrived at the party house I could see it was out of control. The windows were open and guests were leaning out, reminiscent of Noah's Ark, and probably just as noisy. Our knock on the door was answered by a young man who opened the door just far enough to see the blue uniforms before he slammed it shut and locked it. This kind of greeting was seen as a bad omen, and with a gathering this large was almost always met with a show of force. This show was meant to dissuade those who might be considering forceful resistance. But we knew from experience that rational decisions such as these were more often made by sober adults. This house appeared to be chock-full of overheated teenage boys full of booze, marijuana, testosterone, and angst—a dangerous cocktail.

While waiting for the troops to arrive, we backed off into the shadows and talked amongst ourselves about other calls we'd handled that night, about the sleep we were going to catch up on, and, finally, the weather—in that order. Before long we had assembled a contingent of ten squads with a matching number of officers (we ran single-officer squads). The street supervisor, Sgt. Brad Farhaven, took command of this call, since it was deemed to require more than the initial three officers dispatched to the scene. He was wearing his garrison hat, as supervisors sometimes did to gain that extra "command presence."

Officer Lonnie Carson, affectionately known to his brother officers as "BLC" (Big Lonnie Carson), was our largest cop, standing about six feet seven inches, and weighing in menacingly close to four hundred pounds (plus or minus fifty pounds, depending on the diet-of-the-month). A group of veteran officers stood dwarfed by Lonnie as he slapped what looked like a toy flashlight into his catcher's-mitt palm.

As we stood outside telling old stories of past glory, the layer of sweat under our vests grew a little denser and the vests a bit heavier. Nightsticks in hand, we were ready for the order to go. Farhaven looked out at the street, apparently waiting for one more assist squad. Being a prudent man, he wanted this done right, with as few injuries as possible.

A loud crash of broken glass near the house made everyone flinch, and I turned to hear an indecipherable whisper. A fraction of a second later a hard object crashed forcefully against my face and broke upon contact. It wasn't painful, just shockingly abrupt. My head jolted back with the force of the thrust object, and I reflexively cupped my hand over my eye where I felt the contact. All I knew was that some sort of glass object had broken against my face.

The warmth of my hand mixed with the warmth of my blood and the night air, all of similar temperature, so the contrast was minimal. Only the texture, and the quick rush of my blood as it overflowed my cupped hand, clued me in to the seriousness of the injury. Like every fool who can't see the injury they just sustained, I brought my hand down to view what I knew my palm contained. The flow ran unabated from its origin near my eye, down my face and into the abyss of navy blue polyester, where it disappeared. I was afraid I had lost the eye since the blood seemed to be flowing freely from it. There was no way to check my sight at this point since I couldn't see through the blood anyway.

Sergeant Farhaven saw my involuntary metamorphosis from uniformed police officer to *Friday the Thirteenth* victim and shouted, "Okay, we're going in!"

I had unwittingly become the inspiration and mascot for a retaliatory strike that should have been a simple party dispersal. As another officer escorted me to the awaiting ambulance, BLC put his foot to the door and in they went. Seated in the ambulance forty feet away, I heard the kind of shouting and gnashing of teeth one might expect from a massacre of such magnitude. I would have been surprised if any of the dishes or glass items within the house remained intact after our coup d'état.

The first casualty to exit the residence was a now wobbling officer Kevin Thompson, who was being escorted toward our position in the ambulance by a fellow officer. Kevin, too, appeared to have played a supporting role in one of the scary teen-horror movies, as blood streamed down his face. He joined me on the bench in the ambulance and grinned back at me as he considered the irony of our appearance. He told me that once in the house, chaos reigned as police and drunks confronted one another like the Medieval Crusaders confronted the Turks. The last thing Kevin saw was Big Lonnie Carson winding up his flashlight for a grand-slam swing. He assumed BLC missed his target and caught Kevin instead, right on top of his noggin, splitting his scalp to the skull.

We were transported sans lights and siren to Fairview Southdale Hospital where the confident hands of Doctor Justice sewed our heads and faces back together. Minnesota State Trooper Anna Tucker rode to the hospital with us, after assisting our officers at the scene of the party call.

Anna and I watched as Dr. Justice poked, prodded, and finally inserted his gloved finger into the open scalp of Officer Thompson who was mercifully numbed up and could tell, only from our grossed-out expressions of horror, how disgusting his injury must appear. After cleaning the laceration, Dr. Justice sewed Thompson's scalp back together like a maiden darning a sock over a light bulb.

I was next and, after the necessary pain-killing injections, I watched the suppressed expressions of disgust from Anna and Kevin as Dr. Justice now poked, prodded, and inserted a large

Q-tip type instrument into my lacerations, of which there were three. After extracting some small splinters of glass, the doctor assured me that my eye was miraculously unharmed. The lacerations from the broken beer bottle circled my eye like a child's drawing of the sun, with rays emanating from the central yellow star—my hazel iris.

I flinched as I tried to watch the intricate close-up work of the good doctor suturing my injuries. He advised that I close my eyes—not that I might balk at the procedure, but the closed eye stretched the skin and gave the doctor an easier target to mend. With eyes closed and Anna holding my hand, I felt like a child as the doctor commenced with his needlework.

The good doctor was probably biting his lip as the big, tough, uniformed boy-cop held hands with the pretty, petite, girl-cop. You forget how foolish you might appear in these perceived private situations, but the good doctor probably saved scenes like this in his library of memorable follies, reliving them for guests over cocktails on his deck. I wouldn't blame him if he did. He did an excellent job on my face. Sewing the lacerations as he did, using thin thread and a very tight pattern, he left virtually no scars. In fact, when I later retold this story of how I was heroically struck in the face as I stood in the yard, like a moron, with my hands in my pockets, I had no physical proof that the incident actually occurred. Had I known his level of expertise, I would have requested he at least allow for some semblance of a war wound if only to illustrate the story after sharing it with friends during cocktail hour on my deck.

My hand, that trooper Tucker held so comfortingly during the stitching part, was wet by the time the doctor tied his final knot. I could have blamed the moisture on Anna, but that would have been unappreciative and presumptuous. I rubbed my hand on my pants and the sweat disappeared as all things do into the infinite navy blue double-knit fibers. After an acceptable time that would not be confused with a need to vomit in private, I excused myself and visited the restroom. For the first time that morning I looked at my face in the mirror. With sutures, my eye resembled what a woman's eyes probably looked like after applying generous amounts of mascara and then blinking. The area surrounding my eye was already discolored with most of the darker hues of the rainbow and accented by the squiggly centipede-like stitches.

Anna drove Kevin and me back to the BPD. I got home around 0730 hours and sat on the back step of my tiny one-bedroom house by the Minneapolis Airport—that I referred to as "the hut." The sun was beginning its early rhythmic arc across the sky, and the dormant layer of dry perspiration on my chest was liquefying its way back to life. I watched the deafening planes ascend overhead as my two orphaned ducklings followed my bemused Great Dane, whom they'd imprinted on, around my small fenced-in backyard. The sharp, protruding ends of the sutures around my eye bit into the surrounding skin, forcing me to squint, but I was thankful I could still see in stereo.

Some weeks after this adventure, I learned that the pitcher (of the bottle) was a veteran officer's teenage son. I always wondered if he'd aimed for my face as he fired the bottle through the window, or if he just hurled the bottle into the crowd and scored the lucky bull's-eye.

The Chase

While all cops like to go fast, not all cops like to go as fast as other cops and, though there are exceptions to the rule, this phenomenon can be graphed, charted, and categorized in a general way by agency. For instance, a typical FBI agent drives like your grandma. Your basic, local city cop likes to go as fast as the next guy, but your deputy sheriff likes to go a bit faster—but still not as fast as your state trooper. The trooper is the apotheosis of the fast driving cop. Any self-respecting trooper worth the spit-shine on his boots could trade jobs and patches with a professional racecar driver and get along just fine. (The racecar driver might object to the drastic cut in pay, not to mention the less than worshipful attitude toward him.)

Being a local cop on the near bottom rung of the speed ladder, I was not expected to keep up with the troopers, although some of my compatriots made this futile effort on chases. After witnessing the aftermath of countless car crashes, I'd become an ardent believer in sane driving techniques. Like the FBI agents, I was a grandma by nature, preferring to keep it under ninety mph. Any increment of ten mph over that made me feel like I was flying in a machine meant exclusively for land travel. When the vehicle started to shake, shimmy, and wander, my heart tended to pound harder in an attempt to alert my brain to signal my foot to move from its position on the gas pedal to the brake pedal. I'm convinced that racecar drivers and troopers have learned to ignore their brains when they drive at these speeds, since there is nothing logical, intelligent, prudent, or even sane about driving this fast.

Some of my partners loved nothing better than *a good chase,* or at least that's what they said over a couple beers. I never really looked forward to a chase with much relished anticipation, rather I understood that if I were close to one, I would need to join in and do my part until it was resolved.

I noticed early in my police career that there was more to this chase mentality than simply wanting to drive at ridiculous speeds in order to catch the bad guy. There was another kind of madness achieved at the denouement, when the car being chased was brought to a stop, either as a result of crashing, being rammed, or when the driver simply decided to stop, bail out, and make like a rabbit. Now I had been instructed in Police Skills Training that the end of the chase could be the most dangerous phase, and that a "felony stop" should be performed, if practical, at the conclusion of every chase. A felony stop consisted of staying by your squad, using it for cover, as you ordered the driver and occupants out of the car at gunpoint. Once the bad guys were "proned out" on the street, they were handcuffed and placed in a squad. Nice and easy, lickety-split. No muss, no fuss. No one gets hurt.

At the conclusion of my first chase, I was the second car back from the suspect who had lost control of his car and slammed into a culvert. Driving over a hundred mph with a BAC (blood alcohol content) of .20 welcomes this type of conclusion.

Remembering proper procedure, I immediately positioned myself behind the cover of the squad door, drew my pistol, and directed it toward the suspect's driver-side door. I had to holster my weapon almost immediately as every cop in the chase ran past me to the crashed car, dragged the driver out his car window, and started kicking the shit out of him. No one at the scene seemed to have completed the same training I had, or, if so, their adrenaline rush had erased it from memory and replaced it with a montage of scenes from the *Die Hard* movie series. Taken aback by the revelation that no one was following procedure, and feeling like the typical rookie third wheel, I quickly conformed to the rule of, "When in Rome..." and assisted with the arrest.

As more of the veteran officers retired, and departments started punishing officers for unnecessary use of force, chases started being resolved in much less frenetic and painful ways. (Do-gooders with camcorders might have expedited the change as well.) Officers were being trained in the P.I.T. maneuver, which utilizes the positioning of their squads to surgically remove fleeing felons from the roadway with little damage to vehicles involved, and fewer injuries to both suspects and officers.

One of the most intriguing aspects of daily patrol was the ever-present quality of the unknown. One could initiate a routine traffic stop only to find the target vehicle speed up rather than slow down, and subsequently find oneself in a chase. Intoxicated drivers, or drivers with warrants or suspended licenses, sometimes thought the chase was worth a chance rather than the certain consequence of jail time if pulled over. Of course the chance of a driver fleeing grew with the severity of the crime he'd committed, or the number of beers consumed.

In mid-summer 1997, we came across a jeweler on the west side of town who conducted business from his residence, by appointment only. He figured his safety was less likely to be compromised if his customers were required to call in advance to set up their visits. In the early evening hours of a sweltering July day, this jeweler and his wife found themselves looking down the barrel of a six-shooter, as their five o'clock appointment cleaned them out and handcuffed them to the posts of their stairway. The manacled wife managed to free herself from the staircase, run to the window, and get a good enough look at the robber's car to relay the license plate, letter for letter, to the 911 operator who then put it out to the squads.

Being in the right place at the right time is usually luck, and this was no exception. No sooner had the 911 dispatcher put out the description of the car, complete with license plate, than I noted the suspect vehicle two cars in front of mine, traveling eastbound on I-494. Suffering the doubt imposed by circumstance, and the unnatural gush of adrenaline, I asked dispatch to repeat the numbers from the suspect license plate. I then advised dispatch of my coincidental position, but with confident inflection, as though I'd somehow "Sherlocked" my way into locating this suspect. I was quickly joined by another squad, piloted by Carl Nash, who was only a few years into his basket-weave belt. Though we hadn't yet initiated our lights and siren, it didn't take long for the robber to realize that the proverbial jig was up. His eight-cylinder Olds Cutlass moved out like a NASCAR racer out of the pits, and the chase was on.

Pushing hard on the accelerator, I tried to concentrate on both on staying behind this maniac at all costs and calling out the chase, as we flew past other freeway traffic that appeared as stationary objects on an obstacle course.

The driver of the Cutlass suddenly swung his car wildly from the middle lane of the freeway to the exit ramp for Nicollet Avenue South. He adeptly wheeled his way around several cars awaiting the green light and avoided oncoming traffic as he turned northbound on Nicollet through the red. With lights and sirens now blaring our approach, cars moved out of our way and we followed the Cutlass onto the 35 mph city street.

When the Cutlass turned north rather than south, he left our city limits and entered the city of Richfield, which had a "No Chase" policy in effect at the time, frustrating their officers to no end. We turned our squad radios to MNSEF (a radio frequency shared by surrounding agencies including Minnesota State Patrol) so that Richfield PD and State Patrol could monitor our chase and assist with traffic if they were in position.

The Cutlass quickly climbed from the 35 mph it took the turn at, to about 85 mph. Nicollet Avenue turns into a 35-mph residential street north of I-494, and rush hour traffic was just beginning to wane. I could see children and their parents alongside the road in my peripheral vision, which I was just barely able to utilize since tunnel vision at these speeds is an inevitable, and dangerous, phenomenon. Individual objects and persons smeared into the landscape, painting a surreal swath of verdant flora. I heard the trailing comments and shouted curses fall away like birdcalls from a distance, as our squads shot down the street.

This was the point in the chase when the decision to continue or shut it down had to be made. On any other traffic offense or misdemeanor violation, I would have called it off at this point and broadcast the vehicle's description, direction of travel, and speed so that other agencies could position their squads for intercept, but this suspect had held a gun to the heads of the jewelers as he robbed them. I continued the chase.

I felt like the pilot of a runaway train, cognizant that I would not be able to stop my squad for any child who pulled his bike out in front of me. While my brain argued with my foot, which was bearing down on the gas pedal, I unconsciously stopped calling out the chase into the microphone I held to my mouth. Unable to understand my radio reticence, my partner, Carl, took over calling out the chase from his position directly behind me. His slight Southern accent came over the radio, with his inflection just a notch up from its usual, just-woke-up-drawl. And though his voice had a soothing effect, it alerted me to the fact that I was no longer speaking.

"Ah, this is 4832. We're still behind the Olds, northbound on Nicollet at 73rd—about 80 miles per hour or so."

I considered taking my foot off the gas and allowing the speeding vehicle to get away from me. If I decided to end the chase, Carl would have to follow suit since my squad would block him. Surely the suspect would slow down once the lights and sirens faded into the distance, and the public safety would be restored—or would it? Getting away, would this robber figure he had foiled the police and gain enough confidence to renew his crime spree of residential robberies like the one he'd just committed? Looking at the back of his head through the rear window of his speeding vehicle gave me no clue as to what he was thinking, and no gauge of his confidence.

As the debate raced on in my mind, I saw a car up ahead of the suspect vehicle start to move forward toward Nicollet Avenue from its stationary position in a Tom Thumb parking lot. I was back, calling the chase now, and I warned Carl of the movement. I switched my siren to Hi-Lo in hopes that the inattentive driver would hear the siren change and brake before entering Nicollet. But he did not stop. His vehicle came out of the shadows and slowly but deliberately pulled out from his parking spot directly in front of the oncoming Cutlass. Sensing the impending collision, I started to brake so as not to be included in the chain reaction of stunted momentum.

The Cutlass didn't even make it to his brakes but rather smashed like a runaway train into the interloping car, T-boning it squarely into the driver's door and ricocheting off like a bumper car. I could see now that this was not a distracted citizen but rather a Minnesota State trooper's squad, as the low-profile light bar flew from the roof on contact and careened off the street like a rock skipping across the water. I looked in my rearview mirror as my partner's squad screeched toward the rear of mine, sliding as if locked up on ice. He managed to stop his squad just inches from my bumper, and we both exited our squads with guns drawn. The trooper who'd used his car as a roadblock miraculously forced his crumpled door open and stumbled out of his squad on rubber legs, holding his revolver with an obviously broken, bloodied arm.

Carl and I quickly cuffed and stuffed the perp into my squad without incident. Of course, the robber, as usual, was unharmed by the head-on crash. We called for paramedics and they responded almost immediately since they'd positioned themselves in the vicinity, anticipating some sort of injurious outcome. They transported the trooper to the closest E.R., traveling from the scene with lights and siren activated. I'd never met this trooper and never learned the extent of his injuries. The driver's side window of his squad had smashed upon impact and small chunks of the ice-like glass crystals of his window had fallen into his holster, shredding his left hand when he was forced to draw his pistol from it. His deformed left arm was obviously badly broken, the ribs on his left side most likely fractured, and his internal organs within were no doubt perforated.

Carl and I felt we'd done our duty since the cops caught the robber, and justice seemed to have prevailed. We knew we were lucky—no civies got hurt. Back at the police department we listened to the recorded dispatch tape of our radio traffic as we called out the chase from the time I spotted the suspect vehicle until its violent conclusion. When we got to the part of the tape where I quit calling it out, Carl didn't ask why, and I didn't offer—not really knowing why myself.

I didn't hear if the injured trooper was rewarded for his courage or disciplined for his apparent reckless disregard for his own safety. I can't prognosticate what might have happened and I couldn't initially think of alternate resolutions to this chase that wouldn't have involved some crumpled steel and its accompanying bloody tapestry. I thought the trooper a complete and utter fool at the time of the incident, but I've come to question that evaluation.

After I Monday-morning-quarterbacked this incident from every angle, I naturally came up with some options I considered better than the trooper using his squad as a roadblock. He could have pulled out in front of the suspect sooner, and attempted to slow him down by zigzagging his squad as he gradually decelerated. There's no telling how the suspect might have responded to this. He might have tried to get around the trooper and, in the process, taken out a family of roadside gawkers.

The trooper could have simply joined the chase, falling in behind Carl from his intersecting position, and had the chance to drive really fast, living la vida loca, trooper-style. I've come to believe that he saw the squad-car roadblock as the safest means of resolving the chase, and the least likely to injure civilians. After all, there were a finite number of options for ending the chase, and most of them involved bystanders, cops, and the suspect getting hurt. He may very well have been asking himself who these idiot cops were, chasing this idiot driver through a residential area—forcing him to make a tactically inappropriate personal sacrifice. He may have shifted the blame for his painful sacrifice from himself and the local cops and placed it with the robber, who initiated the chase, forcing everyone's hand—a novel idea.

Hell and High Water

With my attention directed to the hoops game, I took a pizza out of the oven and burned my right index finger quite badly. I hollered as I recoiled reflexively and recited a barrage of expletives that would have made even my detective partner Ted, a true cursologist, blush. The crimson diagonal stripe on the pad of my finger shriveled, shrink-wrapping the top of my finger, the nerves beneath it imploding as if they had been saturated in sustained fire.

"Dad?" my six-year-old son Dusty said tentatively, "Are you okay?"

"Yeah," I said, holding my finger under the kitchen faucet. "I burned my finger."

He paused for a moment in deference to my uncharacteristic animation. "You said a lot of bad words, you know."

"Yeah, I know. It really hurt." The embarrassment seemed to make my finger throb even harder.

"You said the S-word, the S-O-B thing and—well, you said the F-word too, and you said we should never say that one."

"No, you shouldn't, and I shouldn't have either." I was starting to wonder if he'd taken notes. "Sorry..."

"And then you said the "Mother——-"

"All right, all right," I said between squeezing and shaking my finger in an attempt to assuage or at least alter the pain, "Are we going to eat this pizza, or what?"

I looked at the throbbing stripe on my index finger and thought of a fire call I had been assigned in the winter of 1984. I'd been off probation for about a year, and pushing a squad on dogwatch for most of my short career. I'd seen more dead people in the first two weeks as a cop than I'd seen my entire life prior, but I still wasn't used to it.

At about 0400 hours on a frigid, sub-zero morning I was called to a working fire at the 8700 block of Nicollet Avenue. As I drove code-three to the area, I saw the tumbling smoke rising in the distance from the swirling flames that shot from the rooftop, lighting the night. The conflagration appeared incongruent against the dark, bitter-cold morning. Several other squads were dispatched to the fire as well, and I could see the flicker of their emergency lights before their squads came into focus. Bobby Landon steered into the complex in front of me and cut his siren.

I grabbed my fire extinguisher, but realized the futility of the tiny apparatus as the flames grew in ferocity. I heard the loud snaps of wood crackling as Bobby and I neared the building. There was a six-foot cedar privacy fence surrounding the townhouse that we needed to jump in order to enter by the front door. Other squads were arriving. Assist officers jumped the fence behind us as Bobby and I approached the front door. As we peered into the living-room window, we could feel the heat from the fire five feet from us. When I approached closer than that, I felt the exposed skin on my face contract from the heat. The living room window seemed to bow inward before it cracked loudly and turned black.

Bobby had managed to open the front door and was shouting over the thunderous roar of consumption that he could see a body inside. I ran beside him and peered into the inferno that was the living room. Furniture, walls, and ceiling were all being devoured. The act of opening the door was feeding the living, insatiable flames, which acknowledged the added fuel with ascending flames and amplified volume that mimicked a cattle stampede.

From the door where we crouched, I saw a body dressed only in underwear, about four feet into the house. Portions of his exposed skin were charred black, while other parts appeared relatively normal. His head was closest to us, as if he had been cut short in his attempt to flee the dwelling. We could take one step into the house and grab his arms, nothing more. Another step further, and we would physically ignite.

"Let's just grab his arms and pull him out!" Bobby shouted.

I nodded my agreement, but thought to myself that the act of actually reaching the man and pulling him out seemed overly optimistic. "On three," I shouted back, and we counted, "One, two, three," and took one giant step into hell. Our eyes reflexively shut as the heat instantly dried them and singed our lashes, eyebrows, and any other exposed hair. I grabbed the man's left arm as Bobby grabbed his right. We pivoted, pulled, and came away with only the slimy top layer of the man's skin, exposing the crimson fleshy layer beneath. We simultaneously turned back into the fire and tried again with the same result. The skin on his arm had the consistency of hot blistering jelly, and we could not get a grip. Frustrated with our failed attempts and realizing time was not on our side, we looked at one another for suggestions.

I hollered at Bobby two feet away from me, "Let's try locking our arms through his armpits."

This action worked well enough to get us out the door. We continued to lose our grip and readjust, but we finally got him out into the small courtyard. I rubbed my gloves together in an attempt to remove the slimy, sticking epidermis that covered them. Another waiting officer threw a wool blanket over him as I checked his vitals. He showed no signs of breathing, yet a thin vapor-like smoke emanated from his nostrils. I took off my gloves and placed my fingertips against his carotid artery. A very faint pulse echoed back against my fingertips—either that or I felt my own pulse against his stiff neck.

I vaulted back over the fence to retrieve my oxygen and vaulted a second time back into the courtyard. Officer Toby Jensen was bent over the victim's body checking his pulse.

He shook his head. "Nothing."

I set the oxygen down beside him as the first fire truck arrived. Firefighters smashed down a section of the cedar fence and entered the courtyard with hoses. Another truck was preparing to spray the interior from the back. Windows were popping, and debris was starting to fall from the roof.

We woke the neighbors in the adjoining townhouses who had not yet exited their homes, and told them they'd need to evacuate until the fire was brought under control. Several young moms carried their pajama-clad toddlers through the snow, staring hard at the object under the blanket. They wanted to know which of their neighbors that blanket covered. We didn't know the victim's name, and we were not comfortable putting him on display. Some neighbors told us that the house in flames was occupied by two guys, a gay couple. According to these neighbors, the two men had lived together in the house for a short period of time and were considered friendly, good neighbors.

The firefighters worked on the house for at least an hour before the structure was completely saturated. They found the second man in an upstairs bedroom still lying on the wire remains of what had been his bed. The firefighters carried him out and laid him beside the man Bobby and I had brought out earlier. The second man was burned black so that he could not be identified by appearance alone. Dental records would be needed to confirm his identity. He lay in the classic pugilistic form the human body is reduced to by exposure to intense heat and flame.

As a result of the firefighters' prolonged hosing-down of the building's interior, the flooded courtyard had become a skating rink. It was a challenge to keep our footing as we baby-stepped our way across the courtyard.

I overheard some soot-faced firefighters speaking in hushed voices about some type of gag-gift, gay trophy found in the bedroom. With that, the scenarios began to unfold. The most popular had the two men engaged in a lover's quarrel, with the first victim found by the door, having intentionally set the fire to murder his partner. His plan backfired when the fire became too intense, and he was overcome by smoke on his way out, dying by his own hand.

Another scenario had one man smoking in bed after sex. The lovers fell asleep and one of the partners later awakened to find the house enveloped in smoke. He attempted to awaken his partner but, having no luck, was forced to flee alone, only to be overcome just short of his escape.

There were others, some suggested only in jest with the punch line centered on some sexual innuendo. We laughed together, firefighters and cops, in the wake of our failed efforts to save the lives of the men and what was left of the structure. Our gallows humor seemed a default reaction to the horrific death we had just witnessed. In the end, nothing was saved.

Even the townhouse was a total loss. Wet charred wood and debris steamed in the freezing pre-dawn, signaling the end.

When the fire department had shut off their hoses and backed up their trucks, the medical examiner was called to the scene. By the time they arrived, the sun was up and the two bodies were frozen to the ground beneath them. Smoke still emanated from the smoldering rubble that had once been home to the two men laid out on the ice.

Exhaustion had set in with officers and firefighters alike, and a quick resolution was needed. Finally, some firefighters asked us to shield the bodies from the growing group of gawking bystanders by holding blankets around them as firefighters used large metal ice-scrapers to pry the bodies from the ground. By the time I cleared the scene my shift had ended.

I arrived home later than normal and noticed a carpet truck parked in front of my house with the confused carpet-layer guy standing by my front door. I'd forgotten about the appointment. As I walked past him, he commented that I smelled like smoke. I told him I'd been to a fire-call during my shift as a Bloomington police officer. He said he'd heard about the fire on the radio, and he paused for me to fill him in on the details. I didn't really feel like talking about it any longer. I felt as though the deaths of the two men had been trivialized enough. I directed him to the job site within my house and collapsed on my bed.

I looked at my bright red, throbbing finger as Dusty and I stuffed our mouths with the store-bought frozen pizza. The pain from that simple burn felt so intense, and there seemed no end to the lingering ache. I thought about the two men in the townhouse and hoped the smoke inhalation had killed them before they suffered the excruciating effects of the fire. I thought about the jokes made at the scene, and the firefighters scraping the victims from their icy anchor points. I knew the comments were the result of frenzied, exhausted workers thrust into life and death, and the subsequent "coming down" from the huge adrenaline rush of our failed attempts to save them. While conflagration had no conscience, we did. As custodians of trauma and tragedy, the seemingly haphazard, vitriolic nature of death took a toll on our compassion.

Dusty smiled at me from across the table as we simultaneously swept dripping pizza sauce from our chins. I licked the sauce from my burned finger. It still hurt—I knew it would take time to heal after it blistered and scabbed over. It was a small, insignificant burn.

AKA Cougar

The city of Bloomington abuts the Minnesota River Valley on its southern border, with the river acting as a physical barrier separating Bloomington from its southern neighbor cities: Eagan, Burnsville, and Savage. About a hundred houses back up to the bluffs on this southern border. Most of these bluff houses on the west side of the city are beautifully landscaped, newer brick mansions, while the bluff houses on the east side are more modest homes built in the sixties, yet with the same stunning views.

There is an imaginary line drawn somewhere near the middle of the city, dividing east from west. Like most Minneapolis suburbs, the city of Bloomington was developed from farmland in the early 1940s and '50s. This development started on the east side of the city and, like a microcosm of our early national expansion, continued westward throughout the seventies. By 1980 most of the farms were bought up, and the now barren, treeless fields were dotted with the unsightly boxes of new residential construction. There remains to this day an elitist snobbery among some west side residents. "West Bloomington" is seen as more professional and affluent than the blue-collar, working-class east side. Real estate agents specify on their Multiple Listing Service whether the property they're listing is in east or west Bloomington, and some residents on the west side even declare West Bloomington on their driver's license, as though it had its own charter.

Though Bloomington police officers are not required to live within the city limits, my wife and I were lucky enough to purchase an east-side bluff house in the mid-1990s, before the prices of these less-prestigious residences skyrocketed.

Living on the bluffs affords residents the best of both worlds—life in the city and abundant wildlife outside the back door. There's an essence of the untouched in the clumps of cedar and the monumental oak stands that make it easy to forget about the city in front of the house.

One of my neighbors brought us a newspaper clipping with a photograph of our property when the foundation was being dug in the spring of 1968. A skeleton was unearthed about ten feet below the surface. Archeologists examined the site and the bones and determined them to be the remains of a female Native American in her mid-teens. Needless to say, the idea of erecting houses over Indian burial grounds did not dissuade the builders from their mission.

There are so many deer in the River Valley that the police department routinely thins the herd to avoid their inevitable starvation. This practice is usually met with cries of animal cruelty from fur-hugger types. These same people seemed to have a ubiquitous presence at car-versus-deer accidents, of which there are about a hundred each year. When the on-scene officer determines that the injured deer is going to suffer a painful, lingering death as a result of its injuries, he dispatches the deer with his shotgun. These are often unpleasant scenes both for the driver who struck the deer and the officer who was required to shoot it (not to mention the deer). Often times the injured deer has suffered one or more compound leg fractures and was attempting, with little success, to flee on its remaining intact legs. Many of the injured deer I was forced to shoot mysteriously abandoned their attempts to flee and simply watched me, scrutinizing my every movement as I leveled my shotgun in their direction. They in their languishing pain seemed to assume their countdown to eternity.

Some of the by-standers at these accident scenes objected to killing the deer, but offered no alternative. When their objections became too adamant, I submitted to them the option of stuffing the injured deer into their Volvo and transporting it to the nearest vet for emergency surgery, but none ever took me up on it.

In addition to the deer, our backyard bluff visitors include squirrel, rabbit, fox, possum, badger, skunk, raccoon, and the occasional coyote. From my deck, depending on the time of day, I can see bald eagles, great horned owls, red-tailed hawks, a wide assortment of songbirds, and the ever gliding turkey vultures who clean up the above-mentioned species when they become carrion. I've even been awakened in the early morning hours by a flock of wild turkeys gobbling as they fed in our back yard. My declawed cats wouldn't last a night outdoors in my backyard, and when one of them sneaks out, we always make a point of finding him before dark.

Reports of mountain lion, AKA cougar, AKA puma, AKA panther, in the River Valley area were rare, but not unheard of. On May 30, 2002, a Bloomington police officer shot a stubborn female adult cougar on a walking path that led to the river valley. She was neither lactating nor rabid, but would not back down to human interlopers walking the path. This unfortunate safety precaution was, weeks later, editorialized in the

Bloomington Sun newspaper under the headline, "Bloomington Police Murder Mountain Lion."

I'd seen a cougar ten years earlier down by the bass ponds on the east side of town while parked side by side, chatting with fellow-officer, Dan Fitzpatrick. I witnessed the animal dart across the dirt road in front of my squad, and Fitzpatrick saw it in his side-view mirror. We looked at each other in shock.

"Did you just see what I think I saw?" I said.

"You mean that mountain lion that just ran across the road behind my squad?

"Yeah."

Neither the police department nor the DNR ever received a report of that wild cat.

In the spring of 1984 I heard that the animal warden had picked up a young mountain lion from a neighboring city that lacked the facilities to contain the animal. The rumor was that this six-month-old cub was being raised to model for the Lincoln Mercury advertising campaign, which traditionally featured a cougar to highlight their eponymous vehicle. I'd seen these commercials with the beautiful wild cat, its gray-brown ticked fur groomed to perfection, lying across the hood of the shiny new car. At the end of the commercial he'd give an impressively carnivorous growl to remind us of the untamed nature of this handsome car. The animal in our shelter had been either unceremoniously dumped in the woods or had escaped and fled. Either way, it lacked the skills of tracking, pursuing, and killing prey, which are normally taught by the cub's mother. This animal was starving to death when our animal warden rescued it.

Being a tree- and fur-hugger at heart, I needed to check out the new inhabitant of the kennel for myself. When things got slow on the street, as was almost always the case after 0300 hours on dogwatch, I surreptitiously nabbed the kennel keys at the PD and skulked over to the City Animal Shelter, a couple blocks northeast of the department. This would need to be a *covert op* since it really wasn't police business, and my supervisor could probably think of something better for me to do.

As I keyed my way into the kennel, the dogs and cats perked up and began their cacophonous chorus of mournful barks and piteous long-winded meows. I scanned the rows of chain-linked compartments until I saw the cougar, which had also awakened and taken an interest in me. With his bright, golden eyes focused on me, he paced in front of his kennel gate moving his mouth, as if meowing like a kitten, but made no audible sound. With this mouthing action, his large canines and smaller incisors were exposed, but he did not appear to regard me as prey. Since humans fed him, I supposed he probably associated my presence with dinner, though hopefully not directly *as* dinner. I approached the cage and, reaching for the hasp, had a moment of rational mental clarity that cautioned me against this course of action but, as usual, I ignored this and entered the cage. I figured a confident all-business demeanor would be met with little fear by the cat. The cougar cub nosed the gate opening as I closed it in his face, and I quickly fastened the dog lead I'd brought with me to the wide leather collar he wore.

He looked dangerously thin, his ribs protruding in pronounced, fine detail. What should have been a sixty-pound cat was probably about fifty pounds. He looked up at me and planted his large paws against my abdomen. His nose came quickly, but only curiously to my face, which he smelled before descending back to all fours, and resumed pacing by the gate. With both claustrophobia and being-eaten-alive-aphobia enveloping my psyche, I opened the gate. The cat immediately darted through the opening. I felt for the first time the power of this weakened cub. He lit from the cage into the space between kennels and jerked me like a fastened balloon behind him. The depths of my poor judgment were becoming clearer as I shouted ridiculous verbal commands like, "No! Sit! Stay! Heel!"

He pulled me from the hallway into the kennel office where the animal warden completed paperwork at his desk and called prospective animal owners in search of their lost pets. The cub's eyes had changed now from those of a helpless, caged prisoner to an unwound predator whose energy did not match up with its sickly appearance. They were no longer piteous, but full of a more robust, quixotic lust for adventure and escape, which I could not *voluntarily* allow.

I quickly checked the door I'd entered by to make sure it had closed completely. It had. He was still a prisoner—though not mine. I was starting to wonder if I was now his. I gently rubbed the thick, soft leather of his ears as I would a kitten's, and he leaned into the affectionate touch and purred, satisfied. He then dismissed it and resumed his mission.

There wasn't much in the office to maintain his interest so he started to eat the animal warden's chair. This concerned me since, up to this point, all my bad judgment had not caused demonstrable injury or property damage. I watched as my "plausible denial" began to be devoured. He ripped the fabric cover from the chair with his front paw, as though it were rice paper. I contemplated the sock I had once mended over a light bulb—but this would be much more complicated.

Using the lead, I pulled him back roughly from the chair as I said, "No," with a tone of authority. He turned back and considered me, eyeing the source of his restraint. This expression was different from both the pathetic one from the kennel and the quixotic delight he'd displayed once freed. This one conveyed a confidence in his ability to control his environment, a physical presence that could accomplish his will, and a virulent annoyance at my interference. He took this expression one step further and expressed a desire to be the dominant presence within the shelter. With brows curled, prepped for battle, and eyes piercingly focused on me as adversary (and a nutritious source of protein), he took a short step toward me and growled. His mouth made the same movement he'd made before when all his *business teeth* were displayed, only now the motion was accompanied by sound and, although this did not match the frightening scream of a full grown lion, neither was it a cat's meow.

He'd made his point. In a grudge match, two out of three falls, no holds barred (and no weapons used by me), I'm afraid he'd have kicked my butt. At a fraction of my weight, and sickly, this would have been a source of embarrassment, but I digress.

I released the pressure on his lead and, as he felt his freedom restored, he lost interest in mauling me and, instead, resumed mauling the chair. Having exposed the inner foam-rubber cushion, he now tore the innards from the chair in large chunks, and proceeded to bat them playfully across the floor.

I knew I had to get him back in his cage, and understood that the cage was the last place on earth he would willingly go. He was free—almost—if he could get past me, and I believe he understood this. Having dogs and cats (and children) at home, I knew the fundamentals of bribery, reward, and punishment. I could see the cat food and, though I knew this food was for the domestic felines in the shelter, I thought it worth a try.

I let go of the lead as he continued to play with the eviscerated chair, and I reached for a handful of cat kibble with one hand. He noticed my action and interrupted his play to check me out. I re-secured the lead and allowed him to sniff my fist that clenched the cat food within it. He started to chew and lick my hand, intrigued but without aggression. I walked back to his kennel, leading him by my fist, and entered his cage with him following. I dropped the kibble into his food dish where it clinked and bounced against the empty metal bowl. I'd tricked him, and it had worked.

I moved toward the gate and started to unlatch it. The cub looked up from his bowl, and in one lightening quick movement, pounced on me before I could exit his kennel. One of the claws on his right paw dug into my left forearm through my uniform shirt. I pushed him back into his cage as I backed out and slammed the gate shut.

His demeanor changed again, almost instantly. The aggressive folds of his facial features dissolved, and his eyes once again took on the expression of the pitiful prisoner. I don't think this was meant to be a ruse. I think this melancholy was a product of his captivity that he could not mask. With no mother, no guardian, and no ability or opportunity to care for himself, the wildness of this presumed wild animal had once again been tasted and then extinguished. He was not a pet, and he was not the independent hunter he needed to be to survive in the wild.

A couple weeks after my urban wildlife adventure, I asked the animal warden, who lounged comfortably in his new office chair, about the cougar's fate. He told me with some degree of satisfaction that the cub had been donated to the Minnesota Zoo, which allows its inmates to live in a "natural habitat setting" with minimal caging or obvious man-made confines. He would be fed and cared for, but he would never experience the glory his species was afforded in the wild. Rather than living his legacy as the feared king of the forest, he would be an attraction. I guessed the fur-huggers who'd objected to our killing the aggressive adult mountain lion and the road-injured deer probably would have been satisfied with this outcome—I probably should have been too.

Hanged

If one more six-foot-four, two-hundred-fifty-pound, red-haired son had squared off with me and demanded I cut his father down from where he was hanging in the basement, I think I'd have done it. All three of the thirty-something brothers had that unmistakable no-nonsense, no-fear, no-bullshit essence about them when they told me to cut him down. If they had sensed any measure of hostility or indifference in my response, their desperation would have acted as catalyst for their grief to evolve into aggression. A five-year officer knows he can either go toe-to-toe at that point or he can use diplomacy. These brothers weren't criminals, and I was running out of toes.

This was my call so I was the boss—although the street supervisor, Sergeant Flowers, could always countermand my decisions. Before the first son arrived, the victim's wife pleaded through muffled sobs that we cut her husband down. Sgt. Flowers was overcome with being human and agreed to cut the electrical cord supporting the husband's dead weight. As his arm reached up, poised with knife in hand, I reminded him that the M.E. needed to examine the knot and the body in *hanged* position to photograph and make a determination whether the death was self-inflicted or homicidal in nature. They tended to be very picky about this technicality and could be quite testy if they arrived to find the hanged one horizontal rather than vertical.

Sergeant Flowers sighed and shook his head in agreement. At fifty-four he was parting his wispy comb-over closer and closer to his left ear. On windy days he wore his hat. He could have retired three years ago but chose instead to add a little gravy to his pension. He didn't need this. Calls like this one made him wonder whether the gravy was really gravy, and whether he truly needed the gravy or was just greedy. With his pack-a-day habit and the paunch getting thicker by the day, he could probably benefit from a little stress relief.

He said he would stay with the body and *requested* I stand at the top of the stairs and dissuade any family members who might be inclined to stampede down the stairs and cut their loved one down.

Officers called to death scenes generally stand around feeling out of place—regardless of our placement. We express our condolences, but are not there to grieve with the family. But it's impossible to remain untouched by the confined tragedy of the moment—the wasted life. My consciousness, especially in my early years, felt like an expanding balloon awaiting the inevitable eruption, as additional family members and friends arrived at death scenes and began their mournful howls of disbelief, grief, and sometimes horror. We stand watch like failed guardian angels beside the crumpled bodies of those who have died unexpectedly—by their own hand. But who could have seen it coming? Our purpose is merely to contain the scene, preserve evidence, and assist the investigators from the medical examiner's office if needed.

In my early years these suicide calls probably affected me more than other critical incidents. I grew to despise the words "committed suicide," since they implied that the victim perpetrated a crime rather than suffered the dismantling effects of mental illness. The distinction seemed petty, but I preferred to say, "He killed himself." I struggled to comprehend the multitude of suicides we responded to. We never saw obituaries that mentioned suicide as a cause of death. Instead they read, "Died suddenly" or "Died unexpectedly," or the fib, "Died accidentally." And who could blame the authors?

At first I considered those who killed themselves to be weak. After all, life was an adventure with hills and valleys, with happiness, failure, and glory. The frequency and the order in which they are dealt was a mystery, but that was part of life's capricious nature—its wonder. To take one's own life and end the adventure prematurely seemed fallacious. Perhaps that's why the word "hanged" itself appears incorrect—a mistake of tense—and the act, an acquiescence to a manic desire to stop the pain and find peace at any cost.

I looked once more at the man who hanged himself earlier that morning while his wife attended church. He'd taken every precaution to keep the area of the laundry room tidy, which it was. He'd drilled a hole in an overhead joist, high enough on the board to support the weight of his lifeless body—about 175 pounds. Heavy-duty electrical cord ran from some plumbing fixtures under the laundry tub, through the hole in the joist, looped around the joist once, and then descended to his stretched neck with a knot tied securely behind the base of his skull. Prior to the actual hanging part, he'd positioned a fifty-five gallon drum directly beneath the hole in the joist and climbed into it. This drum was ostensibly to collect any bodily fluids that might drain from his corpse. As he stood inside the drum, he fastened the noose around his neck so it was tight when he stood straight up on his tiptoes. When ready, he simply relaxed and stood flat-footed, which caused the noose to tighten further, depriving his lungs of oxygen and his brain of oxygen-rich blood.

He was unconscious within twenty seconds or so and died within minutes. This method of tiptoeing one's way to the Promised Land inspired the inquisitive detective to wonder if the hanged one had not been completely sure about his decision to stand flat-footed on eternity road. The tippy-toe method left the much-maligned one the last-minute option to reverse his decision simply by returning to his tiptoes and loosening the noose.

Experienced detectives also knew that this changing of the mind in the final minutes did not always work. Practitioners of autoerotic asphyxiation, the temporary deprivation of oxygen at the moment of sexual climax, are well aware of this fatal drawback. The inability of the mind and muscles to synchronize while suffering from oxygen deprivation resulted in many deaths of teens and young adults who accidentally suffocated to death. In other words, though they enjoyed the simultaneous choking of the chicken and their neck, they did not intend to kill themselves. Often times the confused and embarrassed parents of the hanged autoerotic asphyxiation victim removed the ever-present pornography, along with the occasional black leather lingerie, or cross-dresser's clothing, from the scene and pulled their son's (usually male victims) pants up. These changes made the puzzle more difficult for the detective who later arrived at the altered scene and sensed something amiss— usually in the parents' demeanor. Until the changes were explained, their guilt from rearranging the scene was sometimes read as complicity in the death.

This phenomenon bewildered me—that a parent preferred the police and, subsequently, their family friends and acquaintances to believe their loved one took his own life rather than died accidentally. Shame is a powerful motivator.

Accidental death from autoerotic asphyxiation is rare among the over-thirty crowd and almost unheard of when accompanied by a suicide note. My victim was an obvious suicide. With little expectation of literary accolades, he left a note which stated simply: "Sorry boys—sorry Honey—love Dad."

The first few suicides I responded to, I wanted to know and understand the *why*. I was nearly manic in my search for a note and felt an incongruity of omission if none was found. Like a criminal co-conspirator left wondering why his partner sold him out, I couldn't understand how someone could check out without letting loved ones know why. It seemed selfish.

After my first dozen or so suicide calls, I stopped wanting to know everything. Maybe I understood, not necessarily the reason but that the option was there; that things sometimes got that bad—that pain sometimes became unbearable. Perhaps what I'd perceived as weakness was simply a bow to an overwhelming depression that might have overtaken any of us.

Maybe I was more conflicted by this empathy than the actual death. To empathize or suffer with the victim, rather than with the grieving family, seemed unhealthy. I learned to accept that one could never scribble a simple explanation for such a desperate act.

His wife found the note on a cleared living-room coffee table after returning from church and began to search the house for her husband. Her search ended with the grizzly discovery in the basement laundry room. She called 911 and told the dispatcher that she'd found her husband hanging, but didn't know if he was actually dead. People unfamiliar with hanging death scenes, which would include most folks, often doubt the reliability of the technique when the victim's feet are touching the floor. This threw me off a bit the first time I was called to such a hanging.

Sgt. Flowers and I arrived at the victim's house at the same time and, after hustling down to the basement and checking the victim, we wasted no time advising the anxious wife that her husband was indeed dead. That, yes, we were absolutely certain of it. Though his thinning orange hair was still parted neatly on the side, his purple swollen tongue protruded from his mouth, and a mixture of mucus, saliva, and bile hung from the corner of his mouth and stretched in a stringy liquid bridge to the chest area of his soiled white T-shirt. His slightly opened eyelids enveloped clouded, static eyes—his gaze fixed on a segment of the cement floor about three feet in front of the drum. His skin was cool to the touch, and he had no respirations or pulse. The stubborn resistance of his arms to movement evidenced rigor mortis, and the purple dappling of liver mortis was starting to set in on his extremities. He was dead all right.

As we checked the house for the note and any signs of foul play, the victim's wife phoned some family members and asked them to come to her house. *Something terrible* had happened. Police prefer not to share these death scenes with any more family members than absolutely necessary. The demands to see the body, along with the wailing and gnashing of teeth, are not something you want to deal with. There would be wakes, visitations, funerals, and post-funeral gatherings for mourners to grieve their lost loved ones. The death scene was neither the right time nor the right place.

Prior to any visitors arriving, the victim's wife told us that her husband had been laid off from work a few months before and had sunken into a lingering depression. Their money situation was not as good as it could have been and he felt responsible for their hardships, which were just beginning.

When the first adult son arrived, he didn't know that his father was injured, much less hanging from the basement ceiling. People react differently when surprised with a loved one's death. Somehow it has become socially acceptable to react in a specific manner according to gender and ethnicity. (I'm hoping these grieving norms are not the result of television depictions.) Some people, mostly mature white men, try to mask their sorrow with phrases of disbelief and attempts to manifest a stoic forbearance. The opposite is true for most women, especially black women and many black men. They make no attempt to hide their sorrow, expressing it through loud, pained weeping and shouted expressions of remorse. This actually appears far more natural (and probably aids in the grieving process) than the tough-guy approach.

Upon learning of his father's death, the first son crossed the cultural barrier, shouting loudly, crumpling his entire pain-stricken body to the floor, and pulling his long red hair with both hands. After his mother told him where his father was, the son approached me on the stairs and stated—not asking my permission—that he was going downstairs to cut his father down. I'm a man of average stature, 5'11", 170 pounds (soaking wet, with my boots on), so this son at 6'4", 250 pounds towered over me and had, at that point, absolutely no intention of being talked out of his mission.

I thought how I must have appeared to him as he walked into the house where he once lived. A police officer, an interloper of the worst kind, dressed in navy blue from head to toe with buzzed hair and shiny black boots. This police officer was in his house but acted as though he had some kind of authority, which in fact I did. The police and subsequently the M.E. have a duty to protect a death scene until the investigation is complete. Only at that point is the victim released to the family. I tried to imagine this son's natural antipathy toward me.

In a sincere tone of voice, amalgamating sympathy, compassion, professionalism, and a hint of authority, I told the son that his father's death would be considered a homicide until the medical examiner arrived at the residence and checked the "unaltered" condition of his father. The son slowed his pace a bit as he pondered this slight complication. Then, without looking at me, he continued forward until, like the fool that I am, I blocked his path at the foot of the stairs. I told him that if he cut his father down now, he would never know if his father was murdered or if he took his own life. At this, the son doubled over in agony, crying loudly again. I patted his shoulder without saying anything. When he regained his composure he looked at me and asked when the medical examiner would arrive. The fact that it was Sunday meant the M.E.'s investigator would have been paged out of his residence. He then had to travel to his office to pick up the rig, then continue on to Bloomington, and finally to this house. I told the son succinctly, "He's on his way."

This seemed to be good enough for a temporary reprieve, as the son turned from me and rejoined his mother in the living room. As the pain-filled harmony of their mourning reached me at the stairs, the doorbell rang and another huge red-haired son entered the living room.

Like déjà vu, this son spoke briefly with his mother before shouts of grief filled the house and loud determined footsteps approached me. The second son made the same demand as the first, but before I could discourage him with my pre-planned police rhetoric, the first son came to my aid and discouraged him with the police rhetoric I'd used on him. Amazingly, this worked even better than when I used it. Again I was asked when the medical examiner would arrive and again I advised that he was on his way.

The third son didn't bother to knock or ring the doorbell

but barged right in the front door asking what had happened. He looked to be the youngest of the boys, his red hair much longer than his brothers', reaching his shoulders, and red freckles that speckled his fair features. But he could still have been mistaken for a triplet of the other two. His familiarity with the house made me wonder if he'd only recently moved out.

His mother told him that his father had hanged himself in the basement where he remained hanging as they awaited the medical examiner. Like a soldier rallying the troops he said, "Well, let's go cut him down!"

At this point I decided I would not stand in their way. If they were willing to fight with a police officer to bring what they considered some respect, humility, or humanity to their father, I would not injure them or, more likely, be thrown down the stairs to put a very quick and painful end to the skirmish. As the third brother approached with the other two in tow, I offered one final comment delivered in a sincere tone of capitulation. "You don't want to see your father like this." The third brother looked at me as if he hadn't noticed me until I spoke, but still appeared determined to push past me.

"Trust me," I said, "you don't want to remember him like this." The third brother stopped directly in front of me with the other two behind him. He did not cry. He was seething with anger. He was not just angry that a police officer was standing in his parents' house restricting his movement and giving him personal counseling, or that his brothers had been persuaded to back down and acquiesce to this officer's wishes. He was angry at his father.

He looked at me stricken, and blurted, "How could he do this?"

I shook my head and said softly, "I don't know."

He turned back to his brothers. "How could he do this?"

Now he started to cry. His brothers embraced him. His

mother came to them and they huddled together weeping. They walked back into the living room as a group, their involuntary wailing pained and inconsolable.

I looked down at my boots and released the breath I'd been holding. I thought of the gruesome montage of suicide scenes I'd been called to. The young crack-heads dying alone in their apartments, the ashen, empty alcoholic G.I. bleeds, the seemingly random, cavernous gunshot-to-head wounds. The waste of it all came over me like soured stomach bile rising in my gut. I stifled an impulse to vent my anger aloud, and instead silently cursed the medical examiner for taking so long, my sergeant for abandoning me at the stairs, and finally the boys' father for hanging himself in a trash barrel when he had so much to live for.

Run-Tin-Tin

My partner Mark Sherburn and I were pioneers of the Bloomington Police Department's K9 Unit in 1986. Being first had its ups and downs. No one knew much about what to expect—including Mark and me—but expectations were nevertheless sky-high. We were fortunate to have received training from the St. Paul police K9 trainers who were then, and remain today, some of the best in the business. We also witnessed a different police culture.

The BPD consisted of about one hundred sworn officers at the time, while St. Paul PD had about five hundred. Our sparse numbers fostered a small-town mentality that could be brutal at times. Mistakes made by officers, both on-duty and off, generally became common knowledge and were usually discussed at length behind the offending officer's back. One could feel it in a room gone quiet when entered, or sense it in quick, silent glances. This peer shunning had a profound effect on the bumbling officer and made the job more of a proving ground than an occupation.

In St. Paul, the officers made just as many mistakes, personally and professionally, but the response was different. Rather than whispering behind closed doors and looking away as the subject of their rumors approached, they openly teased, tormented, and taunted the victim—but in a joking way. The malicious shunning was absent, and problems and mistakes were dealt with one day and, usually, forgotten the next. Experienced cops know that the potential to screw up is always there. Shit happens, and sooner or later everyone steps in a pile of it.

My recruit dog, Clyde, was as raw as they came. He was a slender, mostly black one-year-old German Shepherd dog I'd named after the NBA great, Clyde "The Glide" Drexler. (Many assumed incorrectly that I'd named him after Bonnie's partner in crime.) The first day I brought him home from the kennel he bounded gracefully from the kitchen floor onto the counter and started lapping at the kitchen faucet. When given voice commands like, "no," "sit," "stay," or "down," he looked at me with that blank, bewildered stare, and you knew this was his first experience with verbal commands. When he came to the St. Paul dog kennels, his name was "Buddy," a common name for a dog who's never really been named. The owner simply refers to the dog as "Buddy" just like he does with the new forklift driver at work whose name he hasn't bothered to learn.

Tim Jones (RIP), one of the K9 trainees from St. Paul, was familiar with my dog. While working patrol in the "Frogtown" area, he had seen Clyde tied to a tree day and night. Clyde had lived a lonely existence, never having graced the inside of a house. He had no training whatsoever, but he fired up for the aggression testing so was accepted into the class.

The aggression test consisted of a trainer holding the dog on lead while another trainer, the "bad guy" or decoy, as the

Schutzhund trainers refer to them, slunk suspiciously around a corner and taunted the dog from a distance. Depending on the K9 candidates' reaction to the decoy, they were accepted or culled from the group. Clyde demonstrated proper aggression when the decoy appeared, lunging forward and barking ferociously at the interloper. Had he cowered or appeared uninterested he would have been culled.

Clyde had some habits that made me doubtful about his intrepid demeanor during bite work, but I left it to the experts to interpret these personality quirks. On the one hand, he bit like a crocodile during attack work but, at the same time, he was very frightened during thunderstorms, wanting to curl up on my lap until the storm passed. He exhibited a very short attention span when tracking or searching buildings, but this attention deficit was common among young dogs.

I was always encouraged when we stepped to the starting line to do bite work. Clyde stretched his body out toward the decoy, his every sinuous muscle quivering slightly as he anticipated sinking his teeth into the bite arm of the decoy. He focused so intently on his target that he unconsciously refrained from blinking. As the command was given, he sprang forward, a guided missile, his muscled thighs pumping as he ran, propelling him to his target. He could not accelerate fast enough, as the ripped grass in the wake of his strides shot out behind him. Approaching his target he lunged forward for the bite arm and hung on with a vise-like grip that could not be removed by human hands—only the K9 handler could end the attack with a simple voice command. Sometimes when the adrenaline was cooking, the "out" command needed to be screamed into his ears, but this was encouraging. Clyde, like most K9s, loved bite work more than anything—more than sex, food, or rabbit chasing, which could all be real enough distractions once he graduated to the street.

The decoys who ran from and took bites from the dogs were played by other trainees in the class. We all took our fair share of bites. The other trainees were unanimous in their praise of Clyde's bite work. According to them, he bit hard with a full mouth and hung on with tremendous pressure until ordered off. Classmate trainee Mike O'Bannon once ran from Clyde wearing a worn out bite arm with loose stitching. Clyde managed to clamp onto this prophylactic device between the seams, puncturing Mike's arm deeply, resulting in a trip to the hospital and several sets of sutures.

All the trainees had some initial apprehension about taking bites from the dogs, especially early in the program when the dogs were unfamiliar with the bite arms and considered any extremity as equal opportunity. Of all the rookies, none dreaded taking bites more than St. Paul's own, Benny Zucker. Benny had a very strong, hard-biting dog himself, but lacked control of his dog. After missing a couple days of class, Benny showed up with Bell's palsy, a temporary nervous condition with effects similar to a stroke. The left side of Benny's face was temporarily paralyzed. His condition subsided as the class went on and the dogs progressed.

Contrary to what the police department's public relations officer might say, bite work was the most important aspect of K9 training. Everyone involved in the program understood this. If your dog performed poorly on the other, more academic aspects, you could live with that and continue to work on the problems, but if your dog would not bite—he was not going to make it and would be a detriment on the street.

Tim Jones and I ended up vying for "best dog in class" in the K9 graduation dog trial. His dog, Ninja, was exceptional in all aspects of K9 training. The trial included the following competitions: tracking, agility, article search, box work (a simulated building search), obedience, and bite work, which included blank gunfire at the dogs, and handler protection, where the decoy attacked the handler. Of the fifteen dogs in our class, Clyde managed to eke out first place and steal the glory from St. Paul.

But even with trophy in hand, my doubts about Clyde's true potential lingered. His high "play drive," which was beneficial in training, made it difficult to distinguish between immaturity and cluelessness.

Everyone was interested in what these new dogs could do. The K9 program had been funded by the City's crime prevention dollars, much of which consisted of private donations made by Bloomington citizens and local businesses. As K9 graduation came and went, the local newspaper boasted of the dogs' abilities and their start date.

On our first or second day on the street together Clyde and I were called to track a sixteen-year-old boy who had fled his house when officers attempted to serve a warrant for his arrest. It was a sunny summer Saturday afternoon, and families were out in their yards. I was not comfortable with my new partner, feeling like he was, as usual, ready to play but had no idea what he was doing. A police officer with a dog attracted attention, and Clyde was thrown off the track early by inquisitive homeowners and their children who wanted to talk to me and pet the handsome K9. We had practiced tracking with minor distractions, but nothing like this. Having no idea of K9 capabilities other than what Rin Tin Tin did on TV, even fellow officers interfered with the track. Of course, there was no way Clyde could track the suspect with all the contamination, distractions, and interference. I finally put him back in the squad, and officers closed in on the perimeter and found the suspect under a deck Clyde had passed by early in the search.

Directly after the failed track, my boss called me into his office and asked me in a closed door, one-on-one meeting why

Clyde had missed the suspect under the deck. This was viewed as a failure, and some of the recalcitrant veteran officers who had voiced their doubts about dogs in police work would be saying, "I told you so," making my boss look bad. The rumor mill, and the metronome of whispers and glances, started to swing and I was the target. I explained to my boss how dogs were limited by natural physical conditions like cross tracks, interference, and scene contamination. I felt my explanation deteriorating into a rationalization for failure—at least that's what it started to sound like. The success, backslapping, hand-shakes, and smiles were evaporating. The perception of my defensive attitude only made my actions appear that much more like failure.

As we put our time in on the streets, working mostly nights, Clyde proved to be an asset in locating suspects who had fled on foot outdoors or into buildings, but a pattern of behavior that concerned me from the start continued to plague me. Clyde had experienced many opportunities to apprehend (a euphemism for bite) suspects and had chosen not to. He would find them, he might even bark at and circle them, but he would not respond aggressively. So far this had not endangered me, but the potential was there.

The *street* was different from training, even when we tried to make training as real as possible. The main difference was the absence of the bite arm, a protective leather and canvass prosthetic that fit over the decoy's right arm. Dogs could smell the bite arm from literally a mile away, and the training switch in their brains was activated when they made this olfactory connection. Clyde's play-drive switched on with this scent-recognition, and he was ready for action. There was no trepidation involved in practice. I could sense Clyde's confusion when he located a suspect on the street that was not wearing a bite arm. He often turned and looked at me for direction but had no aggressive response to the suspect regardless of my prompting. He'd found the suspect and he was done. Had the suspects worn a bite arm when they went out that night to burgle, Clyde would surely have bitten them—albeit only on the arm.

Clyde also knew the difference between practice and reality from my attitude—my disposition. There was no sense of anxiety on my part as handler during practice; however, when searching a building for an armed suspect, there was a sense of the unknown, and a natural apprehension. Along with these emotions came the release of pheromones, a chemical substance released by animals—and humans—that the K9s picked up on.

My attempts to suppress any emotion on "hot calls" were, of course, futile. Clyde sensed this. He started to evidence this by defecating in the buildings we searched—which really started to annoy me. We began a new protocol of stopping at a park prior to all searches to ensure his opportunity to empty before initiating a building search. Upon being told to "hurry up," which he knew meant "empty bladder and bowels," he looked at me like I was crazy. We then drove to the building to be searched, where I announced my presence to the would-be burglar: "Police officer. I'm releasing my K9 into the building unless you come out now and surrender." I then paused for about ten seconds, drew my pistol, and entered the building with Clyde. Sensing the seriousness of the situation, Clyde sniffed around the floor, and I could tell he was not on the scent of a bad guy, but rather searching for the perfect spot to lighten his load. He then circled once or twice in classic canine form and emptied his bowels—usually a soggy stool at this juncture—onto the floor, which was usually carpeted. As he started to squat I screamed, "Noooo!" at the top of my lungs, literally scaring the shit out of Clyde and the officers at the exits—not to mention the suspect, whose capture had become moot at this point.

This situation progressed and became more embarrassing than the infamous missed track of the boy under the deck. With the pattern of poop came the inevitable rumors, whispers, and glances that became more and more prevalent as the malady continued. Clyde was now pooping in nearly every building we searched, and businesses were starting to call the department and request we leave their offices alone and ignore the burglar alarms rather than stink up their buildings with dog feces. As my frustration mounted, it became more and more tempting during these building searches to direct the gun in hand toward the source of this *shit*.

I told my supervisor that I had lost confidence in my partner and requested I train a new dog, but he always reminded me that my dog was the best of his class and that Clyde's problems were not the result of his weaknesses but, rather, the result of poor training on my part. Our meeting ended with a warning that I bring Clyde up to snuff.

I trained every chance I got, and I had the assistance of many officers who volunteered to help me and act as decoys for building searches—but Clyde knew the difference. He always found the bad guy in practice scenarios and bit him, impressively. I didn't know what else to do. I'm sure there were training techniques I wasn't aware of that might have helped, but I was relying on the methods I was familiar with.

The situation came to a head on a cold January morning, when I was called from my house at 0300 to assist the Richfield Police, who at the time had no canines of their own. They advised our dispatcher that a silent alarm had been tripped at a bowling alley and, upon arriving at the scene, officers had found a forced entry and heard noises within.

I had adopted a new attitude about building searches that was grounded in officer survival—-mine. All my attention in the past had been on the failings of my dog, which left me very vulnerable within these buildings. I decided to search the buildings on my own using whatever skills I'd learned as an officer. I had lost any confidence I'd ever had in Clyde, and saw few options for myself. In retrospect, these lone building searches without the aide of a competent K9 partner were very foolish, but I was guided by the dangerous combination of pride and image.

Upon pulling into the bowling alley with lights out, I found several Richfield officers awaiting my arrival. They had been there for at least thirty minutes since I was called from my bed and had to dress, collect my dog, empty him, and drive to the scene. A Richfield officer at the entrance to the bowling alley showed me the forced, damaged door, and advised that he'd heard what sounded like someone rummaging through the office. It had been quiet for the last half hour.

I brought Clyde, who was pulling eagerly against the lead, to the entrance of the bowling alley, and made my entry warning. "This is the police department. We know you're in there. Come out now or I'm sending in a police canine." I waited about fifteen seconds before I released Clyde from his lead and gave the command, "Find him!"

Clyde ran into the bowling alley and sprinted to the office door. Alone, and with gun drawn, I ran behind him and watched him take a long, audible inhalation from under the office door followed by several shallower sniffs. He then started to bark and scratch at the wooden door, indicating he had found the hidden suspect. He turned to me with an expression of supreme satisfaction. If nothing else, I trusted his nose implicitly. I tried the office door and found it locked.

Thinking we had solved this one lickety-split, and would now treat ourselves to a little burglar "arm-candy," I shouted through the office door ordering the burglar to come out. Clyde continued to bark and jump against the door giving the impression of uncharacteristic blood lust that I found very encouraging. I hoped the burglar would remain in hiding, and give Clyde a chance for his first bite.

I ordered the suspect out repeatedly and finally decided to kick the door and have Clyde charge in and *apprehend* the suspect. Having had the experience of giving a half-assed kick that didn't smash the lock mechanism, I prepared to give it my all. With my right foot poised for destruction, I let go with all my might, booting the door's bull's-eye—right beside the handle hardware. My right foot sailed mightily against—and through—what I now realized was a hollow-core door. My boot shattered both the brittle wood and the intense silence like a firecracker, and Clyde, eyes wide with horror, turned and sprinted through the business and out the door, where baffled cover officers watched his retreat.

I screamed, "Clyde, come!" as I tried in vain to dislodge my foot, which was stuck through the door nearly to my knee. Any attempt to pull it out was met with the painful retaliation of wooden splinters poised at an angle to dig into my calf. I continued to holler toward the entrance, which appeared from my angle to be an exit. After countless commands, Clyde came sulking back into the bowling alley, head down, tail between his legs. He looked at me dancing on one leg with my foot stuck in the door, and started to sniff the floor and turn circles. Knowing the prelude to the poop sequence, I screamed, "Nooo!" but before the word was out, Clyde was hunched over constructing a stinky, steaming log cabin.

Having finally achieved ultimate frustration, I leveled my Smith & Wessen, .45 caliber semi-automatic pistol in the direction of my carpenter's apprentice. I would never have hurt my dog. It was more of a modified hand signal for "STOP IT!" He looked at me mournfully as he pinched off his handiwork prematurely and started eying the exit. Stretching for composure,

I lifted my weapon, and said, in as calm a voice as I could muster, "No, Clyde. Come." He considered the exit again, but wisely chose to join me at the door where I continued my one-legged polka.

Having some concern for the safety of my foot on the suspect side of the door, I weighed my options. They were two: pull my leg out, in what would surely be accompanied by excruciating pain and would no doubt be somewhat messy, or call to the cover officers to enter the building and assist me with the extrication of my foot. In addition to the tools that would be needed, this second option brought with it what would certainly include some embarrassment and ultimately legendary status as a monumental fuck-up.

Coward that I was (am), I chose option number one, gritted my teeth, and yanked my foot back toward my torso. Like a woman in the pushing stage of labor, I screamed as a hundred splintering slivers penetrated my calf circumferentially. A cover officer at the door heard my horrifying scream and shouted in to me, "Everything okay in there?"

"Everything's fine," I lied. "I just...tripped."

Having only moved my stuck leg from the knee to the ankle, I gathered my balance and gave one more pull to regain my foot. I stifled this scream and planted my right foot on the floor beside the left where it belonged. My ankles greeted one another, glad to be a tandem again. I pulled my pant leg up to survey the damage and noticed that, in addition to the inch-long splinters still stuck in my calf and the drips and smears of blood descending from the splinters, my new pair of Rocky boots were scratched and scuffed beyond repair of brush and polish and would never pass a formal inspection again.

Clyde sniffed my ankle and looked up at me apologetically, probably sensing his life was just a whim and a bullet away from spent. I granted him a temporary reprieve and went back to the business of the door, which remained stubbornly intact. Rather than risk my life and another limb, I decided to *shoulder* the door. This, I knew, would also frighten my vacant-bowelled partner so I commanded him to sit and stay before ramming the door with my upper body. The splintering of wood against the flimsy metal handle mechanism was loud enough to frighten Clyde but, sensing the grave danger of retreat, he fought his first impulse for flight and remained trembling at heel.

With the once brave, hollow-core door now defeated, and my steady partner at my side, I shouted to the suspect, who must have been completely bewildered at this point, "Come out now or I'll send my dog in and he will bite you." Doubting the conviction of my delivery, I waited for a reply. After about fifteen seconds a tall, slender teen emerged from behind some metal files with his hands up. Clyde sauntered up to him and circled his legs. I assured the boy that if he continued to cooperate he would not be bitten. I could have given him a written guarantee.

I wonder to this day what Clyde would have done had the suspect charged me with a two-by-four and pounded me repeatedly about the head and shoulders. I'm inclined to believe that Clyde would have quickly opted for the fresh, brisk air outside the bowling alley, but I cling to the romantic hope that he would have come to my aid.

Though a bit dismayed by the comings and goings of my intrepid partner, the awaiting officers seemed unimpressed with my apparent facile apprehension. I walked, limping ever so slightly, out of the bowling alley, looking down at my dog as I wore a mask of confidence and pride that had to be easily transparent. My injuries were covered with navy blue polyester and would never be mentioned on any IOD (Injured On Duty) report.

I extracted the splinters and slivers in the privacy of my bathroom where the shouted expletives echoed only against closed doors and windows. Clyde heard them from his dog house outside where he lay, ears down, tail stuffed between his legs.

Clyde was castrated before his training as a police dog and was never able to reclaim his balls. However, he turned out to be a legendary drug-detection dog, having recovered more drugs and drug money at the Minneapolis/St. Paul International Airport than any dog to date. There was little courage needed to sniff luggage, and if nothing else, Clyde had a magnificent nose. The apprehension at the bowling alley, while suspicious to those officers at the door, was seen as another successful notch in Clyde's collar. Though not an exception to dogdom in general, Clyde was an exception to police K9s and would have been weeded out early in an up-to-date, established program. As a team, we went on to perform countless other building searches, with my private knowledge that our success in finding and apprehending suspects lay exclusively on my shoulders. We also presented numerous demonstrations for a variety of groups.

As a misguided source for PR, K9s were routinely paraded and exhibited in front of civic groups and private organizations—especially those that contributed to the K9 crime prevention fund, which enabled its inception. Of course children were most impressed with the dogs' almost-human response to verbal commands and hand signals. Obedience, agility, article searches, and bite work were the most requested demos, and at the conclusion the children wanted the back-stage pass to meet and pet these wonderful creatures.

While some handlers bragged of their ability to turn their K9's *aggression switch* from on to off, others were more cautious with their dogs. If a dog had been raised from a pup in a house with children, the K9s oftentimes understood the latitude they needed to grant these crawling, pawing, eye-poking, feet- and tail-stepping pains in the ass. Dogs that were not familiar with children considered them annoyances much as they would a puppy that continuously jumped, pawed, and nipped at them, and treated them as such. Adult dogs harassed by exuberant puppies growled a warning and, if unheeded, followed up with a bite, usually to the muzzle—the source of their painful irritation. This bite usually got the message across, and after the puppy recovered from the fear and pain (yip! yip! yip!) he deferred his attention elsewhere. This same treatment was given to a similarly offensive child but with far more serious consequences, usually resulting in stitches and lawsuits.

I was confident that Clyde would not become aggressive with children during these demos since he was very magnanimous with my toddler-aged boys. During one particular Boy Scout demo, I noticed he had developed a routine for coping with the onslaught of rambunctious children. Police K9s, like many dogs extensively trained by one person, typically became one-person dogs, with the handler being that person. Once Clyde had bonded with me during our K9 training, I became his *number one*. Following the Boy Scout demo, when the children were finally invited to pet him, Clyde turned to face me and sat looking directly at my eyes while the swarm of children carelessly but unintentionally stepped on his feet and tail, petted, pulled, and poked him. He never broke eye contact with me and never even acknowledged that anyone else was present, much less attending him.

This worked for us, but I worry about the gambled, misguided altruism of allowing civilians to handle these working dogs. It should probably be enough for citizens to observe the K9's capabilities with the understanding that they are not trained to discriminate between adult and child, nor to accept mistreatment or discipline from anyone other than their handler. The jaw power and teeth of these dogs can be tragically unforgiving.

Clyde's career was mercifully shortened to five years due to a personal problem—my second wife's revelation that she should leave. As a single father with toddlers, the added responsibility of training a K9 became too much. Some of Clyde's personal habits—such as his incessant barking and his in-house sport of "bowling for children" as he scrambled through the house, clawing the wood floors for traction, did not bode well for his future as a pet. Perhaps if we had found more success as a K9 team I would have tried harder to keep him at home, but when I looked at Clyde I saw failure—mine or his, it didn't matter. The bond we established in training had deteriorated. I still cared for him but probably harbored some resentment dating back to a hundred stinky, dangerous, failed building searches.

A married, childless woman who worked for the city asked if she could provide a foster home for Clyde, and her offer turned out to be a blessing for all. Clyde was afforded a retirement life of luxury, living indoors and sleeping between his master and mistress in their bed. Shortly after this change of venue Clyde started to suffer the effects of cancer, and his adopted family spent a great deal of time and money in their attempts to extend his life.

I visited Clyde with my children just prior to his death. He barked a fiery warning as I rang the doorbell, but settled down as my boys and I entered the house and sat down in the living room. Clyde was obviously sick, his ribs protruding from his chest, his slender body gaunt as the brightness in his eyes had started to cloud. Like a car slightly out of alignment, he wobbled as he walked, unsteady on his feet. Clyde sat in front of me and I stroked him along his back, feeling his jagged backbone as my hand traveled the distance from his withers to his flank. To my surprise, Clyde turned and faced his adoptive mother, his eyes locked on hers, repeating the survival technique he'd learned at the Boy Scout demo. Our visit it seemed had become an annoyance to him. He had bonded with his new family and my status as number one had dropped considerably.

The sadness of exclusion and rejection came over me as I considered that perhaps Clyde had forgotten me. It had been several months since I'd seen him; he was suffering from cancer, and taking several tranquilizer-type medications.

Or perhaps he remembered me clearly, our search of the bowling alley in Richfield still lucid in his mind, my pistol leveled at his head, and my voice straining for composure, "No Clyde. Come."

Memorial

It was one of those July afternoons I was glad to be a regular grunt patrol officer, window down, elbow extended, sunglasses on, with the FM radio playing softly, in deference to the squad radio. A gentle breeze made the 85-degree, blue-skied day just about perfect. The Little League baseball fields had filled up, and couples in shorts walked their dogs. My canine partner, Clyde, sniffed at the window cage and jerked his nose in small increments as new uninvited fragrances invaded his small aromatic world.

One of the benefits of living in the town you patrolled was taking your 10-7 (dinner break) at home. It gave you a chance to shed the burdensome gun-belt along with the sweat-caked body armor. I had forty-five minutes to unwind and regroup. On June 12, 1989, at 1600 hours I took my dinner break in my air-conditioned home, just Clyde and me. After wolfing down something quick and easy, I usually watched the news or vegged out on my backyard deck.

Halfway through my break, I heard the dispatcher assign a medical emergency a half-mile from my house. Officers eating dinner were not generally expected to clear their break early unless no other squad could be found to cover the call. This medical sounded serious, and the closest squad was halfway across the city. The dispatcher put the call out as an "unknown medical" phoned in by a woman whose neighbor stumbled into her driveway bleeding profusely before collapsing. According to the caller, her neighbor was last seen mowing her lawn in the backyard, so the reporter assumed the injury was caused by the lawn mower.

As the dispatcher continued to search for an available squad within a five-mile radius of the scene, I decided to take the call. I scrambled into my vest, uniform shirt, and duty belt before taking off in my squad with Clyde.

It had rained for three days prior to this day of cloudless sunshine. People changed when the sky cleared just as they did on full-moon nights. Cops, hospital emergency room medical staff, and detox workers clearly understood this. All my calls had been simple that day. Theft reports, motorist assists, and car accidents, where no one was hurt or quibbling over fault. Nothing could go *really* wrong this day. I was sure the medical would end up being nothing. People always exaggerated injuries that bled.

I arrived at the scene of the medical in less than two minutes and didn't need to check for the address since there was a group of six neighbors standing around a woman who lay on her back with her head on the down slope of the cement driveway. The bystanders waved their arms frantically and shouted at me to hurry as I pulled in front of the house. I glanced at the woman on the ground and reflexively turned again in double-take. The woman bled so profoundly down the slope of the driveway, its wake resembled a water hose left errantly running.

The shouts turned to expletives as a forty-year-old man in khaki shorts encouraged me to "Get the fuck over here!" I felt my pulse rise and fall on my neck, never having experienced bystanders on a medical react so confrontationally. I waddled up the driveway with my medical kit in one hand, and oxygen tank in the other, and knelt beside the woman. The stream of blood I'd seen appeared to originate from the woman's mouth although her entire torso was covered with blood.

I asked where she was cut and the group fell silent. Finally, the homeowner who had called 911 said she only saw her neighbor crumple in her drive moments before, and assumed she'd been injured while mowing her lawn.

I examined the woman closely. She was wearing white shorts and a dark blue midriff, which covered only her breasts. She had long, sandy-brown hair matted around her thin tanned face. I remembered my First Responder training: attend first to A-B-C, airway, breathing, and circulation. I scanned her slender body quickly but could find no source of the bleeding. I paused at her legs believing them to be the obvious source in a mower-related accident but could find no lacerations. Her eyes were open but fixed, frozen in a lifeless stare over the crowd gathered behind me. I felt no rise and fall in her abdomen, or any air exchange by her mouth. She had a very weak, thready pulse at her carotid artery, or maybe I was just feeling my own since it seemed I could almost hear my heart beating as I scrambled to find the source of this woman's injury.

As I asked the group of bystanders who among them could assist me in CPR, the victim produced a voluminous bloody mass in her mouth. I cleared it with my fingers and found the obstruction to be a mixture of tissue and blood. I turned her head to the side so future regurgitants would not block her airway. I had seen a lung cancer victim vomit a sink full of this bloody tissue on another medical. I asked the neighbors if they knew of any medical conditions this woman suffered from, but they knew of none. This woman was dying, her life draining before my eyes. Her only hope was what I might do right then and there to save her.

I repeated my request for help as I turned the oxygen flow to max. Of the six bystanders, it seemed none could assist me. I wanted to say something to them about the worth of their presence at this scene but decided against it. I was, however, growing ever more impatient as they continued with their confrontational chorus of criticisms.

As I placed the mask over her face, I noticed she had regurgitated another mouthful of the bloody tissue. Using my fingers as a scoop I cleared her mouth again and requested via my handheld radio that the assist cars step it up. The futility of my lone rescue efforts only inspired the group of helpless critics to continue their barrage of insults. The two assist cars driving code-three (lights and siren) radioed they were struggling through rush-hour traffic, but promised to redouble their efforts.

The day was lost. Everything had changed. The sun still shone on my back, baking my vest-covered torso in a blanket of sweat, but shadow had darkened this perfect day. The air itself had putrefied with the acrid odor of exposed viscera. The sound of the wind through my window had been replaced by the expressed manifestations of fear and anger.

I placed the mask over the woman's mouth, which filled with blood again before I could deliver the oxygen. I knew a human body contained only five or six liters of blood and, judging from the sanguine stream down the driveway, she had to be nearly depleted. Her fate appeared dubious as my hands floundered from her mouth to her chest, to the mask, and back again in a vicious cycle of futility. I hadn't gotten a single breath into her since I arrived, and knew I was losing her. I turned her head to the side and quickly scooped away the bloody mix before giving her two quick breaths. I then started chest compressions, my hands and arms now covered in her blood.

Though the bystanders could not help me, they must have felt their continuous hysterical shouting to be beneficial or at least better than standing by helplessly, so they continued. I'm sure they too sensed what now appeared inevitable. Their perception of my incompetence had made us adversaries. I was, after all, expected to right the wrong and save her, or at least discover what the problem was. That's why they had called. My powers stripped, I knelt, nakedly impotent.

I asked for someone among them to re-check her body for injury as I performed CPR. Two of the women did a cursory check of the woman but found no external source of the bleeding. I was beginning to believe the cause was internal rather than the external mower accident as reported.

I got into a rhythm of sweeping her mouth, delivering two quick breaths, and then doing the chest compressions. The chest compressions seemed to be having the effect of bringing up more blood and lung tissue into her mouth. Much of the blood and tissue she vomited flowed down onto her chest. Her midriff was soaked, and bubbled with blood, as my hands slipped from their anchor point on her sternum. When I pressed down on her chest, my hand formed a cavity that engulfed the heel of my hand in a puddle of blood. I didn't know if I was doing more harm than good, but knew she would die without oxygen and pulse so I continued.

My first assist arrived in what seemed like a half hour. I later learned it was seven minutes. I told her I could not find the cause of the bleeding so she did a complete body survey but came up with nothing. At that point she took over chest compressions, while I concentrated solely on keeping the victim's airway clear, and delivering oxygen.

At my request, the 911 caller pointed out the victim's house across the street and I glanced over the area between breaths. I noticed dark, football-sized liquid splotches spaced about five feet apart between the victim's house and the driveway she now lay on. It appeared that as she had crossed the street, her every exhalation produced a bloody regurgitation.

The paramedics appeared shortly after the first assist and found the source of her injury in less than a minute. One of the medics cut the victim's midriff off between her breasts, exposing her chest. I could not see the cuts at first. I wanted to deny the revelation that she had been stabbed. At the same time it was akin to a professor explaining a simple mathematical solution to a confused student. Of course she had been stabbed. There in the area covered by her tiny shirt were seven stab wounds in a three-inch group. There were two more in her upper abdomen, and as the medic rolled her over he found one more in her back. There was nothing symmetrical about the punctures other than their shape—straight, almost imperceptibly thin, half-inch lines. Some were horizontal, others vertical or diagonal. I had to look very closely to see them since the paper-thin punctures were no longer bleeding. Once exposed, I could see them open slightly and then seal with each compression—wet, scarlet orifices, evident for a moment and then invisible. A trauma dressing was placed over them and we continued CPR. Detectives would later recover the fillet knife used in the assault.

My concentration wavered as I silently cursed myself for having missed the injuries. Police officers rarely exposed a medical victim's breasts unless the situation demanded it—like this one. We usually left the job to the medics, but I should have done it. Perhaps the presence of the critical audience affected my decision, or maybe I felt it too indiscreet.

I requested detectives to the scene as the medics prepared

the victim for transport. By the time I stood on cramped, unsteady legs, the screaming dissonance of sirens filled the neighborhood as detectives and crime scene techs began to arrive.

I turned toward the medic's rig and noticed the chief of police standing beside me. He looked me up and down with a straight-mouthed expression as if checking my uniform, but said nothing. He would tell me years later that this was the first murder in the city since he took over as chief, and he would never forget my appearance as I stepped away from the woman's body. My exposed skin including my hair, face, and arms were painted with blood. He had been a deputy chief in Minneapolis where homicide was common. He said that moment was a defining revelation for him. Perhaps he thought this suburb could be immune from the blight. Perhaps the shocked neighbors behind me who owned the surrounding upscale two-story homes shared the chief's misconception—his hope.

My assist and I joined the medics in the back of their rig and continued CPR while en route to the hospital. We glanced across the body at one another for a reality check as the ambulance rumbled through potholes or took a fast turn, tossing us off to one side of the vehicle. Without words we telegraphed the futility of our efforts, then we recomposed, repositioned, and resumed our exhaustive rhythm.

Once at the hospital, we peeked into the OR to get a glimpse of the ER doctors' rescue efforts. They were short-lived. The disappointed lead trauma physician quickly pronounced her dead. This doctor found us washing our arms in a large white plastic sink and told us that had the victim received those wounds while lying on the ER table, she would still have died. I appreciated his consideration, but it did little to allay my feelings of incompetence. The victim lay on a stainless steel table twenty feet from us, her tanned body slowly acquiescing to room temperature.

Another officer picked us up at the hospital and drove us back to the scene where our squads remained. The area was still congested with marked and unmarked squads. Yellow crime scene tape stretched around trees and fences in the victim's and neighbors' yards. The street supervisor told me to go home and change my uniform before returning to duty. I walked to my squad, having forgotten about my canine partner who was now lounging in the back seat. He perked up as I approached, sniffing my altered essence, his nose working like a piston.

The victim's husband would return home from a baseball game with his son shortly after I left. He would be greeted with the same scene of disarray until a harried street officer would notice him and ask him to please leave the area of the crime scene.

"What's your name again? You live in that house? Oh, my—I'm sorry to have to tell you this, but..."

If I had to choose between working on the woman, or giving the death notification to the family, I would work on the woman.

The blood ran down my body and collected by my feet as the shower washed me as clean as it could. From the volume of blood coloring the floor of the tub, one would think I was bleeding freely from a serious wound. Like the scent of chlorine on one's skin after swimming in a pool, the faint acrid odor of her life's blood came back to life as it mixed with the shower water. The woman had bled out like a lung-shot deer that continued to run on adrenaline and fear, unaware of the injury and the pain, her terror unfathomable.

The following day the detectives arrested the seventeen-year-old boy who had killed her. He had ridden by her house on his bike, as she was mowing the grass in her backyard, and got the idea to rape her. He surprised her in her house as she returned from mowing and wrestled her to the floor, holding his fillet knife to her throat. He had brought condoms with him. She apparently fought him off harder than he expected, so he stabbed her repeatedly in the chest using both hands in his forceful thrusts. The stab wounds penetrated her heart, lungs, and surrounding veins and arteries. How she managed to stumble across the street with her life pouring from her was a mystery.

The boy admitted his actions without remorse.

Headlines the following day read, "Murder Shocks Suburban Neighbors." The article included eyewitness accounts of the incident by the same neighbors who had shouted at me to save their friend. The neighbors later told police they were uncomfortable with the invasive reporters who amassed at the scene. They couldn't express their fear and disbelief. Those moments in the driveway had changed them. They had watched helplessly as part of their innocence flowed down a driveway and into a sewer drain. They'd never shouted obscenities at a police officer and probably never would again. They tried to make peace with the killing as the victim's last horrific breaths played over and over again in their minds. These neighbors would never look at a teen riding his bike down their street as they had before the crime. They would never leave their doors unlocked. And they would never have the same image of the police—now un-caped and undone.

Q & A

The days of obtaining a confession by beating the crap out of a suspect or sticking a gun in his mouth and terrorizing him are, for better or worse, long gone. The seminal art of interview and interrogation was born of this void, since the more prudent suspects started to opt for their newfound legal right to remain silent. Those willing to talk still preferred to lie, since the adage, "The truth shall set you free," usually backfired, resulting in timely adjudications. In response to this modern civility offered to suspects, interview techniques were studied, researched, tweaked, and taught to detectives with measured success.

Schools dedicated solely to the art of interview and interrogation, such as the John Reid School, teach reliable, sophisticated, sometimes convoluted methods of eliciting a confession. I remember my first such school where the instructor proposed we think of the interview process as a game, with a winner and a loser. If the interviewer secured a confession he won. If not...

There was never a shortage of suspects with whom I could practice; in fact, I had a barrage of sexual perpetrators to hone my techniques on, along with attendance at two nationally acclaimed schools of the art. And while this training was useful, the first interview I sat in on taught me more than everything I had learned from all the schools, books, and videos.

Oddly enough, this first interview was not conducted by an old salt who had performed hundreds of career interviews, as one might expect, but rather by a young detective who'd only been assigned to Investigations for about three years. As I was starting my Investigations career, Matthew was leaving Investigations and returning to the street.

There are few people with the ability to speak with anyone about anything, at a moment's notice, without preparation or collected intelligence. The few who can, possess a naturally effusive, outgoing personality with acumen for interpersonal communication. The Bloomington Police Department has a handful of officers who possess this quality, and they represent the ideal, the kind of interviewers the rest of us aspire to emulate. They can quell a raging domestic, talk a suicidal gunslinger out of his gun, or convince a drunk twice their size to rethink fighting his way out of imminent arrest. Most of these gifted cops could have used their gift for more prosperous endeavors, but decided instead to be cops. Matthew was one such cop.

The first Criminal Sexual Conduct case left casually strewn on my desk involved a fifteen-year-old boy who'd sodomized a nine-year-old retarded neighbor boy. Josh was not your typical fifteen-year-old suburban child. In addition to having scraggly sideburns, Josh was a strong-willed, manipulative, physically well-developed boy with a chip on his shoulder and a very dysfunctional family. His uncle was believed to have been sexually active with all members of Josh's family, and I would learn later that Josh and his older sister had a long-term incestuous relationship. With all the sexual activity in Josh's life, it was not surprising that he would go outside the family, especially to a vulnerable victim, to enhance his growing appetites for both sexual satisfaction and domination.

We really had no training program for new detectives, but I knew enough to interview the victim before the suspect. Tim was the first in a long line of mentally retarded victims I would have contact with as I continued investigating sex crimes. I spoke with Tim and his mother at their townhouse, which was adjacent to the suspect's residence. Speaking as though his mouth was filled with marbles, he told me enough that I could schedule a forensic interview with the specialists at Cornerhouse. These interviewers were trained to elicit details from sex abuse victims using open-ended questions. Tim told them that Josh took him into the woods by his house and pulled his pants down; that Josh then put his "wiener" into his butt, and it really hurt. Tim said that he told Josh to stop, but he wouldn't. Tim's nervous stammers and his continuous habit of averting his eyes signaled his shame. Even after being assured that he had done nothing wrong, Tim felt guilty and embarrassed, as though he had some complicity in the sex act. Tim could not articulate any further details, but his disclosures were enough for a probable cause arrest.

I got another detective to join me at Josh's house, where I planned to arrest him for a felony sexual assault. I knocked on the door and was greeted by a young man who was as tall as I, a bit heavier and stronger, with an unshaved growth of blond beard and mustache. I asked him if he was Josh, and he said he was. I told him he was under arrest for criminal sexual conduct and I started to handcuff him. He said he was alone at home and asked if he could call his mother. I secured the cuffs, and after dialing the phone, I held it to his face. Josh told his mother that the cops were at his house arresting him for *some-thing*. He then handed the phone back to me and said that his mother wanted to talk to me. I had seen this coming. I really didn't want to talk to her, since her role as Josh's enabling defender was well known among officers. But since Josh was a juvenile, I was required to advise a parent of the custodial arrest, so the contact was inevitable. I held the receiver to my mouth and explained that Josh was under arrest for the sex assault of a child in the neighborhood, and that she could visit her son in the Juvenile Detention Center downtown. I hung up the phone, cutting off the Wilma Flintstone protestations that flowed from the receiver.

I drove Josh to the Bloomington Police Department and allowed him a bench in the Tank. Now what do I do? This was as far as I'd planned this gig out. He looked at me through the bars and I looked back at him—I told him I'd be right back.

I knew the interview should come next but I had no real strategy for it. I had witnessed other detectives perform interviews with limited success. Individual detectives seemed to have their own style. Some chose to chisel away at a suspect's alibi using unwavering persistence as their hammer, while others gave up too early. Still others floundered away with nonsensical questions and antics that did nothing to advance their case or gain rapport with their suspects. I had yet to develop a style of my own.

I played out the likely sequence of this interview in my mind:

Did you do it?

No.

Yes you did.

No, I didn't.

Yes you did!

Fuck you!

I went looking for help and found Matthew in his office. He was familiar with Josh's near-legendary status in the world of juvenile crime. Josh had been arrested for sundry property crimes along with a bully fistfight-type assault.

"Need help with the interview?"

"No, I just want to see the master at work one more time."

"Perfect answer, let's go."

I briefed him on the case as we walked back toward the jail. Josh's mother was waiting for us at the counter and forbid us any interview with her son. Matthew assured her that her son would be whisked downtown to the Juvenile Detention Center at our earliest convenience and that she could visit him there. He was gracious, polite, and very convincing.

I voiced my disappointment to Matthew that we would have to forego the interview process and simply make the best case based on Tim's very limited statement. Matthew smiled a perfect Cheshire cat's grin and told me to get the interview room ready.

We sat in the completely empty, whitewashed interview room on old, gray, fold-out steel chairs. Josh alternated his gaze between the ceiling and the floor. He pushed his muscular chest out of his tight white T-shirt and splayed his legs in front of him in a mock attempt at something like confidence, but he was scared shitless. Matthew told him in as mild-mannered a voice as he could muster that he had the right to remain silent. Josh said he understood his rights per Miranda and that he would waive them and talk to us. Actually he just grunted after each of Matthew's questions but we took these as "yes" responses.

Matthew had a quality of relaxed confidence. His appearance, being shorter than average and a bit soft in the middle, fostered little fear or intimidation. He limped slightly when he walked, claiming an old hockey injury. He laughed loud and often but was not averse to intense debate when he thought the matter deserving. When Josh braved eye contact with Matthew, all he saw was a man who knew the last scene in the last act of the play.

This agreement to talk with us was, to Josh, an act of bravado. He needed to show us that he was not intimidated. As career criminals cycled through revolutions of the criminal justice system they gave up all pretense of eristic battle with detectives and begged off the interviews. They had learned through experience and their lawyers' advice that silence worked to their advantage. Every decent attorney, and most crummy ones, advised their clients not to utter a single word other than what was necessary to complete the booking forms. Luckily, some criminals think lawyers and cops are stupid—and some of us have indeed demonstrated this quality from time to time. These arrestees, along with the ignorant and the few who are truly innocent, continue to talk with detectives.

Matthew wasted no time in getting to the crux of the matter. He told Josh that he knew what happened already and just wanted Josh to explain *why* it happened. With the detective's hands tied in so many knots by the rights of defendants, the police are forced to play the cards we're dealt and use circumstance to our advantage. With an unsophisticated young man, ignorant of both the law and the camouflaged temerity of the police, these flaws would be used to benefit the detective. But there were hurdles. The most blatant was getting a young male to admit that he'd had sex with another male. The rape part was almost incidental. For a fifteen-year-old boy, homosexuality, even if consensual, was more taboo than forced heterosexual sex. Getting a teenaged boy to admit taking part in any kind of homosexual activity was like pulling teeth, but Matthew had a plan.

Just as improvisation represents the pinnacle of talent in a musician, the same is true of its use in the art of interview and interrogation. Matthew saw the obstacle to a confession and the method to defeat it, seemingly simultaneously. Without taking his eyes from his subject he started softening him.

"You're worried what people are going to think because you butt-fucked this guy, aren't you?"

"I didn't butt-fuck nobody. I ain't no faggot."

Matthew leaned forward in his chair. "Listen Josh, I know you're not a faggot. Just 'cause you fuck somebody up the ass doesn't make you a faggot. Richard and I have both fucked lots of guys in the ass and we ain't faggots either. Hell, we're both married."

Josh looked up from the floor at Matthew. I bit my lip and turned away from Josh.

"You know we're not going to tell anybody what you say to us, but we need you to say it before we can tell the judge that you came clean with us. It's important to the judge that you tell us the truth. Now, like I said, we know what happened. We know you butt-fucked this kid and the judge is going to know it too. You think we're all idiots?"

Josh looked back down at his feet.

"Josh?....Josh!"

"What?" Josh replied with restrained hostility.

"You think we're stupid?"

"No."

"You think the judge is stupid?"

"No."

Matthew pulled his chair closer to Josh, and Josh leaned back further in his.

"Josh, look at me."

Josh looked at Matthew for a moment before returning his trance-like stare to the spot on the floor, five inches in front of his feet.

"Josh, I know you butt-fucked this kid. My partner,

Richard, knows it, and the judge knows it. Are you going to stand in front of a judge and tell him you didn't butt-fuck this neighbor kid? 'Cause if you do, you'd better prepare yourself for some serious shit. Judges don't like being fucked in the ass—"

"What?" Josh interrupted, having missed the metaphor and having thought the charges had been multiplied to include a judge.

"They don't like to be lied to. I don't mind that much, but judges take it personally."

"I don't give a fuck," he spat defiantly.

"Well, in that case, I can't really help you," Matthew said, never allowing a moment of composure. "I think I know what the hang-up is, and believe me, no one's gonna think you're a faggot cause you fucked this kid. We've all done it. It's no big deal. I'm sure the judge fucked some kid in the ass when he was your age. That isn't gonna be the problem. The problem is gonna be you lying to the judge."

Matthew moved his chair to within a couple feet of Josh's outstretched legs forcing Josh to bring his feet in toward his chair.

"Josh," Matthew said raising his voice, "Let's stop fuckin' around."

"I ain't fuckin' around," Josh shouted back.

Matthew shouted back at him, "Well then, quit acting like such a little pussy and tell me the truth. Be a man!"

"I am telling the truth," he continued shouting. "I did not butt-fuck no retard neighbor!"

Matthew relaxed, leaning back in his chair and replied in a calm, measured voice. "I didn't say anything about the neighbor being retarded. Did you, Richard?"

This was my chance to participate! I shook my head—no.

Josh was flustered. He shouted back at Matthew, "Yeah you did!"

"So you know why we're here, Josh. Let's drop the bull-shit, okay?"

"Fuckers," Josh spat under his breath.

"Josh. Let's end this. This is a waste of your time. You're worried about looking like a fag when you should be worried about how the judge is going to treat someone who can't admit when they make a mistake. Can you admit when you make a mistake, Josh?"

Josh nodded his head—yes.

"Do you think you might have made a mistake, Josh?"

Josh shrugged his shoulders.

"Let me clue you in, Josh. Fucking a retarded kid in the ass is a problem, lying about it is only going to make it worse."

Josh sat motionless without responding.

"This thing happened didn't it, Josh?"

Silence.

"It happened didn't it, Josh?"

Silence.

"Didn't it, Josh?"

Silence.

"Didn't it?"

Josh moved his head in a barely perceptible nod. I wasn't sure if the movement was in response to Matthew's question or just an involuntary movement associated with respiration, but Matthew pounced on it.

"Good for you, Josh! It feels good to tell the truth, doesn't it? Welcome to manhood. I'm proud of you Josh, and I'm sure the judge is going to appreciate the honesty. Now let's go over exactly what happened."

Then it flowed, like a new Christian at a revival, *for the truth shall set you free.* Josh started slow. He minimized the sexual contact and rearranged circumstances to sound as if they'd been walking in the woods for nature appreciation only, when he'd tripped and his penis accidentally ended up in Tim's rectum. It didn't matter. The room was bugged and his skewed confession had been recorded.

So, how did Matthew do it? How did he get a boy to admit something the boy had solemnly swore to himself never to reveal? He actually utilized a combination of skills taught in the interview and interrogation schools, but Matthew never made it to those schools. He knew instinctively what was necessary. He measured Josh's weakness, his macho bravado, his lack of sophistication and his fears, and capitalized on them. Those skills in combination with Matthew's rapport-building skills, his timing, and his persistence broke down Josh's defenses. It was a game to Matthew, and he was determined to win. The used-car world would never know the one that got away.

This interview ended up being pivotal in both the felony juvenile court proceeding and in the court-ordered sex-abuser therapy.

Josh never again admitted to *anyone* that he'd had any sexual contact with Tim. He denied making a confession to detectives until the recorded interview was played in court. Some of the jury did not appreciate Matthew's methods, objecting to the language and the raising of his voice at one point with a *child*.

What they didn't understand was that Josh was on the road to becoming a freight-train-type sex-abuser, the kind that overpowers his victims and viciously drags them out of sight, rapes them, and, with time, fear and panic would probably kill them. He wanted to dominate his victims as he'd been dominated when he was smaller. Of course he denied ever being sexually abused. That would include admitting to being dominated, to more homosexual contact, and that could not be rationalized away. Not at fifteen.

The interview was allowed into evidence and Josh was found guilty of the felonious criminal sexual assault.

Josh never admitted the sexual assault in therapy. He said the cops tricked him into confessing. He was forced to stay in therapy twice as long as the judge suggested because of his refusal to admit his mistake. When he was finally released, his mother moved him out of state and called to admonish me, at high volume, for ruining her and her son's life. She said, "I'm moving somewhere, where you'll never be able to fuck with my son again."

She slammed the phone down before I could say, "Buh-bye."

Mandatory Pain

Billy C's years investigating child abuse were divided between the years he performed the job as an alcoholic and the years following his recovery. I only knew him in his recovery years when he performed his job admirably. Like many recovering alcoholics, he was on a permanent health kick. He started each day at his desk, dissecting then devouring three oranges. His day-to-day attitude was surprisingly upbeat and, when interviewing a child or a suspect, he always tried and usually succeeded in putting his subjects at ease.

The sex abuse cases involving children were usually the most traumatic, and liable to drive just about anyone to drink. Even so, the child cases never seemed to get the same attention as similar cases involving adults. As for the discrepancy in recognition between detectives working adult rape and assault cases, and those working child cases, Billy didn't seem to care. But he was aware of it. He once commented to me that if I stuck with child abuse investigations, I would become an outsider among the other investigators. He may have been right.

Our deputy chief at the time once asked me after a lengthy absence, "You still working as a diaper dick?"

Billy informed me early in the learning stage of my child abuse investigations career that most of our abuse reports came from individuals designated by profession as "mandatory reporters." This group was comprised of professionals who worked with, or had professional contact with, children on a daily basis. The most prolific of this group were teachers, cops, doctors, nurses, dentists, clergy, and daycare workers. In my ten years working child abuse cases, I received reports from individuals in each of these professions but made an interesting distinction. Of all the groups listed, teachers and daycare workers had the most frequent contact with abused children, but seemed the most reluctant to report. Not all teachers, of course. Some educators, most notably one elementary school principal in our city, were a constant source of reliable, accurate reports of abuse.

Many teachers were uncomfortable reporting child abuse because they felt they were alienating themselves from the children's parents. They knew the report would foster permanent hard feelings, and the chance always existed that they could be mistaken and making a false report. After making this report, the teachers realized they would continue to see the suspect parent and might be in contact with them for years to come if the parent had younger children, siblings of the current victim. Being a *rat* or an *informer* was not a title they wanted attached to their name and reputation. I believe I shared this trait of concern about how I was perceived by others before becoming a police officer (whereupon I was despised equally by all), so I was somewhat sympathetic.

These considerations should have been secondary to their assigned requirement to report suspected abuse, and they legally had no choice in making a report since they are *mandated by law* to report. The identities of child abuse reporters are supposed to have a cloak of protection since their names are considered private information, but teachers know that the suspect parents can easily figure out who the reporter is. This apprehension and fear of involvement results in some unreported abuse. As a result, I saw some horrendous cases that never should have gone as far as they did.

The issue of mandated reporting is complex but crucial to children's safety. There is no better illustration of both the complexity and the necessity for reporting than the sex abuse scandal of the Catholic Church in 2002. One wonders how many mandatory reporters neglected to report their suspicions, or their knowledge, of abuse, and thus allowed the abuse to snowball.

A social worker I came in contact with at Jefferson High School called me one afternoon from her new job at an elementary school within the city. There was a note of urgency in Deb's voice when she said she needed me to meet her ASAP in the school nurse's office. Part of the urgency had to do with the hour of day, since students were scheduled to be dismissed about an hour from the time she called. The other part pertained to the seriousness of the situation, since a trivial case could have waited until the following day.

I arrived at the Elementary School ten minutes before the final bell. Deb met me at the door, and quickly escorted me to the private area of the nurse's office. Two black boys, brothers, six and eight, were being examined by the nurse. Deb asked me to examine Anthony, the smallest brother who was clothed at the time in blue jeans and a white, long sleeve T-shirt.

Anthony was small for his age, very cute, with a shaved head and fluid, dark brown sullen eyes. I asked him if he was almost ready to go home for the day. His soft brown facial features signaled his timorousness, as he looked back at me without reply. I told him I was a police officer and needed to check him over to make sure he was all right to return home. He shook his head in tacit understanding.

Usually, the first thing I asked a suspected child abuse victim was to take off their shirt so I could check their back for signs of injury—abuse. But in this case Deb asked me to start with his arms, which were covered at present by his longsleeved shirt. I pulled his left sleeve up and was momentarily dizzied by the damage I witnessed. I reflexively pulled up his other sleeve and saw the injuries were not limited to the left arm. I pulled his shirt off and saw the injuries were spread uniformly across his torso, disappearing into his pant line. He pulled his pants and underwear down at my request and I observed the complete picture.

He appeared as I envisioned a slave of the early nineteenth century might look after being brutally lashed with a bullwhip for some perceived serious infraction. Not just on one occasion, but repeatedly—for weeks. Whip marks, most likely the result of an extension cord, literally covered his body from the shirt line at his neck to his ankles. These marks were not generously spaced as one might expect; rather, they were very tightly grouped. His arms alone probably had hundreds of such marks, overlapping, raised, and corded like vines, crossing at angles that suggested a struggle to escape the beatings. There was not a single square inch of his torso that was not streaked with these marks. Different slash marks were in various stages of healing evidenced by textural and color contrast. Many of the marks were already scarred; others were scabbed over, while others were freshly abraded. I'd seen a lot of bruised children; belt marks on butts, finger-grip marks on biceps, knuckle bumps on foreheads, split lips and slap marks on cheeks—but nothing like this.

Deb advised me that his mother would be at the school any minute to pick him up. This case was complicated by the fact that the family did not live in Bloomington, since they had moved to Brooklyn Center a year before but continued attending Bloomington Schools. I put Anthony's shirt back on and asked him to finish dressing while I checked his older brother. Drew took a step back as I approached him and offered that he had no injuries. Deb confirmed this, advising me that she and the nurse had already checked both boys thoroughly. She needed me to examine Anthony's injuries independently since I was the only professional at the school with the authority to place an emergency hold on a child.

As Anthony zipped up his pants I could hear a woman shouting in the adjacent main office, demanding to see her children. The principal was stalling for time in an effort to help us, but her attempts were of no avail as the door designated *private* crashed open and a woman entered.

She took in the scene quickly. "You boys get out here," she shouted, indignantly. "We're going home." She glared at the three of us, and fixed her gaze on me. "What are you looking at?"

I was caught off guard, probably staring at her as if she wore a red suit with horns and carried a pitchfork. It wouldn't have mattered what this woman looked like, or what her demeanor was. I assumed she had caused the injuries to Anthony and I could not make peace with that. What kind of anger resulted in this kind of brutality, and was it just anger? Or was it some deeper visceral form of evil? There was a difference in my mind. She happened to be an attractive thirty-something mom whose essence suffocated every emotion other than anger; she carried with her a cat-spitting, retaliatory attitude of disdain.

"Hold up, guys," I said to the boys. Then to her, "Are you the boys' mother?"

"What do you think? I'm here picking them up."

"What's your name?" I said, taking out my pocket notebook.

"Fuck you!"

I thought of a fitting reply but reconsidered and swallowed it, preparing myself instead for the certain tirade and possible physical struggle I assumed was forthcoming. I considered the shouting match that would certainly ensue if I entered into a debate, so instead I mustered my most authoritative tone—which for me was entirely ventriloquistic— and stated, "I'm taking the boys to a shelter for—"

"Oh no you're—"

"I am. If you interfere I'll be taking you to jail—and I might be taking you to jail anyway." My last statement was threat only, since neither Deb nor I had been afforded sufficient time to conduct a decent interview with the children, and with the victim-fear and reticence typical of children, they were not offering anything up. Though I strongly suspected, I didn't know for certain that this woman had caused Anthony's injuries. Another legal concern was the fact that the incident did not occur in the city of Bloomington, and so was out of my jurisdiction.

"Well, you're not taking Drew!" she huffed.

"I'm taking both of them," I replied.

"Drew hasn't got one mark on him unless you put it there," she said. "How can you take him?"

So though she didn't ask, she had an implicit understanding what this was about. Her statement regarding Drew's lack of injuries bordered on self-incrimination.

"Why is that?" I asked, truly wanting to know the answer. "Why all the whippings to Anthony and none to Drew?"

She said nothing in reply but held her hand out for Drew. "Come on, baby."

Drew took a step forward before Deb grabbed his hand and positioned him behind me. He did not attempt to pull away from Deb. I spoke into my police radio requesting a uniformed squad come to my location for the transport. I added through 10-code that I might need assistance with my situation as well.

"I'm taking both boys on a health and welfare hold to St. Joseph's Shelter in Minneapolis. You can leave now. You've got no other business at this school."

"You can't—"

"There's a squad on its way here now. If you're not gone when it gets here I'm going to arrest you for trespass." I didn't really care at that point whether the arrest I threatened to make would be legal or not. She had every right to be at the school to pick up her children. I decided I would arrest her only if she interfered or attempted to grab one of her children. She studied me, her hands defiantly gripping her hips before she turned away. "I'll be coming to pick you up, Drew. Don't you worry." And she walked toward the parking lot, never having acknowledged Anthony's presence.

I hoped she wouldn't return with a large, muscular, angry husband/boyfriend type with a chip on his shoulder and a glove compartment full of traffic citations—at least not until my backup arrived.

Deb and I completed our reports and forwarded them to Hennepin County Child Protection and to the Brooklyn Center Police Department. I phoned the investigator there and briefed him personally on my observations. I never heard from him again.

This was a fairly simple case. At least one of the children, maybe Drew rather than Anthony, once safely out of harm's way, would tell investigators the source of Anthony's marks. That suspect, most likely the boys' mother, would be charged with Felony Malicious Punishment or possibly with Felony Third Degree Assault, or maybe both. Either way, she would need to petition the court and prove that she would do whatever the court required to get her children back.

If Family Court offered her the possibility to regain custody of her children, she would be required to attend anger management therapy along with parenting classes and, most likely, a psychological screening coupled with personal therapy. Even then, she would have a Child Protection field worker assigned to her who would monitor her progress and the welfare of the boys.

The boys would initially be placed in temporary foster care, and remain there until their mother made a commitment to complete the above requisite conditions to have them returned to her.

I got the feeling that Anthony's mother would not even attempt to regain custody of him. She would fight to have Drew returned, but I believed she had only hatred for her younger child. Perhaps this contempt was transferred to Anthony from another source, such as Anthony's biological father. Whatever the cause, there appeared to be no love bond between mother and son but, rather, something foul, the result of some wreckage in the past, the pain and malice of which were redolent only with Anthony.

My hope was that someone seeking permanent foster care or perhaps a relative (although that was tempting fate) would find Anthony and show him the kind of parental love so lacking in his life—someone whose hands would caress his back, covering the scarred map of his pain in a blanket of love. Perhaps that kind of love, the kind all children seek and need and deserve, could dissolve the horrific memories of fear and pain, violence and hatred that had been his sustenance. That kind of love was his only hope, his only prayer.

Something troubled me from the moment I saw Anthony's injuries: the apparent obviousness of them. Anthony could not possibly have hidden these injuries throughout the school year, and even if he managed to conceal the actual marks by wearing long sleeves every day, he could never mask the pain, day in and day out, of his freshly inflicted abrasions. He was forced by convention to sit, his buttocks on a seat, his back against the chair, his arms grabbed in play by classmates at recess. I wondered how much he'd suffered because someone was afraid of being embarrassed or labeled an informer.

On Billy C's last day, a group of detectives took him out for—what else—a doughnut, to send him off. Billy was apprehensive about retiring. Like most cops he wondered if he'd put enough away to survive financially. After all, he was still comfortable with his job, having established countless contacts and friends throughout the child protection/child justice system in his lengthy career, making the decision to go that much more difficult.

Billy lives in another state now but makes an annual pilgrimage to the BPD to visit his friends. After eight years of retirement, he could be the poster boy for *early* retirement. We call him the "bronze god" in reference to his year-round tanned and sculpted body. He enjoys talking about his many volunteer and recreational pursuits, claiming to be busier now than in his working days. He makes a joke about missing the job and comments on the scattered pile of cases on my desk, but he doesn't ask for details.

Lazarus Eyes

I was surprised to see a man with no feet roll his wheelchair into my office at Jefferson High School with a teenage girl in tow. The man introduced himself and his daughter, Fay, who sat quietly on one of my steel office chairs, averting her eyes. Fay was a very pretty girl whose reticence suggested she'd outgrown the need or at least the desire for her father's accompaniment. Upon being introduced, she flicked a glance of acknowledgement my direction, and quickly turned away.

The position of high school liaison officer was not a highly sought after job, since these detectives not only carried the standard case load of an investigator, but also had to contend with the day-to-day problems at the school. The liaison job was considered the bottom rung on the Crimes Against Persons Unit ladder, and most detectives started with this job on their way to becoming robbery/homicide detectives. It was not uncommon for a line to form outside my office as students, parents, social workers, school personnel, and the like came to report their cause or question. Some days it seemed the Beatles reunion concert would come to town before the bell mercifully signaled the end of day. I shared a temptation most principals must have, of closing my office door and turning off the light.

I broke my annoying habit of looking at people's mouths when they spoke rather than their eyes, as I was drawn to Fay's flicker of a glance. Being stuck in the awkward hot-box of consciously diverting my attention from her father's legs and being drawn to Fay's eyes, I found myself alternating my gaze from the ceiling to the blank report forms on my desk. Like a child, my eyes tended to follow my curiosity without benefit of mature oversight.

Fay's father said he wanted to make a police report. Apparently Fay had been the victim of a violent assault at the hands of a man she had just met the day before, when she went AWOL from school for an unauthorized jaunt to the Mall of America. Fay rolled her eyes as her father said this and, again, something about her eyes drew my attention. This time I decided to just stare. Fay was slender, with red hair and a body that, much to daddy's chagrin, hadn't waited for the rest of her to mature. Her facial features were thin and made to look thinner by the pageboy cut that framed her face, while both her jeans and sweater fit snug to her body. As I continued to stare through the silence, Fay turned to me and finally—and purposely—surrendered the secret of her eyes.

Set behind too much make up and too thick an application of mascara were her shining copper eyes—but something was wrong. She had no *whites* surrounding her brilliant light-brown irises. The usual contrast of white and color was absent, with the white having been replaced by enveloping blood-red orbs that made her appear like an alien on the first *Star Trek* series with its really bad special effects. I knew what had caused the gross discoloration to her eyes and wondered if she knew how lucky she was to count herself among the living.

Having allowed me this revelation, Fay turned back away from me without a word. Her father noticed our connection, but rather than explain the cause of Fay's trauma, he talked about her attitude.

"She never tells us what's going on. I didn't know she was skipping school. First we get a call from the school, and then we get a call from the Minneapolis Police."

I was suddenly struck, remembering how I felt on a recent trip to the doctor with my seven-year-old son whose eardrums were nearly perforated from infection. The doctor continued to ask me how my son felt, rather than asking him directly. Fay's father and I were doing the same thing.

"Let's have Fay tell what happened," I interjected.

"She won't tell you. She wouldn't tell the Minneapolis Police—hell, she won't even tell her mother and me."

I looked at Fay, who looked at the wall, and I looked at her father, who looked from Fay to me, and back to Fay.

"Would you mind if I talked alone with Fay, if that's all right with her?" Then to Fay, "Would that be okay, Fay?"

She shrugged her shoulders, still facing the wall.

"That's fine with me," her father said. He cranked one wheel of his chair, spinning it toward the door, and wheeled himself out of the room.

"Why don't you come and sit in this chair," I said, indicating the chair directly in front of my desk, "and we can talk." I knew this act was going to be about as simple as trying to make your girlfriend smile as you break up with her.

Fay nodded and switched chairs. She looked at the top of my desk, which was littered with reports and photographs under glass of my wife and two boys. My boys had been instructed to make goofy faces for the camera and so were pulling on their eyes, sticking out their tongues and laughing at the same time. She finally smiled, "Those are cute."

"You should see them when they try to look silly."

It took her a moment, but she finally looked up at me with a small smile.

"Are those your boys?"

"No, my boys are really homely," I said with a straight face.

"Shut up," she said, stifling a laugh.

"All right." I tried to find the proper attitude; serious, but not so serious that Fay would be afraid to open up. "Just so you know, I'm not the slightest bit interested in why you skipped school or about getting you in trouble for that. I'm thinking we have bigger issues." She nodded, and her frightening eyes started to well. "Just to make it easy—for me, why don't you start at the beginning and just keep going."

She nodded as she sniffled. "I met this guy at the Mall a couple days ago and—"

"Time out. Describe this guy, including age, race, height, weight, and all the other stuff."

"He was about thirty and—"

"Thirty! What were you—" I stopped mimicking her father, and invited her to go on.

"He was about your size, with darker hair and a little thicker around here." She indicated her torso with both hands. "I met him by the arcade and he started talking to me and my friend, Sheri. Well, we kind of hung around with him that night and he—he kissed me and gave me his phone number."

"Did you call him?" I scribbled notes as I spoke.

"I called him that same night and he agreed to pick me up here at school the next day."

I shook my head, forcing a non-judgmental expression and invited her to continue.

"He took me to the Mall again first, and he bought me some clothes, and then we went to his apartment somewhere in south Minneapolis. The Minneapolis Police have the address, and then we were just sitting on his bed watching TV."

"Were you comfortable with that?"

"Um, kind of, I guess, at first, but then he started kissing me, and he was kissing me really hard—you know?"

"Yeah. Did you tell him you were uncomfortable with that or anything?"

"Yeah, I told him to stop! But he kept going and then he started feeling me and stuff and—"

"I know this isn't fun, but you need to be specific about what he was feeling."

Fay nodded, her eyes a frightening harbinger of what was sure to come. "Well, everything. He was grabbing my breasts and then he stuck his hands down my pants and started touching me down there."

"Did his fingers penetrate your vagina?" I asked, attempting to gauge the degree of sexual assault.

She nodded yes, took a cleansing breath, and continued, wanting now to tell her story. "Then I started fighting with him and he backed off a moment and I saw him smile. That scared me more than anything—it scared the shit out of me. He was enjoying the fight. It was like that's what he was waiting for. Then he grabbed some handcuffs from I don't know where. He just had them all of a sudden, and he put them on behind my back."

"You must have been scared to death."

She nodded and started crying into her hands. I pushed the Kleenex box closer to her and she grabbed a couple. After she blew her nose and wiped away her tears, she continued with her story, struggling to speak through her sobs. "He pulled my pants down then and had sex with me—there was nothing I could do." Her language capitulated with the telling, as if it was happening again and she was feeling the same helplessness.

"What happened then?"

"I thought it was over and that he might let me go because he started taking one of the cuffs off. But after he took that one off he dragged me over to the radiator—you know, one of those old ones that stick out of the floors in all the rooms. He locked the one free cuff to that and then he started strangling me. He put his arm around my neck like this." She demonstrated, her elbow under her chin with her arm around her neck. "He just kept choking me. I was fighting for a while, kicking him, but then I couldn't, and I knew he was just going to kill me."

I shook my head. "You better get to the happy ending part of why you're sitting here with me rather than taking up refrigerator space somewhere else."

"I don't know. I guess he thought I was dead. I woke up on the floor with my arm stretched over to the radiator, and he was gone. I had no idea how much time had passed, but it was still light out. The radiator was near a window and I had one free arm so I opened the window and started screaming for help. Somebody yelled back up at me after a while, and then the cops showed up about fifteen minutes later."

"Did you go to the hospital?"

"Yeah. The doctors said they're going to have to do some more tests, but they think I'm going to be okay. They said I could have some damage to my eyes and possibly to my brain."

"I'm sure you'll be okay," I said, in an obvious attempt to placate. "Let me see your eyes."

Fay leaned over my desk and forced her lids wide open. Her eyes were aqueous like blood-filled crystal balls. They looked like you could touch them and wipe the blood away, or at least smear it. The skin around her eyes was a pointillist's study of a raccoon mask, as hundreds of tiny red hemorrhages dotted the living canvas of her smooth skin. Her neckline under her jaw shared the same dotted pattern along with some minor bruises. "It's called petechia. Did the doctors tell you that?"

"I don't—yeah. Maybe. I don't really remember what they said. They just..." She shook her head.

"I've seen it on other choked victims, but their eyes were never this bad. There was always a little white left."

If you squeezed someone's neck hard enough and long enough, the blood vessels within the eyes, face, and neck started to hemorrhage. This much damage was fairly unheard of, unless the victim lay on a stainless-steel table, staring rheumy-eyed at the ceiling of the morgue.

Every time I saw Fay after that, I knew there existed a merciful God. Beyond the simple miracle of surviving what her assailant considered the coda to his orchestrated *Executioner's Song*, and what probably amounted to coming within seconds of ending her life, she now appeared happy. Her father told me Fay didn't have any real friends. He said she had grown distant from her former group, and complained that she couldn't feel part of their self-absorbed, snotty elitism.

I hung around one of the exit doors at the final bell so I could see my *frequent flyers* off for the day, and I noticed Fay laughing and tagging along with some new girlfriends who obviously enjoyed her company. Perhaps sometime in Fay's life her father had witnessed her triumph at something she'd struggled with interminably. I hoped he'd felt the same satisfaction then that I was feeling at that moment. Seeing her smile was answer enough for my greatest concern.

It took a long time for her eyes to change back. She wore sunglasses for a while, but her outward appearance returned to normal. She always waved or said goodbye to me when she saw me at the door, and updated me from time to time on the criminal case.

After interviewing Fay the day her father brought her to my office, I made her repeat it all in much greater detail into a tape recorder for a formal statement. I wasn't sure why she'd decided to confide in me. Perhaps the uniformed officers at the scene appeared too officious or ominous, and perhaps her parents wore that ubiquitous "I told you so" expression that made the telling feel more like expiation than the impassioned cry for support and compassion she needed.

This would be a Minneapolis case rather than Bloomington, since though they had met in my jurisdiction, the actual crime occurred in Minneapolis. I sent the taped statement off to Minneapolis and briefed the lead detective. They had been staking out the apartment since finding Fay, but the suspect had not returned.

The day after Fay's statement, the man came back to his apartment building with a blond teenage girl whom he'd met earlier that same day at Southdale Mall in Edina. She was holding hands with him, smiling and laughing when the police surprised them and took him into custody. I wondered if he remembered Fay's discarded body when he walked toward his apartment that day. Perhaps he would have brought this victim to a different room. Perhaps after having his sadistic appetite whetted, he would skip the charade and get right down to the pain. Whatever the case, he seemed unconcerned and unaffected that he was reentering what he believed to be a death scene with a decomposing corpse.

Fay and I got our subpoenas for court and were prepared to testify, but the case ended up settling when the man agreed to a plea of a lesser sentence for first degree Criminal Sexual Assault and second degree Attempted Murder. Like most of the students I dealt with as victims or witnesses, I never saw Fay again after graduation.

Thursday the 12th

From my desk at the high school I fielded a variety of complaints, many times in the form of notes from parents. *"My son's car was legally parked yesterday when it received this ticket. Please take care of it." "Bus #995 has an incompetent driver who does not come to a complete stop at stop signs and sometimes uses the 's' word or even the 's-o-b' word when avoiding near collisions. Please see to it that he's fired—ASAP."* I was reading these notes to Sean McElroy (Mac), the civilian hallway/parking lot security guy, when I unfolded the last of them, written neatly in longhand on a full sheet of notebook paper: *"I've grown increasingly uncomfortable with a neighbor boy, Tad Jenson, who's on the JV football team. His family lives next door to us and Tad has a crush on my daughter, Tracy, who is a JV football cheerleader. You see the problem. After asking her to prom, and being turned down, he's been giving her dirty looks at games she's cheering. He even came into our house unannounced. I feel he should be removed from the team."*

"Man, they think you got the power all right, don't they?" Mac said.

Mac was a fifty-year-old ex-trucker whose own two teenage daughters attended high school in another city. He always wore cowboy boots with his faded Levis. His long silver hair and full matching beard made him look like an itinerant Grateful Dead fan. Along with this look, Mac had an easygoing, natural manner that endeared him to the students.

"Yeah, they always seem to think that since I'm a police detective I can fix tickets," I said, "and that I would even if I could. It kind of negates their purpose doesn't it, if you write 'em and then I cancel 'em?"

"Ah, who gives a shit? I don't care if you cancel them. What about that last note?"

"What do you mean?"

"It's the same old story isn't it? Boy meets girl, boy wants girl, boy asks girl, girl turns boy down, boy stalks girl."

I noted his seriousness and laughed, "I don't remember stalking any of the ones on my wish list, do you?"

"Fuckin' A-right I did," he said, staring me down, dead serious.

I bit my lip, not really knowing how to respond to this without insulting him. I silently considered how complete his background check had been for this job. "Relax, Mac. What about your daughters?"

"Shit. I know the same thing is going to happen to them," he grumbled. "The only thing different is that I'll be waiting for these guys with a shotgun on the other side of the door."

"Whoa there, big fella. You don't want to get yourself into any trouble over some lovelorn lad who's infatuated with your daughter."

"The hell I don't," Mac said, rising from his chair as the overflowing well of self-righteous indignation mixed with his blood, invigorating him. "I don't give a rat's ass what they do to me. No one's getting near my daughters!" He turned from my office with a huff, and headed down the hallway, cutting short our usual half-hour BS session by about twenty-five minutes. I could live with that today. Now I could make my calls.

With our debate on the cheerleader fresh in my mind, I decided to call that mom first. Many of the west-side families were well enough off that the moms could stay home rather than work. Such was the case with Tracy's mom, who answered the phone on the second ring. I told her I was calling in response to her note, and that she'd have to take up Tad's position on the football team with the coach or the principal—that I only dealt with criminal problems. I suggested that if her daughter could not handle being around Tad at the games, that maybe she consider switching her cheerleading talents to another sport.

"I didn't really want to get Tad into any criminal trouble, but I don't think my daughter should have to switch sports because of him. She likes cheering football."

"What criminal trouble are you talking about, Ma'am?"

"I mean with him sneaking into our house, and the knife."

"The knife?" I said, wondering if I'd mixed up my messages. "I remember you wrote something about Tad entering your house unannounced, but you didn't say anything about a knife." There was a long silence on the line. "Ma'am?"

"Well I didn't want to get him into trouble. His parents have been our friends for a long time, before Tad was even born."

"I understand. Tell me what happened with the knife."

"Well, you know that Tad asked Tracy to the prom, and she just didn't feel like going with him. She said it would be like going with her brother. They've been friends since they could crawl."

"Uh-huh."

"Well, the same day she turned him down I saw him walking out behind our house right around dusk. I didn't know what he was doing. He couldn't have known it, but Tracy had to stay after school for a Yearbook Club meeting. Those meetings always run long. Normally, she would have been home right after cheerleading practice. He knew she didn't have cheerleading practice that day. He rides the same activity bus home with her after football practice."

"So he thought she was home, right?"

"Right. Anyway, I saw him walking through our backyard as I was doing the dishes."

"How did you know for sure it was him?"

"He always wears that same beat-up green, down-filled jacket. I knew it was him right away."

"Were you the only one home?"

"Yes," she said. "My husband had taken our younger son to soccer."

"Okay."

"So then I hear our garage door, the service door, open and I figured it was Tad, but usually he would have come to the front—"

"Had he ever entered unannounced by the garage?"

"No—never," she said, sounding more concerned at my concern over the door. She waited for me to say it.

"Go ahead."

"I heard some rummaging around in the bathroom by the stairs, and after a couple minutes I decided I'd better go see what he was doing." She paused.

"Uh-huh."

"So I walked into the bathroom and I could hear him breathing in the shower, but the curtain is pulled. I said, 'Tad, what are you doing?' but he doesn't answer, so I pull the curtain. Well, I have to tell you, he gave me quite a start. He's standing there in his green jacket, but he has a mask on—"

She had me after, "I could hear him breathing in the shower." I interrupted, "What kind of mask?"

"Ah, well, you know, like the kind with the eye and mouth holes. A knit cap, the kind hunters wear when it's really cold. But his was black."

"Okay," I said. "What did you do?"

"Well, I saw the mask and I backed up a little and I saw he was holding a butcher knife in his hand."

"A butcher knife?" I asked, wondering if she'd seen *Friday the 13th* too many times.

"Yes, I recognized the knife as one from Trudy's set."

"That's Tad's mom—Trudy?"

"Yes. I recognized it right away. I've been at their house socially, many times. So I said to Tad, 'What are you doing with your mother's knife, Tad?' But he just stood there. He stood there for the longest time behind that mask—there in the shower stall. Just standing there with the knife."

"What did you do?" I asked. Then, without allowing her a reply, "Were you afraid?"

"Well, like I said, I've known Tad since he was a baby, but the mask and the knife were a little unnerving. I asked him to take it off, but he just kept standing there. I think he was embarrassed. I finally reached over and took it off him."

"What did he do?"

"He looked down and he didn't say anything for a minute, and then he asked me if Tracy was home. I told him to give me the knife, and he handed it to me. I told him Tracy was not home and that he should go home. I told him not to sneak into our house again and that his mom or dad would have to pick up the knife."

"That was good. You handled that well. You probably don't get much practice at that sort of thing."

"No."

"So then did he just leave?"

"Yes. I walked him to the front door and he left. I knew he wouldn't tell his mother so I called her, and Jim came right over to get the knife. Jim was very concerned and said he would take care of this. He's very strict so it seemed like enough. I just—it didn't seem right or necessary at the time to call the police. I know it probably sounds crazy now. When I think about it at night and all the things that could have happened I just...whew."

"Yeah. Well, now the cat's out of the bag, and I'm going to need to talk with Tad."

"Will he have to go to jail?"

"I don't know," I said quite honestly. As a rookie detective I'd never handled anything even remotely similar to this. As far as the shower scene was concerned, it had ended much better than the shower scene from *Psycho*, but it could have been just as bad—or worse. I considered what I had as far as a crime was concerned. Was it a prank, a burglary, a threat, an attempted rape—murder? Of course I couldn't prove any of these things. Tad was the only one who knew his true intentions when he stepped into that shower stall holding a butcher knife, breathing hard under the mask, his thoughts a whirlwind of emotion. He couldn't deny his presence, but he could feign a simple prank.

Jim and Tad walked into my office the following morning at my request. Jim was reluctant to leave his son alone with me and asked what my intentions were. I told him that I already knew what happened, but that it was important in the juvenile justice system for the child to admit his misconduct. Judges took into consideration such things as forthrightness, remorse, attitude, and honesty. When suspects reached the age of eighteen our justice system considered these virtues virtually irrelevant, since the system was forced by sheer numbers to focus on simple guilt or innocence.

Jim wanted to avoid the whole criminal justice court thing if possible, preferring instead to handle it within the family. I understood what he meant and sympathized with him. I told him that there could be some criminal consequences, but that Tad's status as an honest juvenile, willing to take responsibility for his actions, would be taken into account by the judge who in turn would most likely mandate only court-ordered counseling. Jim argued that if that was the case, he would simply take Tad to counseling on his own and we could avoid court altogether.

I was balancing here atop a slippery slope of diplomacy, since Jim had every right to tell me to take a hike, and then leave my office with his son. (I'm sure if he had it to do over, he would do just that—emphatically.) If he had, I would have attempted to charge Tad with something like misdemeanor disorderly conduct, but it would have been tough to get him charged with no intent. Had he been a stranger rather than the next-door neighbor kid, a felony burglary would have been a cinch. I needed Tad to tell me his thoughts as he stood breathing behind the shower curtain.

I told Jim that it was important for Tad to understand the serious implications associated with entering someone's house with a knife, and that all well-intentioned families offered to take their kids to counseling, but unless it was court mandated, the families usually found a convenient excuse to quit going. Jim looked me up and down, and reluctantly capitulated.

"So you don't think Tad will have to go to jail?"

"No," I said. "I don't think so. I'm not going to arrest him today, regardless of what he tells me."

"Do you think we need to get an attorney?"

This question spurred the moral dilemma that always left a bruised conscience. As the lead detective, I was the last person Jim should have been asking for legal advice. If I said yes, then the attorney would advise his client—Tad—not to talk with me, and I would have no case. If I said no, I was lying, since an attorney could save Tad from experiencing the true, crushing power of the legal system's hammer. Tad needed to feel that blow in the worst way. In the long run, his taking responsibility now for his very deviant behavior could save him from a life of wrongs he might not be able to forgive himself for, not to mention time lost in prison. The adult legal system would offer him no sympathy.

"I'm not really the right person to answer that, Jim. You know you can always call an attorney for advice. That's what they're there for."

Jim considered my reply as he looked at his son seated beside him. Tad was a bigger kid than I'd imagined after talking with Tracy's mom. This tenth grade boy-next-door was probably 5'11", 180 pounds. He had short blond hair, blue eyes, and was wearing a clear expression of wanting to be somewhere else. I'm sure his father saw this too.

"Okay then," Jim said. "I'll leave you two alone and, uh, Tad—just tell Mr. Greelis the truth." Jim nodded to me and conveyed in that nod his trust in my interceding on his son's behalf, which was not at all my intent nor my job. A free radical cell of betrayal ricocheted through my brain as Jim closed the door behind him, leaving his son at my mercy. My portrayal of trust and integrity facilitated Jim's decision to leave his son in my care. I would use that trust to get Tad to tell me his intent in pulling a mask over his face and wielding a knife in his neighbor's shower. I told myself there was a goal at the end of all this artifice, and that goal encompassed a greater good. It even had, at its core, a belief that dealing with Tad's problem now would actually serve him in the end.

I told Tad that I already knew what happened and that I was proud of him for having the guts and fortitude to come to my office and tell me the truth about what happened. I told him that everyone makes mistakes and that I had certainly made more than my share, but it was the brave few who could admit their mistakes and be willing to make amends for them. I was tempted to recite my favorite Shakespearian verse here since it fit so well: *Cowards die many times before their deaths; the valiant never tastes of death but once.* The insinuation of impending death probably wouldn't have served my cause, so I thought it better to keep my Shakespeare to myself.

The only true part in my little preamble was the segment about me making a lot of mistakes, but the difference between his mistakes and mine was that, while I may have engaged in some petty mischief bordering on major mischief that I got away with, I never holed up in my neighbor's shower outfitted like an evil Zorro—not even on Halloween. The part about him being willing to come and tell me the truth was, of course, a bunch of BS. I'm sure if he had his druthers, he'd have been miles away from my office, riding his horse at full gallop as he turned back to measure the distance between himself and the posse.

Tad nodded his head, a bit proud of his doing all those good things I'd mentioned.

I asked him to please humor me in repeating the events of the day, since I already knew what happened. He slumped down, a little disappointed that he'd have to participate, and cleared his throat.

"Want me to just start from the beginning?"

"Yeah, wherever you want."

"Well, I suppose that would be when I asked Tracy to the prom." He looked up at me for my approval.

"Sure that's fine," I smiled, "perfect."

"Well, I wanted Tracy to go with me. She's really the only girl I've ever really liked, you know, and she just really shot me down, you know."

"Yeah, Tad. That's one thing I know about. In fact if I was an expert on anything—it would be on getting shut down by chicks. So yeah, I know how that feels. Were you pretty bummed out after that? Did you ask her to think about it or anything, or was that just the end of it?"

"She seemed pretty sure—in fact, she said she was already going with someone else."

"Yeah, I see what you mean. Tell me about what happened that night after school." He looked at me like I had asked him to recite the Gettysburg Address in Chinese. "You know, the whole thing at Tracy's house."

"Oh yeah," he said as if it had slipped his mind. "Well, so I was just going to go over and talk to her and stuff and so I grabbed my jacket and walked out the back door."

"Did you bring anything else with you from your house?"

Again, the *surprise question* expression. "Oh, yeah. I just saw the knife there on the counter as I was leaving and so I grabbed that on my way out."

And why not? He had his coat and mittens, why not a butcher knife to complete the outdoor accouterments? Wouldn't that be included with the winter ensemble in the L.L. Bean catalogue? I decided not to ask him just yet why he chose to bring it, and why he'd left out the mask.

"Okay. Then what did you do?"

"Well, I decided to surprise her so I went around the back and into the garage door."

"The big door or the service door?"

"The service door. They keep that one unlocked."

"How do you know that?"

"Oh, you know, we're always borrowing stuff from them and they borrow our stuff sometimes, too."

"Okay. What did you do next?" I asked, as if he were recounting his summer vacation.

"Well, I walked in the house and I was going to go into Tracy's room, but then I heard Mrs. Skofield in the kitchen and I kind of panicked."

"So what did you do?"

"Well, I started looking for a place to hide—"

"Did you want to talk with Tracy alone?" I asked. "Was that the thing?"

"Yeah. I just wanted to be alone with her. So I finally went into the bathroom and I was just going to wait until Tracy's mom went upstairs or something. I don't know."

"What happened next?"

"Well, after a while, maybe ten minutes, Mrs. Skofield comes in the bathroom and starts talking to me, and then she tells me Tracy's not home, and so I just went home."

And that's all I can remember. I'd heard that so many times, I prepared myself for the two-hour interview, where I try to get him to remember little by little the incidental little parts about the mask and knife. Then, in keeping with tradition of the boilerplate memory loss, he feigns those parts of the incident have conveniently flown south of his recollection.

"Where were you in the bathroom when Mrs. Skofield came in to talk with you?"

"Um, I was in the shower, I guess."

"And what were you wearing?"

"I had on my green winter parka and my jeans."

"Anything on your head or—" I looked at him, conveying that I knew the answer I was fishing for "—anything like that?"

"Oh, yeah. And I had the mask on, too."

I smiled and shook my head yes, to let him know he had responded correctly. "And what did that mask look like?"

"Oh, you know, the kind for ice fishing and stuff like that."

"Describe it for me."

"Well, it was black and it fit over my head."

Now I wasn't sure if he was intentionally blocking or if he just had a fashion dysfunction like so many men, young and old. "If you were asking for a hat like this in a store, how would you describe it?"

His patented blank expression returned. "Just a hat, a winter hat with, ah, with the holes for the mouth and eyes, I guess, you know?"

"Yeah. I think I know what you mean now." Dentists have it easier than this. "Where was the knife when you were talking with Mrs. Skofield?"

"Oh, I was just holding that at my side."

"Oh, okay," I said, as if all interlopers who hide in their neighbor's showers probably hold their knives in a similar fashion. "Tad?" I said, waiting until he looked up at me. "What were you going to do with the knife when you talked with Tracy?"

"Oh, I don't know. Nothin', I guess."

"Well, why did you bring it then?"

"I don't know. I just decided to at the last minute."

"Did you want to have sex with Tracy?"

"Yes," he said, his spontaneous honesty startling me.

"Is that the main reason you went over to her house?"

"Yeah, I guess."

"Was the knife for just in case she didn't want to have sex with you."

Tad paused a couple seconds. "Yeah."

The interview automatically moved to the series of questions investigators used to soften up the confessor, to make it easier for the suspect to spit it out. "I think I've gotten to know you a little, Tad, and you don't seem like the kind of person who would hurt someone you really care about. I know you weren't going to hurt Tracy, right?"

Tad nodded his head—yes.

"I'm thinking you were just going to hold the knife by Tracy so that she knew you meant business. Is that right?"

"Well, kinda," he said.

"Tell me what you mean, Tad. I don't mean to put words into your mouth," I lied.

"Well, I just had it in case she said no. I was only going to hold it up by her if she said no."

"Where were you going to hold it, Tad?"

"By her neck," he said, confidently.

I couldn't believe he was giving me these details, and I was shocked at the violence of his plan. I started to wonder what his plan was for Tracy's mom. He knew she would be home, and he must have known she would intercede on her daughter's behalf.

"Okay, and let me know if I have this right. You would only have used the knife if Tracy refused to have sex with you. Is that right?"

"Uh-huh," he agreed.

"And the only way you would have used the knife and cut Tracy's neck would have been if she refused to have sex with you after you showed the knife to her. Is that right?"

"Uh-huh," he said.

"You know, Tad, you thought this out pretty good. I can tell you're the kind of person that doesn't leave much to chance. Am I right?"

"Yeah, I guess," he said, his pride showing through.

"What was your plan for Mrs. Skofield—I mean, if she interfered with you and Tracy?"

Tad shrugged his shoulders.

"I don't believe that, Tad. You've been very thorough in your strategy. Would you have used the knife to stop Mrs. Skofield if she interfered?"

Tad hesitated a moment before nodding his head yes.

Tad and his family would traverse the sometimes capricious world of juvenile justice, and Tad would spend a few days in juvenile detention after all. No one imagined how messed up Tad truly was. There would be complicated Orders for Protection specifying how far from Tracy Tad had to stay while in school. Tracy's family let the excuse of "old friendship" go out the window when they learned of Tad's true intentions. They wanted Tad locked up, and anything short of that was a miscarriage of justice. In addition to long-term probation, Tad would receive loads of court-ordered counseling for a variety of aberrant inclinations. Other than the infrequent notes from Mrs. Skofield demanding that Tad be imprisoned for life, I never heard Tad's name come up again with any criminal connection.

The morning after Tad's interview I told Mac the security guy that Mr. Skofield could have come home to a very messy scene involving the stabbing deaths of his wife and daughter. What he wouldn't have known, at least not right away, was that the stabbings would have been incidental to the sexual assault of Tracy.

"I've seen Tad around, and I'd have never guessed it. He seemed like he had his shit wired fairly straight."

"Well, he's a strategist, I'll give him that. You know it's like everything else in life—it all comes down to sex."

Mac laughed at our ongoing axiom. "Amen. It sure seems to be true around here."

"This school is but a microcosm of the world, Mac. You know that."

"You are so full-a-shit."

"Yeah?" I asked, knowing full well that I was indeed full of shit on this subject and most others, but I wondered at the same time if I might be accidentally right. It happened from time to time. The sex theory certainly seemed plausible, since almost every violent crime and a host of property crimes had, at some level, a gender conflict or, at times, an obvious sexual nexus. Besides the myriad blatant sex assaults and child sex abusers, domestic assaults are, by their nature, sex related. Homicides inspired by petty jealousies, ex-lovers, or outright extramarital affairs are common motivations. The male sex drive, unencumbered by conscience or logic, evolves from a romantic craving to a runaway semi, with no brakes, on a downhill run. And only after the crash (post-orgasmic stage), does conscious thought return and, with it, a plethora of creative alibis. Had Tad decided to kill Tracy's mother as she opened the shower curtain, the sex relation would have been difficult to flesh out, but it would have been there, like a taproot feeding the visible, healthy vine.

Mac paused conspiratorially. "Well, just in case you're right, my wife and I aren't taking any chances with our daughters." Mac smiled at this, leaving me hanging.

"You mean with the shotgun greeting for all your daughter's suitors?"

"Well, that too." Mac leaned in closer to my desk as if the room might be bugged. "Just in case our advice doesn't *take* with our daughters—every morning we crush up birth control pills and put them in their orange juice."

My jaw dropped, and I laughed, "You're kidding, right?"

"Fuck no, man. If we offer them birth control pills after

telling them to remain abstinent, it's like saying we don't really expect them to obey—"

"Which you obviously don't."

"It's not that we don't trust them. It's just a little insurance."

Making Canoes

We padded our way through the double doors of the medical examiner's O.R. like ghosts to a cemetery, our surgical shoe-covers dragging ethereally on the tile floor. With rubber-gloved hands, I carried only my camera bag into the brightly lit room. Def Leopard's "Animal" blared from a boom box on a counter near the back of the expansive room. I don't know if I was expecting Barber's "Adagio for Strings," or what, but this music didn't seem to fit. No one else seemed to notice the music or the acrid odor, as they moved about the room making preparations for the examination.

Of the four stainless steel tables, two were occupied. The table in front of me supported the nude body of my murder victim. Two tables from him, a man I believed to be a pathologist was bent over his work, blocking it from my sight. I approached the table and peered around the man to find him stripping tissue from the chest of a human fetus no larger than a squirrel. I stifled my revulsion and asked the assistant what the doctor was doing. She told me matter of factly that the tiny body was a "crack baby," delivered dead, several months prematurely. The mother was to be charged with some lesser crime than murder.

I turned my attention to the man who lay supine on the center table. His clothes were laid out on the vacant table beside him. His brown polyester pants were scuffed at the hip, most likely from his final fall to the pavement after he was shot. Otherwise the pants evinced only his occupation. A brown leather gun belt lay atop the pants; it too bore scuffmarks from the fall, predominantly on the side of the empty holster. Beside the pants and gun belt lay a tan short-sleeved uniform shirt, with the shoulder patch insignia of the armored car service he'd worked for. The shirt was disheveled and presented a hole in the left breast, surrounded by a dark burgundy stain emanating from the flaw. Beside the shirt lay underwear briefs and tan socks. I photographed each item of clothing.

My mind filled in the vacancy of the absent wallet, which I knew had been photographed at the scene by the crime lab. I had noticed the bloody wallet when I surveyed the scene of the shooting. The medics most likely removed it from the victim's trouser pocket to identify him, as he lay motionless on the parking lot pavement. How it ended up soaked in a pool of blood, I could only imagine. Perhaps the wallet occupied that space on the pavement prior to the blood, although that would not account for the complete saturation of it. The wallet had some girth to it, yet the victim's photo, which presented on the top of the clear plastic pockets, smiled through the barely translucent sanguine film. Perhaps the medic had opened the wallet to the I.D. and then placed it on the victim's chest where it became soaked. Either way, I was struck by the irony of the framed smiling face on the driver's license photo, soaked in his own blood. I was thankful that this item could be kept as evidence rather than returned to the victim's wife who would find the irony more painful than intriguing. The blood-soaked keepsake would be an agonizing reminder of her husband's fate.

The pathologist, Doctor Ames, entered the room right on schedule. Apparently there were several posts scheduled this morning. There was no time for dawdling, and he would allow none. I can only describe the man generally since his scrubs covered most identifying features. He was small in stature, about 5'5", and appeared to be in his forties. His scrubs fit loosely and did not tighten at the gut. He moved through his surroundings with the quiet confidence of a man with nothing to prove. He had no reaction or comment to the loud rock music. His gray hair curled over his skullcap in the back, and small spectacles rested on the blue paper facemask, which covered the bridge of his nose.

He introduced himself and maneuvered a triangular wheeled ladder beside the stainless-steel table supporting the victim. Noting my camera in hand, he invited me to follow his photography sequence as he stepped up the ladder for a better vantage point. After several flash photos his assistant rolled the victim's rigid body over, so his back could be photographed. The doctor finished quickly and descended, signaling that it was now my turn. I quickly climbed the ladder, braced myself on the handles, and leaned out over the body. I peered through the viewfinder of my 35mm Nikon FE 2 and adjusted the manual focus on the 35-80 telephoto lens until the victim's entire body came into view. The immodesty of death filled the rectangular confines of my camera as the forty-year-old denuded corpse lay face down on the cold steel table. I photographed his entire back to show the position of the projectile exit wounds in his back, and then his body was returned to a supine position. The air tube that the medics had used in their attempts to revive him still protruded from his mouth, and the leads from the heart monitor remained attached to his chest.

After our initial shots, the M.E.'s assistant hosed off the body and scrubbed the dried blood away with a sponge. Pink residue flowed sparingly from the bullet holes down the side of the body and disappeared into several strategically placed drains in the table. The wounds would not continue to bleed since the heart was silent. The victim's remaining blood followed Newton's law of gravity as evidenced by the lividity on the victim's back, buttocks, and heels of his feet. The injuries appeared less traumatic without the cause-effect relationship manifested by the accompanying blood. The projectile intrusions could now be examined and photographed. I replaced my 35-80 telephoto lens with a 1 to 1, 100 millimeter macro lens. I often thought injury photos taken with this lens captured detail better than the human eye.

At this point, I departed from the pathologist's sequence and photographed only the injuries, of which there were three. I waited for the doctor's cue, then started from the bottom and worked my way up. The lowest injury was a through-and-through bullet wound which entered the victim's left breast about two inches above the nipple and exited the back just below the shoulder blade. The assistant advised me that the bullet had fallen from the victim's back when his shirt was removed. All that velocity, moving at a speed of approximately 1,200 feet per second, and it didn't penetrate the thin cotton shirt. I later learned that this phenomenon was fairly common with shooting victims.

With my camera approximately one foot from the chest injury, I could see into the wound one half inch before the surrounding tissue closed around it in an attempt to stave off the blood flow. Aside from the almost imperceptible stippling around the chest wound, it was nearly impossible to tell whether the victim had been shot in the front or the back. Exit wounds were generally larger than entry.

The next injury was a superficial bullet wound, which grazed the left side of the victim's head. This bullet first took a chunk of the victim's left ear before it traveled between skin and skull and finally exited about two inches behind the ear. Incidentally, this bullet continued on its course, smashing though the rear passenger window of a passing car before it lodged on the rear deck.

The final injury was a bullet wound to the right side of the victim's forehead. This projectile grossly deformed the victim's forehead but was isolated to that specific area. The bullet had fragmented on impact, causing extensive skull, tissue, and brain damage. The shiny, red, orange, and yellow tissue, disrupted and torn by the bullet, appeared more the result of blunt object trauma than from such a small projectile. If one placed a patch over the orifice, the face of the victim would not appear unnatural or traumatized. And though the victim had died a horrifying violent death as his assailant stepped from the shadows and assassinated him, his eyes and mouth lay quietly shut, conveying the kind of posthumous peace we see at funeral visitations. This appearance was most likely compliments of a compassionate ER doctor. And though it certainly made no difference to the corpse on the table, or those responsible for determining cause of death, a gaping mouth and eyes frozen in fear might have had a disquieting effect on me. His tranquil appearance made me wonder what his final thoughts might have been as the gunman raised his pistol and fired it into his face. After falling to the ground in the parking lot, police found the victim's holster still snapped, suggesting he never saw it coming.

Believing the chest wound had missed the heart, the pathologist offered a theory that had the victim received only the chest and grazing head wound, he would most likely have survived. Another "ifa-woulda-coulda" that wasn't to be.

Dr. Ames lifted the eyelids of the deceased with a gloved thumb and studied the eye with a small flashlight, which reflected only the dull, waxen, unwavering colors of the iris. If the eyes were truly the windows to the soul, this victim's soul was long gone.

Without further delay, the pathologist began the post with the "Y" incision in the chest. That first cut through epidermis and the yellow fat beneath was always so deliberate. I wondered if doctors performing open-heart surgery on live patients were as swift and confident with their initial incision.

Dr. Ames spoke into a microphone as he worked, describing his procedure and observations. His conversational tone could barely be heard above the music.

I have seen both methods of removing the frontal ribs and breastplate, and have concluded that the operation of the pruning sheers is most impressive. The first time I saw them used, I presumed the saw to be out of service but later learned that it was this assistant's preference. I assumed with twentieth-century technology that an electric saw would fly through the ribs like a circular saw through paneling, but the pruning sheers in the right hands were actually faster, quieter, more efficient, and eliminated the possibility of spray.

The skilled hands of the pathologist carefully cut away and removed the heart and lungs. He displayed the bullet's path by placing a pencil through the holes in the organs created by the round. The demonstration proved his earlier deduction correct. The round penetrated the lung and missed the heart. He explained the resultant effect of that injury on the victim. He next cut around the victim's face and pulled it up and over the skull. His assistant sawed around the crown of the victim's skull until he completed the circle and removed the top of the skull, lifting it off like a tam. The brain stem was then cut and the organ removed.

Samples of each organ were taken by slicing off thin sections of each respective organ, including the brain, with a long serrated knife. Dr. Ames followed the bullet's path through the brain, locating and removing three curled bullet fragments along the way. These fragments, along with the intact bullets recovered from the victim's back and from the car, were placed in evidence containers to be inventoried.

The masked group then proceeded to the viscera, where the contents of the bowels would be removed and examined. I knew from previous experience that the foulest of odors would now be released. I always unconsciously attempted to adjust my breathing to prepare for this but there was really nothing you could do. I took an unspoken tip from the professionals in the room and attempted to breathe normally. There was, however, no getting used to this smell.

With the last of the intestines removed, the victim's body cavity was virtually empty, bearing a remarkable resemblance to a canoe. I don't know how old the expression of "making canoes" at autopsy is. One of Joseph Wambaugh's characters from *The Delta Star* introduced me to it in my pre-police years, but as I stared at the empty shell on the table, the expression struck me as surprisingly accurate. The collarbones and pelvis served as thwarts with the first uncut ribs on the sides acting as gunwales, and the back ribs acted as cedar strips. The victim's skin, stretched over the ribs, provided the canvas shell.

The pathologist filled a Glad Bag garbage can liner with the victim's organs and placed the bag nonchalantly in the victim's abdominal cavity. The skull, face, and thorax would all be pulled back in place and sewn back together where needed. The cornucopia of guts, though mixed together in the trash bag, would remain in the general vicinity of their origin. His empty body, dissected and gutted, would be its own disposable receptacle.

The man, a hollow shell on the table, had been reduced to his lowest element. What was once a man was now a carcass, skinned, gutted, and restuffed, to be sewn back together. These professionals around the table interrupted the transitory station in the shell's progression from death to dust. Somewhere along the way they hoped to find some truth that would allow me to award some justice for the shell who in life had been husband, father, son, and worker. He had earned $8.75 per hour to guard his company's cargo.

Observing this body with its chest splayed apart like a novel left carelessly open, I contemplated my own mortality, as all who view this procedure surely must do. Blemishes and other physical shortcomings, that in life caused self-consciousness, were open for inspection. The male genitalia would remain in its position at death, lifeless tissue to be observed and examined. There was no other surgical procedure so intrusive, invasive, destructive, and complete. Insides would be outside; faces would be rolled over skulls, whose tops would then be sawed off. Sections of viscera, organs, and bone would be sliced off and set aside for further examination. In viewing these procedures, I could not help but compare them with the day-to-day labors of a butcher.

As I stared at the empty shell before me, I realized that if I died a suspicious death, a detective would be present at my autopsy taking photos, asking questions, and struggling through the stench of my dissected bowels. In the end, I too would be made into a canoe like the cadaver before me; my bow and stern, gunwales and thwarts, would be covered and put away for storage, or even burned. Ultimately, when all was said and done, the body's final condition didn't much matter, since this canoe was simply a vessel.

Over the Edge

I was awakened at 0230 hours on a Saturday morning when my boss called me to investigate a *jumper* at the Mall of America (MOA). With only a hundred and twenty sworn officers, the detective division could not fill the night shift and relied on an on-call detective to handle the after-hours critical incidents. My sergeant sounded tired, as I'm sure he was, since he too had been awakened. The street sergeant had phoned him to request a detective to the incident scene. All suspicious deaths needed an investigator to assist the medical examiner in determining the cause of death. As my sergeant filled me in on the details, I started to resent the cozy position my wife had assumed after handing the phone off to me. My resentment then transferred to my sergeant, who after advising me of the assignment, would probably return to his bed and curl into the same envied position as my wife.

I heard little of what he said other than the apparent death of someone at the Mall, and that I should meet the street sergeant on the third floor of the east parking ramp.

I dragged my butt out of bed and used both hands as a cup to splash cold water on my face. Whether it heightened my low level of consciousness or just fueled my aggravation, it seemed to work. As I toweled off the water I wondered who the moron was who started that repulsive cold-water wake-up tradition. I complimented myself on remembering my gun, and glanced at my wife as she mumbled something into her pillow to me, probably some endearing comment. I mumbled something back to her and walked out.

There was no one on the roads at 0240 hours, but I still piloted my vehicle like the grandma I was always accused of driving like. The early August humidity greeted me from the stale vents of my vehicle's air conditioner. It would take a couple minutes before the *ice-cold air* would kick in and cool me off.

Basking in the splendor of self-pity, I took a moment to berate just about everyone involved, directly or tangentially, in my bad fortune of being called out. Those culpable, in my skewed reasoning, included my wife, my sergeant, the street sergeant, the street officers, the dead guy, and all the idiots who go to the Mall to get drunk and get laid. I thought it a fair assumption that the dead guy was most likely intoxicated, and that the opportunity of getting laid would somehow play a part in the saga.

The Mall of America is an abomination of cement, glass, color, space, and energy. No one thought the Mall would draw the numbers that actually showed up each day. The city's population of about 100,000 was doubled almost daily by visitors to the Mall and the surrounding hotels. People came from everywhere. Buses from all around the country, visitors from around the world, continued to come. After all, it was as the slogan purported, "A place for fun in your life."

As I drove by the east entrance I saw a couple of police officers standing around some debris on the pavement of the ring road, which circled the Mall and acted as barrier between the shopping center and the parking ramps. Judging by the thick, burgundy puddle of blood on the ring road, someone's night did not end up as the slogan promised. The telltale signs of medics having arrived, treated, and transported someone gravely injured, were evident at the scene: plastic bags that once contained breathing masks, bloody trauma dressings and their torn receptacles, and of course the plastic gloves used by the cops who administered first aid to the victim. The paramedics had wasted no time transporting this victim to the hospital. When I finished my survey of the scene, and Hennepin County crime techs concluded their evidentiary examination, MOA maintenance would remove the debris and scrub away every sign of misery that contradicted the Mall's blissful slogan.

An officer at the hospital advised me via my police radio that the victim had been identified by family as Patrick McGovey and that McGovey was brain-dead, awaiting the family's decision to turn off the respirator. I winced at the thought of changing roles with the victim's parents as I acknowledged the radio transmission. Mall security officers informed me that the first responding police officers were waiting for me on the third floor of the east parking ramp, directly above our position.

On the third floor of the ramp there were two groups of officers. The first group stood around a two-door Saturn with its roof, hood, and trunk smashed in. The other group stood by the presumed site of the fall. The street sergeant flagged me down from the Saturn. Sergeant Bach had been working dogwatch for a long time. At fifty-five his hair was still sprinkled with some gray; the remainder had evolved to stark white. In crisis or routine, his demeanor remained unflappable, evidencing his time on the job.

Bach delivered a two-minute, nutshell scenario in perfect Joe Friday monotone. He said our young, male-adult victim had been drinking at the American Sports Bar when he was challenged by another young male adult concerning his intentions with the other's girlfriend. There was some posturing and pushing before the bouncers escorted both club-cruisers out of the Mall. McGovey was allowed to call a female acquaintance for a ride since he was too intoxicated to drive. After making the call, McGovey played secret agent, and followed his adversary to what he thought was his car. As it turned out it was not his car after all but, having thought it was, McGovey climbed atop it and stomped on it like an angry bull, causing about a thousand dollars damage. This roof dance was picked up by Mall security camera monitors, and security personnel were dispatched to the ramp. The rest of the story was speculation.

Bach thought McGovey heard the approaching security vehicles and fled from the ruined car to seek a hiding place. With the ramp nearly empty, McGovey could find no place to hide and so, in desperation, climbed over the third floor railing and hung from the outside edge of the ramp.

There was evidence to support Bach's theory. Two sets of finger marks could be seen on that cement ledge directly above the spot where McGovey landed on the ring road. The finger marks clearly showed an individual's fingers pointing in toward the ramp from the outside edge of the ledge and evidenced the weight the fingers bore, since a simple touch would not have left such distinctive marks.

Either security personnel remained in the area longer than McGovey was able to sustain his weight from the ledge, or he simply could not pull himself back up after they left. I never seriously considered the option that McGovey let go of the ledge intentionally, since there was no background or evidence to support this conclusion, and it could never be proven. This unlikely eventuality would remain an implausible, unspoken possibility for his family.

The security officers who checked the car did not see or hear McGovey hanging or falling from his position. Blood drawn from McGovey by hospital staff would later establish his BAC (blood alcohol content) to be .28, which is dangerously high. This high level of intoxication surely played a part in the incident on the ramp.

I tried to imagine receiving the wake-up call his parents got from Fairview Southdale Emergency requesting they come immediately to the hospital regarding their son. Then the panicked rush to the hospital, where they would see him lying lifeless, with his crushed head wrapped in blood-drenched trauma dressings, with intubation tubes protruding from his mouth and nose. Doctors who knew would tell them their son would never have another conscious thought. "Brain dead" was the layman's term. First experiencing this hell surrealistically from his bedside, they would then have to participate in his death by allowing doctors to discontinue life-support to their son.

As they watched their son lie motionless and listened to the forced-air respirator breathing for him, perhaps they saw him again as a toddler asleep in his crib, pale skinned, small fingers clenched in soft, pudgy, pugilistic fists, his hair a lighter shade of blond and wispy thin, trusting his every step, his every breath to his parents.

I could only imagine how Patrick's parents felt. As a father sharing custody of my two boys, I understood separation and emptiness. My children started splitting time between their mother and me when they were one and two years old. The first nights were the worst when empty beds forced visions of the nighttime ritual of prayers, books, songs, hugs, and kisses. The absence of this physical contact and the emptiness of the house in their absence manifested in me a restless loneliness. As of this writing, my boys are twelve and thirteen years old, and their school bus driver cannot be expected to know which days they spend with me, and which are spent with their mother. From my living room window I see the bus stop at the corner and open its door. The days my boys don't step off the bus remind me of those first nights when I entered their bedroom and stared trance-like at their empty, made beds.

After saying their goodbyes, Patrick's parents allowed nature to take its course and their son died quickly. Then they wanted answers.

A natural consequence of a loved one's death, especially the accidental death of one's child, is to seek the cause—the fault—the *blame*. Rare is the family that can accept a deficiency in their kin as being responsible for their loved one's death. This case was no exception.

I returned home that morning at 0515 hours to find my wife in the same position I had left her in. I snuck quietly back into bed and lay on my side, facing away from her. I had about forty-five minutes before my alarm would ring, signaling the start of my day. I would have time to shower, shave, and return to the office where the report from this case would lie prominently on my desk. I was tired, but I didn't bother to close my eyes. The images would be the same open or closed.

"How was it?" my wife whispered from beside me.

"Young kid—too much to drink—he's dead," I mumbled.

She gasped. "That's terrible. What happened?"

"I'll tell you about it in the morning."

"It is the morning."

Later that morning I attended the autopsy. Young people always appeared out of place as they lay denuded and jaundiced on the medical examiner's stainless steel tables. The cutting away of flesh and bone seemed contradictory on such a young man. Logic implied that anything resembling surgery should have as its aim the saving of a life rather than the determination of the cause of death. The discarding of the visceral organs into a garbage bag gave a ring of finality to the process. The left rear portion of Patrick's skull had the consistency of moist, spongy toast. Upon removal and examination of the organ, one could see the massive bleeding on the brain, consistent with a fall from that height—no surprises for the M.E. or me.

I had no evidence of foul play in the death of Patrick McGovey, but Patrick's parents suspected it nonetheless. MOA security had a reasonably good video of Patrick stomping on the car, but there was no camera directed to the spot on the ramp from where I believed Patrick had fallen.

Following Patrick's funeral, I received several calls from people in attendance offering their suspicions of non-accidental death. The funeral served as a forum to vent speculation and deny the possibility that a life had been wasted through too much drink and the resultant poor judgment.

Most of the speculation centered on the possibility that the boy Patrick was chasing had doubled back and thrown Patrick from the third-floor ramp, only there was no evidence that anyone else was in the area when Patrick fell. Neither the MOA security guards nor the surveillance cameras captured any footage that supported this claim. The other scenario had Patrick hiding in the ramp when the first two MOA security officers arrived. Having found Patrick in the ramp, they either threw him over the side of the ramp (there is a four-foot guardrail) or upon noticing him hanging from the ramp, pried his fingers off or stepped on them, causing him to fall. This version doesn't coincide with the fingerprint evidence. There are no other marks near the prints that evidenced any kind of struggle or trauma directed to Patrick or his fingers. Neither was there any motive for MOA security to treat Patrick with such malice.

Patrick's parents were still not convinced so, in an effort to spread the blame, they decided to sue the MOA for having served their son alcohol after he'd become intoxicated. Patrick's father owned and operated a bar in Minneapolis and, as a result, was familiar with Dramshop laws. The family enlisted my help in proving their case, and I went so far as to question the bartenders on duty the night of Patrick's death.

The Sports Bar at the MOA had several hundred patrons per night, perhaps even a thousand or more on weekend nights. The bartenders had certainly been coached in having no recollection of serving our recently deceased young friend, and may in fact have had no memory of him, but this was not acceptable to the grieving parents.

I believe Patrick's father realized the truth without having verbalized it, but not Patrick's mother. I could sense her grief coupled with the unquenchable desire for a scapegoat. She would never accept Patrick's culpability in his own death. That responsibility needed to come from elsewhere.

There comes a point in every investigation where there are simply no more leads to follow up, and no one else to question. No one else's blood or DNA was found on Patrick's body or clothing. There was no evidence to support the theory that someone else had caused his death. Though the victim's family was still not satisfied, the case had come to completion for me. As new cases continued to mount on my desk, I finally told Patrick's parents I was closing the case, calling his death accidental.

I expected some opposition to ending the investigation. I was assured by Patrick's mother that my supervisor would be contacted, and I would be ordered to return my attention to the investigation of her son's murder. My boss did not see it her way.

I was contacted months later by a private investigator hired by Patrick's parents to find the true cause of his death and bring the killer to justice. Perhaps this kind of tragic reality could only be accepted when it was someone else's, or when it excluded the kinds of pain that couldn't be assuaged with any amount of grief, support, or time. The P.I. told me the results of his investigation mirrored mine, and for this conclusion he was fired and replaced by another P.I.

I watched the bus as it pulled into my cul-de-sac. It was the first week of school and like the bus driver, I sometimes confused the days I had my boys, since our even split was based on their mother's convoluted nursing schedule. The door to the bus unfolded and they stepped off. Sometimes they put their arms around each other as they walked to our house. Other times they raced, their backpacks bouncing against their backs as they ran. I watched them until they scrambled up to the doorstep. I opened the door, and they crossed the threshold. Now they were safe.

Special Affect

As I drove to the incident scene, the suburban landscape appeared strangely peaceful. Aside from the minimal traffic, the city seemed almost deserted. We are made hermits by Minnesota winters, going out only when necessary. But one by one, some of the hermits died. I recalled how dumbstruck I was as a rookie, seeing all the day-to-day dead people. Prior to my first days on the job I had never seen a fresh corpse in its final natural state—and I don't mean a casket. I remember being in awe of the situation—the finality. These people were really dead. Their adventures had ended, and their passing had become part of my experience. I didn't want to be the FNG caught staring at the corpse but sometimes the moment got the best of me.

The body count at times seemed staggering. I never realized how many people died every day. Not just your decrepit, living fossils, but people of all ages, ethnic groups, and income brackets. The corpses mounted all over the city to the point where I was finally forced to consider my own mortality—even in my immortal twenties.

As a Christian I considered the dead body just that—a corpse. The lease was up for this body and the tenant soul was seeking new lodgings. This new lease on life, or death depending on how you looked at it, was more than just morbid curiosity to me. It was a demonstrable step from this life to the next, and though it seldom appeared glamorous or noble, it was that person's final revelation and, therefore, momentous.

My boss had briefed me by phone when he called me out from my home. He described the incident as a "shotgun suicide." His description of the victim brought back a virtual slide show of past gruesome pictures stored in my death-scene-images library, scenes I'd been to, photographs I'd taken.

When I pulled up to the house I got the feeling that I was the last to arrive. Parked over the dirty remnants of melting mounds of snow were an array of emergency vehicles including Chevy Suburban rigs from both the Hennepin County Crime Laboratory and the Hennepin County Medical Examiners Office. Marked and unmarked squad cars lined both sides of the quiet suburban street, some with lights left errantly flashing. Oftentimes during critical incidents, the initial responders left their vehicle's flashers on to serve as a locator beacon for subsequent responding squads and emergency vehicles to drive straight to the squad.

The ever present line-up of curious neighbors stood precisely on their property lines peering at the interlopers, suggesting various scenarios back and forth. They waited for the friendly officers to make eye contact so they could ask them what had happened. The officers, however, looked anywhere but at the neighbors, hoping to avoid the reply that was often misconstrued as less than cordial, since it was unprofessional to tell the neighbors of a death prior to notification of the family. The sum of two and two could often be arrived at without asking, by adding the police and the crime lab to the medical examiner and the body within the bag.

Being the local jurisdiction investigator, I took exception at having to identify myself by badge in my own city, to the group of *brown shirts* (deputies) in the doorway. My supervisor, Sergeant Helms, scrambled his way through the living room, which was crowded with uniformed professionals videotaping, fingerprinting, and processing the scene, until he arrived at my position by the door. The thermostat within the house must have been set stiflingly hot, which was not uncommon for rental property, and this small two-bedroom rambler was made warmer with the addition of each investigator.

Helms' hairline was beaded with a raised outline of sweat as he advised me of the abundance of *biological evidence*, a euphemism for blood and gore, in the bedroom where the death presumably occurred. Due to the weapon of choice—a shotgun—there would be far more color at this scene than others where smaller caliber guns were used.

Our victim, he explained, was a special-effects artist for Hollywood and had worked on several feature films. Most of the effects he'd created were of the creature or horror film genre. Throughout the living room where I stood, there were displays of incredibly creative head and body molds of various sci-fi goblins and demons.

My boss ran interference for me as he negotiated his way back through the uniforms to the room where the victim lay. He pointed out blood spatter on the hallway walls and on an eight-fingered latex hand, mounted on a small table just outside the bedroom where the victim lay. The fresh blood on this monstrous prosthesis had descended down the fingers, and then stopped, cooled, and formed dulled darkened droplets prior to reaching the mounting base.

The victim lay on his back just inside the room. He looked

to be in his late twenties, wearing black shorts, tennis shoes, and what was once a white T-shirt. His head was grossly deformed by what appeared to be a point blank, large caliber gunshot wound to his mid-forehead, just above his eyes. The blast had the effect of parting the two spheres of his brain, displacing and dispersing them on the surrounding walls, ceiling, and floor. His eyes thankfully remained in his skull but protruded from their sockets. On closer examination I could see that his left hand formed an "O" with the thumb and fingers where he most likely held the barrel of the shotgun against his forehead. Stippling—gunpowder residue—peppered this hand, lending further credence to its close proximity to the barrel upon discharge. If this theory was accurate, his other hand would have been responsible for pulling the trigger, a simple enough action.

The shotgun in question lay at the victim's feet. It was an off-brand, short-barreled twelve-gauge with a cheap black plastic handgrip. Its discount, unappealing appearance had had little impact on its effectiveness. Loading this simple weapon, charging it, and pulling the trigger produced the desired explosion of gunpowder and gas, causing the discharge of penetrating pellets. I had to believe the victim understood this. The device in question was probably the most common gun used in this country, and the mechanics were simple enough. Though an accidental discharge could not be ruled out, it was doubtful.

One of the victim's running shoes had blood spatter on the bottom, and the other did not. It was possible the victim had supported the butt of the shotgun with his knee or rested the heel of this foot on the mattress, thus exposing the underside of his shoe. Nearly every exposed surface in the room had some sort of biological spatter on it.

Sensing someone watching me, I turned and noticed my own image in a small rectangular mirror on the wall beside me.

I stared at the reflection and noticed my flushed expression of surprise, along with what appeared to be light orangish brain tissue, which descended almost imperceptibly down the mirror at gravity's whim.

The victim's wallet lay casually open on a nightstand beside the bed. His driver's license had been extracted from a plastic pocket within, and sat indiscriminately atop the split black leather halves. His first name was Jack, and the short smile on his DL photo appeared the accidental result of something the photographer said, rather than any inclination to appear happy. I looked back and forth from the photo to the supine victim's face and noticed both the resemblance and the grossly deformed trauma the gunshot had caused.

My partner, Ted, who met me in the victim's bedroom, was born and raised on a Wisconsin farm. He continued to commute from Hudson, considering Minnesotans to be "mud-ducks." He was assigned as lead investigator to this case, and it was evident by his short monotone responses, his all-business demeanor, and his heavy perspiration, that he'd been at the scene for some time. He told me the victim's body was discovered by two female friends of the victim, both in their mid-twenties. According to them, they had walked in on the death scene sometime after the event and attempted to rouse their friend, Jack, by gently nudging him with their feet. They didn't want to get any other part of their body or clothing soiled. They then went out on the front step for a smoke, discussing between exhalations whether or not their friend had just pulled off the best effect of his lifetime, or if he was truly dead—or both. They checked on Jack again after their smoke and decided he was either really skilled at remaining motionless or he was truly dead.

They called 911 and went out for another smoke. Ted's voice inflections and eye rolls signaled me that he was not impressed with the two. A squad car had been called to transport them to the police department to make formal statements. One of the girls mentioned that her boyfriend, Chad, lived at the house with Jack, and may have been home earlier that morning. Dispatch had advised Ted that Chad had in fact called them from a friend's house in Coon Rapids about an hour after the incident to report the shooting. Chad was requested to come to the Police Department.

Videographers from the Crime Lab waited outside the bedroom door with an annoyed essence, expressed only by intermittent heavy sighs and a lack of comment and eye contact. We got the hint and got out of their way as we stepped precariously around piles and puddles of biological gunk.

Ted gave me a tour of the house, which culminated in the basement where the victim divided one half of the large unfinished space into his effects laboratory, and the other half into a marijuana-grow operation. (It may have been the housemate's marijuana for all we knew, but they assured us it was the deceased, and he was in no position to deny.) Aside from the very slim possibility of the drug rip-off homicide, we were not that interested in the grow operation. Ted advised the narcotics detectives of the plants, and left that aspect to them.

Some of the special effects projects in the basement were much more interesting than the marijuana plants. There was a fully intact, life-sized human skeleton dangling from a joist that required detailed inspection to determine whether or not it was real. A six-foot-square section of one wall consisted of an unframed latex structure with numerous non-human, expressive heads protruding from it. On a nearby workbench sat dozens of half finished projects, more creatures and critters bearing teeth and tentacles and talons.

As the temperature of the house heated to a shirt-drenching scorcher, Ted and I decided to return to the police department and interview the fleeing Chad, since he did not seem *right* somehow.

Ted spoke to Chad's girlfriend first, who told him that Chad had actually found the body prior to her arrival at the house, and so she couldn't really tell him anything about the discovery of the body. This scenario was a little different from Ted's initial conversation with her at the scene. Chad's girl-friend had just unwittingly made him suspect.

We watched Chad in the interview room from a remote monitor, which got its picture from a surreptitiously mounted miniature video camera. Chad looked very nervous as he fid-geted with his fingers and tapped his feet, awaiting our entry to the interview room.

There could never be any variation in the good-guy, bad-guy routine for Ted and me. Ted is the kind of guy that would give you the shirt off his back in a snowstorm, but he can also be an ornery, belligerent, sarcastic, argumentative curmudgeon. I, on the other hand, play a wimpy bad-guy. So, in classic tra-dition, Ted raised his voice and intimidated, while I befriended the weakened man and offered him hope. In this case our job was made simple. We asked him about the gun, about the time he arrived at the house, why he had left the house without reporting the shooting, and about his relationship with the deceased, who as it turned out was not only an acquaintance, but was responsible for collecting his rent, which was then for-warded to the victim's father, the landlord. We also asked him about a blood smear on his jacket, and a blood smear on the hallway wall.

Yes, there had been some arguments, he said between snif-fles. Yes, he had been late on some rent payments, but it did-n't seem fair that Jack didn't make rent payments directly to his father, the landlord. He did move Jack's body slightly to retrieve some keys from his pocket and must have transferred the blood on the hallway wall when he left. Yes, he had handled the gun on several occasions and knew how it operated—but no! He didn't kill his friend.

Ted and I left the room presumably to allow the witness to compose himself. (This was my—the good-guy's—decision rather than Ted's.) We watched Chad wipe his nose on his leather jacket sleeve and snort the rest of the ever-flowing snot back in his nose. Chad was a very weak man, prone to suggestion, and we realized with a bit more pressure we could quite possibly get some kind of admission or confession from him, even though we were pretty satisfied he had nothing to do with his friend's death.

We returned to the room and asked Chad point blank if he and Jack were handling the gun when it accidentally fired and killed Jack. An accident was much easier to admit than an intentional killing. He denied this accident scenario between blubbering and coating his sleeve with more snot. We believed him.

I observed the medical examiner's movements, as he deftly performed the post-mortem on Jack the following day. I was convinced by (among other things) the victim's final resting pose, the positions of the victim's fingers, the victim's hands, the gun powder residue, the entrance wound and the surrounding blood spatter, that the gunshot wound was self-inflicted rather than murder.

I spoke to the victim's father that same day, and he said he did not suspect anyone of killing his son. He said Jack had been depressed and had alluded to taking his own life in the past. He confirmed the medical examiner's suspicions about some of the scars on Jack's body being self-inflicted knife wounds. There were probably twenty such thin scars on the undersides of Jack's forearms. Apparently Jack had frequently mutilated his body, cutting shallow lacerations into his flesh with razor blades and other edged weapons. One of the wounds appeared to be a deeper laceration to his neck. His father recalled this neck scar to be the result of a previous suicide attempt.

The victim's work evinced a preoccupation, or at least an overriding interest, in eliciting a shocked, frightened, disgusted response. I wondered as I reviewed the death scene photos if Jack had indeed staged this scene, if he'd thought about the contrast of his projected body fluids and brain tissue on the white bedroom walls, of the form the blood spatter would take on the ceiling and walls, and gravity's subsequent rendering of that picture. He could have killed himself in a much less dramatic manner and, though it was a spectacle, it demonstrated the affect of a very lonely, disturbed young man.

As with all the dead, this one resulted in a police response, a report, and the M.E.'s cause-of-death determination, which in this case would read "self-inflicted gunshot wound." Unlike most death, which takes its victim by surprise, stealth, or conspiratorial illness, I thought this death experience to be the result of great care and premeditation, of apocalyptic finality. With it came another set of images to be stored away somewhere behind my conscious thoughts.

I was reminded of this case years later when my three-year-old son, Henry, fashioned a pistol from Duplo blocks complete with handle, barrel, and a blue, one-block-trigger. He lay in bed with this multi-colored toy examining it with great care, moving it from hand to hand as I prepared him for sleep. Noticing his intense concentration, I stopped and watched him as he studied the gun's design, its heft, and its smooth texture. After this brief, admiring consideration he turned the gun on himself, pointed its blocked barrel at his forehead, and said, "pa-kissh!" Then he looked at me and smiled.

Shoe Horny

While I probably couldn't name five people in my fifth-grade class, my wife has kept in contact with the same clique she went to grade school with, and they get together every year for a reunion Christmas party. My wife and her friends have mostly type-A personalities and are very adept at commingling with new faces brought about as a result of divorce and first-time marriages. These new spouses and boyfriends appear at the Christmas gig each year, and each year I'm treated to the conversational ice breaker, "So, what do you do for a living?" After mustering as much enthusiasm as I can fake with my type B-minus personality, I reply that I'm a sex-crimes investigator—to which the usual semi-innocuous follow-up is, "You must really see some weird shit." That, of course, is an understatement. Weirdness is the rule. The scary part is that the more weirdness you see, the less weird it becomes. I suppose the desensitization keeps those in the field from falling from the precipice of semi-sanity into the murky chasm below.

Last year's "new spouse" at the party was a computer programmer named Darryl, and he deftly feigned true interest in my career. Most likely he was just glomming onto me because he didn't know anyone, but I could sympathize, having been in his uncomfortable shoes several years earlier. I knew his next question before he asked it, and, sure enough, after another gulp of Grain Belt he blurted it out. "So what's the weirdest case you've ever had?"

The Shoe Guy came to mind straight away, but I decided not to tell Darryl his story because I didn't think people really wanted to know about people like him. His case made the news at six and ten, and his picture was shown in brilliant color for all the world to see, but little was said about his true eponymous passion. The TV audience was led to believe that, rather than a sex offender, the man pictured was some kind of burglar who entered his victims' houses under the ruse of being a ceramic tiler.

After all, primetime TV feeds its audience a stereotype of sex offenders, portraying them as masked villains jumping out of the bushes after buxom college co-eds (Ted Bundy actually used this method with some success), but sexual assaults by strangers are truly the exception. Your garden-variety sex crime, not counting those committed against children, involves familiar men and women who are under the influence of something other than love. The nearly deaf, overpowering, unstoppable, unquenchable, male sex drive is locked into overdrive and all the "no-no, please stop" protests are going in one ear and coming out the zipper.

Psychologists, sociologists, therapists, and other mental health professionals attempt to label each of the sexual perversions (now called paraphilias) suffered by men. (Women supposedly suffer from paraphilias as well, only we almost never see reports that confirm this.)

Fetishes are paraphilias that involve sexual attractions directed to parts of the body other than the genitals, or to objects. We've all heard jokes about foot fetishes and wondered how someone could truly be sexually turned on by someone's feet.

The Shoe Guy, as the name implies, went one step further than (or one step behind) the foot fetish. He was, as the name implies, attracted to shoes—women's shoes. I've heard of *shoe* fetishes, but rather than homogenize the paraphilia into some latinesque foot-fungus-sounding malady, I chose rather to refer to him simply as—the Shoe Guy. There very well may be some medical technical term for such a dysfunction that would allow the paraphiliac to take refuge in the presumption that, since his perversion was named, it must be a medical or physiological *condition* rather than a simple perversion. If there is such a term, I'm not going to use it.

Some sociologists, psychologists, psychiatrists, and sex therapists would like us to believe that these paraphilias are temporary conditions suffered by otherwise normal individuals and, as with other conditions, are curable. The new Sex Offender Registration laws contradict this presumption in that, if the offender was cured, why do we need to keep track of him for an additional ten years after he'd served his time and been rehabilitated, and why do we need to warn those in his vicinity of his presence?

The theory, that one predisposed to a particular paraphilia can be changed through therapy, is absurd. Think of your sexual orientation. Could someone convince you to change it? If you're heterosexual, could any amount of therapy change your sexual orientation to a same-sex attraction? Could it make you change your sexual attraction to children? To shoes? To children's shoes? You may learn to answer the therapist's questions so that he believes you've changed, and you may somehow foil the "erect-o-meter," but have you truly changed? Did Pavlov's dogs salivate because they liked the sound of the bell?

The sad truth, especially when considering pedophiles is—once a pedophile, always a pedophile.

The Shoe Guy presented far less a threat to society than any pedophile, but he did have his dangers, and I don't just mean to shoes. His case was brought to my attention via the usual route—an officer was called to a residence where a concerned citizen wished to report that a crime had occurred and, as such, needed to be handled by the authorities, the cops in this case. A report was made, and videotapes and other physical evidence were handed over to the friendly policeman taking the report.

Good videos of a perp committing a crime are the kind of evidence detectives and county attorneys fantasize about, when they're not fantasizing about the kind of things they normally would. These videos sometimes showed a perp as he robbed a bank or convenience store, snatched a purse, or pocketed a CD. Good videos, however, are the exception. The quality of surveillance videos is typically horrible. They most often utilize time-lapse recording to allow the videotape to continue on for hours, causing recorded movement to appear choppy, since there are usually four seconds or more between each frame.

The videos handed to the friendly policeman taking this report were shot at normal SP speed, producing an excellent, sharp, full-color image. The reporter in this case was the perp's wife, who *stumbled* upon the three videos under the front seat of her husband's truck. They had no title so she thought she'd better check them out prior to recording over them. What she saw on these tapes shocked her more deeply than her recent discovery that her husband was having an affair. (This same realization might have had something to do with the thorough search of her much-maligned husband's truck and the garage).

Further investigation by the wife produced an unusual scrapbook and a metal toolbox with a peephole drilled in the side to accommodate a video camera capable of covert recording.

This scrapbook, the toolbox, and its contained video camera were also handed over as evidence to the reporting officer.

Back at the police department, the report and accompanying physical evidence were summarily dumped on my desk. For a busy detective, videotapes elicit ambivalence. They take a long time to review—three videos could take two days depending on which speed they were recorded, and are usually of such poor quality that the footage is seldom beneficial. So I was less than thrilled when the reporting officer deposited the report, the toolbox, the scrapbook, and the set of videos on my desk.

"You gotta read this one," he said. "And let me know about the tapes."

With that, I scanned the report and my interest was piqued. The report documented the reporting wife finding the videos and checking their content. She advised the reporting officer that her husband was a self-employed ceramic tiler who usually worked remodeling jobs in established homes. She said she had found the scrapbook and toolbox in the garage.

I opened the scrapbook and found family snapshots that included several young women pictured alone or with others. Most of the women were photographed unprovocatively in swimming suits or underwear. Beneath the pictures, taped to the page, were small cellophane bags containing what appeared to be pubic hair. There were handwritten notes beside each bag with comments like, "Cunt hair from Jane Doe's sweet pussy." There were about fifteen such pictures and corresponding pubic hair with notes. The reporting wife stated that most of the women pictured were extended family members or friends.

This was uncharted territory for me. It was very different from simple pornography. In fact, it was not pornographic at all. It did entail some degree of invasion of privacy if it could be proved that the hair contained in the bags was actually the pictured woman's pubic hair, and that the perp had retrieved it from their beds without their permission. This, however, would entail DNA testing and, for the misdemeanor crime of Invasion of Privacy, it would not be cost effective. Depending on what the videos from the secreted camcorder contained, I was looking at a relatively insignificant misdemeanor case, involving a typically vengeful wife suffering the effects of betrayal.

With my curiosity now on an equal plane with George's, and with videotapes in hand, I padded straight away to our modest Video Center, which doubled as Tech Detective Jason Scheid's office. His office, which accommodated two seated people comfortably, contained two high-end VCRs and a monitor. I told him I had videos in a yet-to-be-determined sex case and needed to check them on his VCR, which had slow-motion, forward, and reverse, with printer capability. With Jason's curiosity also whetted, he inserted the first video, and we sat down in front of the monitor (sans popcorn or doughnuts).

The first video was recorded from the camera within the toolbox. The vista was partially shrouded by the narrowly drilled peephole, giving the viewer the sense of focusing through the wrong end of a telescope. It appeared the handler of the toolbox brought it into a house and set it down on the floor. From that position the only subject it could record was—*shoes*. This tape was agonizingly boring with only the occasional foot striding in and out of the camera's field of vision.

The second video greeted us with a parcel of mail bearing a woman's name and a Minnetonka address. The camera then took us on a tour as it scanned the unoccupied house in choppy hand-held fashion before it was placed to rest on a stable surface, probably a dresser in the master bedroom. From this vantage point the camera began recording a series of events that would be repeated in many different homes throughout the metro area.

The lone star, cinematographer, videographer, and director of these videos was a medium built, thirty-five-year-old male, about 5' 8", 160 pounds. He had dark-brown medium-length hair, and a full dark-brown mustache, which offered contrast to his thick pale skin.

The master bedroom scene opened with a close-up groin shot of our star, masturbating. Without fully ejaculating, he masterfully managed to work out a bead of semen, which clung on the tip of his penis like a raindrop on the tip of a leaf. He then took earrings from a jewelry box on the dresser and slipped the spike of the earring intended to penetrate an earlobe, through the drop of semen and into his urethra. At that point he posed narcissistically for the camcorder with the earring adorning his dick. As he backed away from the camera and allowed the rest of his body into the viewfinder, we saw that he was dressed in women's clothing, in this case, a lovely, black evening gown. He mixed and matched earrings, replacing those he *used* back in the jewelry container. He maintained a serious, all-business expression as he exchanged jewelry.

Jason and I were struck with a sense of disbelief but were unwittingly drawn in and entertained. Though the director's intent was probably geared to the erotic genre, we were finding the content to be hilarious. There was a suspense unfolding that could never be predicted since we had no idea what our *star* had in store. We assumed correctly he was in the house of a client and had taken a break from his hectic tiling to unwind in his own special way. He had been invited into the home so he couldn't be considered a burglar, and unless he stole the women's clothing or jewelry he *wore,* he could not be charged with theft. We could tell his motives lay elsewhere.

The jewelry scene stopped as abruptly as it started while our star set up the next scene, which began with a distant unfocused view of a single object. The telephoto capability of the camcorder was then utilized to bring the subject of the video-grapher into closer relief. It was, as it appeared from a distance to be, a black pump. A woman's shoe. Jason and I looked at one another a little perplexed as the shoe was shot from several angles, giving it a thorough consideration. The camera stopped once again.

When filming resumed our star was seen in profile, dress hiked up over his waist, straddling the previously videotaped black pump and sporting an erection. Jason and I saw the writing on the wall and in a manner befitting mature professional investigators, we loudly summoned anyone within shouting range to hurry into the video office to see what was sure to come.

As six additional investigators, both male and female, sandwiched themselves into the tiny office, our star positioned himself over the innocent, unsuspecting shoe. To the many shouts of encouragement from the audience, our star inserted his penis into the shoe and began humping. As he was about to ejaculate he craned his neck to the floor where women's panties lay just in front of him. Without using his hands he scooped the panties into his mouth like a snapping turtle devouring its prey. Panties in mouth, he raised his body just over the shoe so his ejaculation into the shoe could be seen and recorded. This act, commonly used as denouement in porno flicks, was but a segue to the following and final epiphany.

Using a syringe, our star collected his ejaculate from the shoe. He then spread his seed about the house inserting his semen into unused tampons, onto toothbrushes, lipstick and other facial cosmetics. As the coup de *gross*, he emptied the syringe into an opened wine bottle, then recorked and replaced it in the refrigerator.

As the grossed-out group of voyeuristic investigators prepared to leave the office, the video continued with another parcel of mail, a tour of a different house, more women's clothes, the jewelry, the shoe, the sex act, and the collection and distribution of semen. This sequence was repeated ad nauseum and no one made it past the first video but me. I needed to watch them all in their entirety, in case an additional crime was recorded.

The first two tapes were more and more of the signature sequence, but the final tape contained something else. This third video was recorded from an elevated, secure position, most likely a false ceiling, over a small rustic bathroom. The camera was focused on the toilet. I set the playback speed to fast-forward and, sure enough, several women entered the bathroom and used the toilet. The reporting wife later confirmed that the recorded bathroom scene was from their own cabin in northern Wisconsin. Once again, I was dealing with a minor crime that outraged the women recorded, but could only be considered a misdemeanor, and turned out to be well beyond the statute of limitations.

On a tip from his ever-helpful wife, Detective Sergeant Mike Bergey and I arrested the movie man as he left a job in Plymouth. At the time of his arrest, I thought I could charge him on a host of crimes ranging from burglary and criminal damage to property, to adulteration of food, and invasion of privacy. I didn't tell him right away what he was being arrested for, and he didn't ask. I almost didn't recognize him. He looked much different in person and dressed—in men's clothing. His light-gray hair and mustache evidenced a lengthy passage of time since the videos were recorded.

Sex criminals are often thought of as the most egregious offenders of our sensibilities, yet we in the field find that there is no shortage of them. As Shakespeare said in *Richard II,* "Some of you with Pilate, wash your hands..." I don't know if sex crimes have always been this abundant and simply underreported, or if the proliferation of sex in every aspect of life, from music to TV and advertising, has ultimately influenced us. Has America turned into the United States of Sodom and Gomorrah? Have our sophistication and technological advances perpetuated a philosophy of Machiavellian immorality? Perhaps our culture has become so selfish that there is no guilt in acting on our sexual impulses. With each case it seemed new answers or a lack of them came to light.

The Shoe Guy had little to say to me about the videos. Seated in the small interview room I felt uncharacteristically claustrophobic in such close proximity to my suspect. I could only concentrate tangentially after having watched his relentless assaults on the shoes. I defensively tucked my recently-shined, brown loafers under my chair as I began the interview. He admitted he'd had a problem with shoes about fifteen years ago, but had not done anything similar since. He said he didn't understand the *shoe thing* and apologized for all the spreading of his seed. I asked him about his provocative experiments as a vintner but, as luck would have it, he'd conveniently forgotten his days of wine and semen. I told him it was a moot point, since the recipe had been saved for posterity on film. I had a hard time believing he could put this life-consuming fetish to rest, but I had no proof of any recent shoe business. He said the tapes were at least fifteen years old, and his aged appearance seemed to confirm that.

Being outraged, or at least flabbergasted by what I'd witnessed on tape, I attempted to charge him with some kind of felony. As I discussed his case with the Hennepin County Attorney I found that nothing he did fit any crime listed in the Minnesota State Statutes. Even the adulteration of the wine was not considered a crime unless he intended to harm the consumer. My shoe friend agreed to an AIDS test, but the results came back clear, so there could be no intent to cause harm. The Invasion of Privacy crimes had long since fallen beyond the statute of limitations. Astonishingly to me, the Shoe Guy walked out of our police department never to be charged, much less convicted of, any crime related to his extra-curricular tiling hobbies.

I think of the Shoe Guy from time to time when I get a new case involving some different guy exhibiting a new (to me) paraphilia. I don't know how the Shoe Guy got started; he was either too embarrassed, or too frightened he'd be charged with something else, to tell me.

I worry that there may be more paraphiliacs among us than we could ever imagine, but then I'm paranoid. Most fetishes have little effect on *uninvolved others* and give the public little need for concern. I believe we tend to trust those we know and assume them to be *normal*—whatever that means. Of course, the word and the condition are relative. I'm sure the Shoe Guy's friends had no idea about his "hobby." The same psychologists who replaced the word *pervert* with the condition *paraphilia* want us to believe that there are no perverted sex acts, just different ones. Maybe they're right.

One of the most accomplished serial murderers in modern history was a Russian named Andrei Chikatilo, who admitted to fifty-three murders but probably committed many more. After his arrest he told police that he started his crime spree by simply exposing himself. He said he would never have progressed beyond that if he had been caught, since he was terrified of the publicity and punishment that would have resulted from his arrest. But he wasn't caught. The victims he'd exposed himself to didn't think these incidents serious enough to report. Encouraged by the laissez-faire response to his exposing incidents, he then progressed to frottage, and finally to kidnapping, rape, and murder, followed by the dissection and ingestion of his victim's breasts and genitals. (This sequence would later be imitated by others, including Jeffrey Dahmer.)

I considered my new friend Darryl's question about the weirdest case I'd encountered as a sex crimes investigator, but decided against relating the Shoe Guy case. Instead, I told him about a recent case of a man whose ten-year-old daughter surprised him in his basement study as he stood dressed only in his estranged wife's bra, his vacuum cleaner hose securely attached to his erect penis—and running.

Lacking Virtue

Seated at my desk, I heard the one radio call that elicits a universal cringe among police officers—baby not breathing. My boss heard it too and came into our office to request that we stick around until the verdict was in. If the baby responded to rescue efforts, it would be transported via ambulance to an emergency hospital and detective involvement could probably wait. On the other hand, if the baby died, we would have an unexplained death, which would require an immediate investigation. There was nothing quite like interviewing grieving parents when they knew, though it was never suggested, that they were the primary suspects in their baby's death.

Bobby Landan had been the first officer on the scene, and he did everything right. A twenty-year veteran who knew the drill, he ran from his squad to the house. He knocked once and announced his presence before entering and repeating his announcement. He rushed into the house and was met at the stairway by the father of the baby, who had just descended the stairs after getting off the phone with the police dispatcher. He cradled his lifeless daughter in his arms, her chubby white legs splayed in repose.

Bobby took the baby and placed her on a nearby dining table. He hurriedly touched his hand to her chest and felt a tiny, but still encouraging, rhythmic beat. He leaned over her face and watched for the rise and fall of her chest, and for the soft exchange of air from her mouth to his cheek. Sensing no response, he started rescue-breathing for the baby, placing his mouth over the infant's mouth and nose and delivering small puffs of air. Sergeant Pierce arrived shortly after, and seeing that Bobby had started breathing for the baby, he began getting the baby's medical history from the father. The medics arrived minutes after Pierce, who then advised Bobby of their arrival.

Bobby ran to the ambulance in front of the house while breathing for the baby he held. He handed the infant off to a medic in the back of the rig who quickly took over respirations with an infant ambu-bag.

Having heard no further updates on the radio, I decided to drive out to the scene and see for myself which way the verdict was leaning. Bobby was inside the ambulance when I arrived, assisting the medics who were working frantically to stabilize the infant. Sergeant Pierce was talking with some concerned neighbors who stood a comfortable distance from the rig. The baby's father, James, stood at the rear of the rig, looking in at his tiny, five-month-old daughter on the adult-sized cot.

I asked him if he was the baby's father. He turned to me and said that he was. His bottom eyelids formed crimson reservoirs of pooled tears. I introduced myself and asked him what had happened. He told me he had gone in his infant daughter's bedroom to change her diaper after she awoke from her nap, that she was happy and smiled as he changed her, that she remained on the floor where he changed her when he left the room for a couple minutes. When he returned, his daughter was motionless and not breathing. He said he knew CPR and attempted to breathe for her, but after a short time with no response, he called 911. According to James, there had been two previous instances of Alex losing her breath, and after each instance, they brought her to the pediatrician but no cause was ever determined. In both previous instances he had been alone with his daughter when she suffered the temporary asphyxia.

As I spoke with James, the medics finished their attempts to stabilize Alex and prepared her for transport to Children's Hospital in Minneapolis. James asked them if he should ride in the back of the rig with Alex, and a medic offered him a seat beside his daughter. James considered it shortly before opting to drive separately. His decision surprised me, but I didn't read anything into it at the time.

I'd seen far more dead babies resulting from "baby not breathing" calls than surviving ones. I drove from the scene in an elated haze, the kind of mental state where you forget your destination and even that you're driving. My unmarked squad piloted me home where I typically ate lunch with my wife, who officed out of our house. I called her up from her basement office and told her I had some exciting news.

I described to her how Bobby Landon, whom she was familiar with, had just saved a five-month-old baby's life. Having a two-year-old, and feeling we had serendipitously triumphed over the SIDS threat, these baby calls aroused an eerie empathy. My wife wanted all the details and was very excited, and proud of Bobby. She too had heard her share of such incidents turning out the other way.

Bobby found out later that afternoon that the Investigator position he'd applied for had been given to a younger, more inexperienced candidate, but that was just the beginning of the day's irony.

At about 2000 hours that evening, Patrol Sergeant Warner called me at home after a nurse from Emergency Care at Children's Hospital had phoned him to report that the infant girl that Bobby had saved earlier that day was in critical condition, and there were more problems than the mysterious apnea episodes. The cause of the baby's respiratory distress was no longer a puzzle for the emergency doctors. They had found that in addition to her respiratory failure, the infant had subdural hematomas—blood on the brain—old and new. She also had retinal hemorrhages, three broken ribs, and a fractured tibia. Babies' bones are typically resilient—even difficult to break.

The doctors at Minneapolis Children's Hospital were not fresh out of medical school, nor were they general practitioners taking a whimsical spin at pediatric maladies. They were the finest pediatric specialists in the state, very skilled at distinguishing child abuse from accidental and non-preventable injuries. They concluded that the injuries this baby sustained were the result of child abuse, not just one impatient, inexplicable moment of rage but several uncontrollably violent incidents over a period of months. The fresh blood on the brain and the retinal hemorrhages evidenced severe trauma that definitely occurred that day, probably minutes before James called 911. The old blood on the brain, the broken ribs, and the fractured tibia were older. How much older? The infant was only five months old. All of her injuries had most likely been sustained within the past couple months.

Our jubilation over the saved life had turned to ambivalence. Bobby had saved the baby's life, but now the question was: "From what? Or whom? And to what end? What would be her quality of life?" The nurses said Alex had suffered indeterminate permanent brain damage and loss of sight. The severity of these injuries would not be known for years, when she could be properly tested.

The father, whose tears pooled in the wells of his lower lids, and who declined the offered ride with the ambulance, was now suspect. He was really more than just suspect. He had told police that he had been home alone with Alex from the time his wife left for work at 0830 until he called 911 at 1100 hours. Doctors with expertise in "shaken baby syndrome" said that Alex could not have looked normal to her mother or anyone else after receiving these injuries. They said the injuries had occurred abruptly and that Alex would have been totally unresponsive immediately following the trauma.

The nurses interviewed Alex's mother and father separately. James reiterated what he had told police and Alex's mother could only say that she had handed Alex off to James in the morning when Alex was normal.

After these separate interviews the doctor spoke with mother and father together and told them that unless Alex had been involved in a severe auto accident or had fallen a great distance, her injuries were the result of being violently shaken. Even the car accident and the fall would probably not have caused the severe retinal hemorrhages. Both mother and father, prior to this interview, told the nurses that Alex had suffered no accidental trauma since birth.

The mother later told me that, once informed of her daughter's condition, she experienced a whirlwind of evolving emotion. She first stared at James with disbelief, then uncertainty, followed by dismay, disappointment, and finally disgust and anger as she shouted at him to leave the room.

The following day, the story of the saved baby, now doomed to a life limited by brain and sight injuries, swept through the police department. I arranged for the mother and maternal grandmother, whose house the family resided at, to come to the police department and give statements. I called the hospital and tried to locate James to get his statement, but he could not be found. I left messages with all links at the hospital and with James' friends. Finally, at about noon, he called me from a friend's house. He said he had been advised by friends not to talk to police, and so would not be making any statements.

To find the address, I reversed the phone number he called from. I was shocked by the resultant address, which looked like it was mistakenly taken from my Christmas card list. James was staying with a friend who lived with his mother, one half block from my home. I was familiar enough with this family to know that they were decent people. Two of my partners went straightaway to the house and arrested James for PC (probable cause) first-degree felony assault. This police invasion of the neighborhood was probably not seen as being very neighborly, but James was only a baby's breath away from being a homicide suspect.

In the meantime, one by one, the extra chair in my office began to fill with police officers and detectives who wanted to share their two cents on this case. Without exception, the conversations began with that officer's opinion of what should become of the suspect father, and without exception their judgment allowed for a very unpleasant punishment. Some wanted to reinstate Minnesota's ban on capital punishment while others opted for James to be drawn and quartered.

After offering their severe judgment, the officers with children told of how they had been tested by their own infants, who cried at length without cause, and stretched the limits of their fatherly patience to the point where they had to do— *something*. This *something* ranged from placing the crying baby back in their crib, while the father regained composure, to taking the baby for a drive, to calling family or friend and pleading for help. All of the options were, of course, better than shaking the fussy, helpless infant. All the police officers understood how a father could lose patience with the infant, yet none had a scrap of sympathy for the young father in our jail—nor did I.

Perhaps this microcosmic group of cop fathers was really passing judgment on themselves for the rage they realized was, at times, just a flash away. Perhaps some of them had gone so far as to bring their screaming infant to their own face, twisted and flush with anger, before regaining that fleeting flicker of their own composure. That distance between blind rage and violence was often too short.

I remember the subject of shaken baby syndrome coming up at the baby classes my wife and I attended when she was pregnant. Our class was presented with a film in which the actors staged an incident of shaken baby. The narrator advised that many expectant parents would have their patience tested by colicky babies. Of course, most of the parents dismissed the possibility, thinking this malady was another one of those problems that "other people" would be forced to deal with.

I ended up being one of those *other people,* tested by both my first and second sons. I understand the frustration of being unable to relieve a screaming baby of his or her pain. Like a rope slowly uncoiling, fraying from a weight too heavy, I felt the strained limits of my own patience. The word *uncomfortable* perfectly defines the condition of colic, since the baby simply cannot be comforted. Once the parent accepts that his infant is, at times, inconsolable, he or she can start dealing with the ordeal of caring for an otherwise healthy baby. Unfortunately, this acceptance is far easier said than done. An infant's nonstop crying seems to provoke an almost instinctive, primitive, unsettling anxiety among most people.

All those who knew James said he was a model father when in their company. Whenever he became stressed with the baby, he simply handed her off to his girlfriend or her mother, who took over comforting the baby. No one, not even the baby's mother, thought it suspicious that each instance of apnea occurred when the baby was alone with her father.

Apparently James, like many mothers and fathers, was a master of concealing or camouflaging his anxiety. I'm sure he believed his loss of composure to be a forgivable act that would never happen again. That space between control and rage having grown smaller and smaller until it disappeared exploding into unrestrained violence. With time, he could probably convince himself that he was not responsible for his actions. After all, he had been someone else when composure left him.

While his tiny, five-month infant girl stared blankly into a pain-induced haze, James stared up at the dirty tiles on the ceiling of our jail, his thoughts, no doubt, on rationalizations, excuses, defenses, and lost time.

Cry Rape

The medical staff at night appeared like worker bees, moving from here to there with purpose, natural and uninhibited. There were no extra movements in their walk or supplemental mannerisms added for anyone's benefit. Their actions, like feral animals, were less planned, less narcissistic. They were less on-stage than their daytime counterparts. Like the cops working dogwatch, the medical staff was on duty for eight hours in darkness while everyone else—the normal people—slept. And like the cops, they experienced more aberrant behavior during their shift than day-watch and mid-watch combined. I knew the routine after working my first three years in patrol on dogwatch. As a detective now working *days*, I didn't miss it.

It was a slow Sunday morning in the ER. At 0615 hours there were only two groups awaiting service, and neither looked like they were suffering from anything serious. Some of the weary-waiting read magazines, while most craned their heads up from rows of uncomfortable couches to watch television screens mounted from the ceiling. Both groups glanced up at me and contemplated my presence as I approached the charge nurse. Without the briefcase I could have passed as patient or visitor, but its attachment marked me as some responding professional. My badge and gun would have been a dead give-away, but they were concealed under my baggy polo shirt. My gun's only possible purpose in my present state of semi-consciousness would be that of an anchor should I somnambulate into the water.

The charge nurse checked her chart and told me which rooms the two victim women were in. As she continued to type, she directed me with a head-nod and glance to the entrance of the ER, where I had conducted numerous interviews and photographed injuries many times before. She said the SARS (Sex Assault Response Service) nurse had been paged, as I had been, and was on her way.

I entered the sanctum sanctorum and tried to guess the function of the actors by their scrubs. The doctors were easy, wearing blue scrubs and stethoscopes, although a nurse or nurse practitioner could sometimes mimic the doctor's duds and throw you off. There were various scrubs designating different nurses, surgeons, techs, and custodians. The uniformed cop at the end of the shiny wide hallway was far easier to peg. He saw me coming and managed a smile. A *friendly*, a brother. I knew the feeling. His shift ended in forty-five minutes, and my arrival meant that he could now ditch me, and head for home, having been properly relieved.

Rare was the hospital staffer, especially on dogwatch, who made a cop feel welcome, or even acknowledged his presence. Sometimes it seemed we were considered a necessary evil, since all sexual assaults needed to be reported to the police. I felt like we were viewed as the source of too many bumped, bruised, or K9 bitten patients who, according to them, received their injuries from some nasty cop who beat them indiscriminately.

The medical staff probably heard this story so often, they started to believe it.

Whatever the reason for our presence here, we caused some of them to write another report or walk from here to there. No one on dogwatch wanted any extra duties, especially this close to quitting time, and since we were on their turf, they would assist us when they were good and ready—or even better, they might allow their relief to assist us after shift change.

There were exceptions. Nocturnal brethren of shift work, cops and nurses, often met in the dark and mated as like-species. These nurse-cop relationships made for preferential treatment at the hospital when you could find some other cop's spouse working as a nurse.

No "friendlies" tonight. Officer Willitz stood in the hallway between the two victims' rooms. He acted as guardian, and liaison between the police and medical staff, but aside from scratching out the initial offense report, his main purpose this morning was to make sure the victims didn't run off before they were treated. He told me that both victims believed they had been drugged and raped. He pointed to the room on the left and whispered a warning about any direct contact with *that one*. She was apparently a bit hostile.

A coward at heart, I went in the other room first. An attractive Caucasian brunette in her mid-thirties looked up from the tissue-covered examination table where she sat. I introduced myself as the detective who would be handling her and her friend's case, and pulled out my little notebook. In response to my salutation, she said she had a very painful, throbbing headache, different from a hangover—more intense. She thought the pain was the result of a drug given her surreptitiously by the man who had sexually assaulted her and her friend, Brenda. Being a linear thinker, I asked her to start from the beginning.

Jill started her story, defining her relationship with Brenda as best friends. Both were married with children who played together. The previous night was "ladies' night out" for the two of them. They had rented a hotel room across the street from the Mall of America and brought in a cooler of beer. Their itinerary included a few warm-up beers at the hotel, followed by dinner at one of the Mall's finer dining establishments, and finally some old-fashioned bar-hopping on the Mall's fourth floor.

The evening had progressed as planned until they went to the American Sports Bar and started dancing. An athletically-built black man in his late twenties or early thirties approached the two as they danced together and started dancing with them. He seemed more interested in Jill and, as the night went on, he and Jill continued to dance, while Brenda watched from the sidelines. Brenda told him at one point during the night that he was really cute. He told Jill his name was Marcus, that he'd attended the University of Minnesota where he'd played varsity football, and that he presently sold cars for a dealership in Apple Valley. He wore a blue polo shirt with the dealership logo on it, but she couldn't remember which one it was.

She remembered dancing and drinking with Marcus but did not recall leaving the Mall. She said he tried to kiss her a couple times while they danced, but she did not allow it, and he did not persist. She thought she remembered being out in front of her hotel with Brenda and Marcus as Marcus tried to bum a cigarette for Brenda from some hotel employees on a smoke break. The next thing she remembered was being awakened by Brenda who seemed terrified, so much so that she couldn't catch her breath to speak. She finally managed to tell Jill that she awoke to Marcus rifling their dresser drawers. She yelled at him, and he fled the room. She paused and then said between sobs that her groin was very sore and she felt like she'd recently had intercourse. Brenda was wearing only panties and a T-shirt when she awoke, and did not recall taking off her clothes. Jill said she awoke in the same clothes she'd worn the night before, that her pants were zipped up and her belt fastened. Her shirt and bra were also intact and she felt no pain, or hint of sexual contact. Jill added that she had to talk Brenda into both calling the police and telling her husband what happened.

I spoke with Brenda next as she sat more on the small of her back than her butt, reclining on the exam table between stirrups, which projected outward, foreshadowing her eventual exam. What soft lines her face may have possessed had calcified into expressions of anger. Her attitude and demeanor were colored by humiliation and shame.

"I suppose I'm gonna have to tell this story again," she said, annoyed. "Who are you?"

I told her I was the assigned detective and she would probably have to repeat her story to the SARS nurse when she arrived, and then again to the county attorney and whoever else she chose to tell.

"My husband already asked me everything you could possibly think of," she said, with a hint of exasperation. "He's on his way here from the hotel." She rolled her eyes as she started to get up. "I'm gonna go find this guy myself, and kill—" She squatted, wincing. "Oh, my ass hurts!"

"Let's leave the killin' to the police," I said, facetiously. "First things first, you need to have your exam and—"

"Are they gonna be checking everything—if you know what I mean?"

"Yes," I said. "That's what they do. We need that physical evidence for charging in case we don't have any luck tracking him down and killing him."

She acknowledged my sarcasm with a faint smile, but continued, dead serious, "Don't worry about that. You guys just tell me where he is and I'll take care of him."

"I'm sure you know it doesn't work that way."

She fidgeted on the exam table, trying to get comfortable. "I just wanna kill that guy. I can't even sit down. Are they gonna look at my...you know...my butt, too?"

"If you feel like you were assaulted there—yes."

"Well," she said, "I was obviously—assaulted—there."

"And vaginally?" I asked.

She looked at the ceiling. "I'm having my period now, but yes, vaginally too."

I asked her to start from the beginning as Jill had, and she reiterated most of what Jill said, but remembered even less. She alluded, without saying out right, that Jill was enjoying the attention Marcus was showing her. Brenda too spoke of an uncharacteristically intense headache and admitted to drinking about five or six drinks over the course of the evening.

Brenda's husband, Tom, arrived at her hospital room with the SARS nurse as I was preparing to leave. He was suffering the classic symptoms of a sex-assault-victim's spouse. He knew he had to ease up on the inquisition with Brenda or she was going to lose it with him. At the same time, he obsessed over questions that needed answering, so he turned to me: "What was this man doing in their room? Was he invited? By whom? Was there any consensual sex? Is there such thing as consensual sex when someone is drugged or drunk? Did these memory drugs really eradicate one's memory? Is it really possible to have intercourse and not remember it? Did the suspect use a condom? If not, was she in danger of contracting AIDS? Am I? What kind of drugs did people like this use? Did these drugs produce any side effects? How and when are you going to find this miscreant and bring him to justice? Could drinking too much alcohol have the same effect? How long do these drugs stay in the system and why hasn't someone taken some blood from my wife yet?"

Tom was an intelligent, successful businessman, but he was not prepared to be the compliant *rock* his wife needed at present. The security he'd built for himself, as he attained his upper-middle-class status, had been breached, and there seemed to be no way to get it back. I answered his questions and advised him to ease up on the interrogating and, "just be there for her." I also advised him to make sure his wife did not attempt to clear this little matter up on her own with a bullet, since she seemed perfectly willing at the moment. Strangely enough, that homicidal-justice emotion was uncommon in my dealings with sex assault victims.

I knew what Tom *wanted* to believe, but there was a vast expanse between the scenario of a suspect jumping out of the bushes, forcing sex on the resistant young women—and the scenario of his wife and her friend getting drunk and inviting a young stallion back to their hotel room. Tom was clearly not through lamenting about this, and would continue quizzing his wife until he was satisfied. His taut brow signaled his serious doubts about the propriety and innocence of the "ladies' night out" scenario. Having met his wife, I could tell that Tom would need to walk on eggshells or would be wearing their contents.

I shared some of Tom's doubts about the scenario given by the women. Though there were specific details of the night's progression, the momentum changed at times, and deletions in memory and content, especially at the hotel room, were overly opportune. Most glaringly, if this suspect had planned on drugging these women and having his way with them, why would he tell them his name, his personal history, and his present employer complete with polo-shirt logo? Perhaps all he told them was fabrication, part of his convoluted plan—but I had my doubts and so did Tom.

My next stop was the Country Suites Hotel—the scene of the crime. Uniformed police officers and Hennepin County Crime

Lab technicians met me at the hotel room and processed the scene. The estimate of consuming a couple beers before heading out to dinner had been conservative to say the least. The small bathroom wastebasket was full of beer cans, and the remainder of the twelve-pack littered most surfaces of the room. An empty bottle of Tequila shared space with the cans in the wastebasket. Also of interest was $115 in cash, lying in plain sight within a dresser drawer. This amount was within twenty dollars of what cash the victims believed they had stashed at the hotel. This recovered cash diminished the theft motive since, if the suspect was going to steal their cash, why not take the entire amount? Thefts of under $500 only constituted a misdemeanor. Finally, Brenda's used tampon was found on the bed near the pillow where Jill slept.

The Crime lab took some partially consumed beer cans to test for drugs, along with the bed sheets and the tampon. I left the hotel with the other police, and caught up with my family in church, halfway through Sunday service. I noticed that my boys had skipped their morning shower and they probably ascertained the same of me.

My Monday morning voicemail greeted me with a deluge of successive despairing messages from Tom. (Oddly enough, throughout the course of the investigation, I never heard from Jill's husband.) Tom had been working the two scenarios over in his mind all day between a near-constant onslaught of questions to Brenda. He wanted to know if I believed that his wife had been raped, plain and simple. It mattered to him what I thought.

Before I returned his calls, I phoned the SARS nurse and asked that she brief me regarding her examination. Her serology exam of Jill produced no detected semen from vaginal swabs taken at the hospital. Semen was found on Brenda's vaginal swabs, but not on anal swabs. Brenda's vagina and anus were both violently torn. According to the SARS nurse, the tears were due to vigorous unlubricated intercourse. This sexual experience had not been a pleasant one, but if the victim was unconscious during the infliction, the pain would not have been noticed until consciousness was restored.

My next consult was with the crime lab, which found no evidence of "date rape" drugs. They did find, however, that both Jill and Brenda had twice the legal limit of alcohol in their systems—and that was the result detected *six hours after* their last drink.

I called Jill and Brenda and informed them of the findings. Brenda said that her marriage and Tom's physical safety were in jeopardy since he would not stop interrogating her. She asked me if there would be any charges, and added that Tom had threatened divorce if no charges were filed. I explained to Brenda that it was the responsibility of the county attorney rather than the police to charge cases, that police were merely fact-finders who forwarded these facts to the county Attorney so that they could form an opinion of intent, guilt or innocence, and that space between. I knew her next question before she asked it. It was Tom's question. Did I believe that she had been raped? Yes, I did believe that she was helpless when Marcus helped himself to her unconscious body, and that was considered Third Degree Felony Criminal Sexual Conduct, punishable by up to twenty years in prison.

Tom said something in the distance, and Brenda turned away from the phone and told him that I thought Marcus should be charged with a felony for raping her. The next voice on the phone was Tom's. "So you really think he raped her?" he said, as though I had just said this to placate Brenda out of pity.

"Yes, Tom. Her vagina and her butt were all tore up. No one consents to that. She did not consciously allow that guy to do that to her—that makes it criminal."

"So you can get this guy charged?"

"Well, we're not even sure who or where this guy is, and I always like to hear both sides of the story—so let's wait until we hear from him."

Tom had a lot more questions and he varied his volume and inflection as Brenda came and went from the room he was in. His off-balance, topsy-turvy world had been almost righted for the time being. He wasn't entirely satisfied, and probably never would be, but he saw a ray of consolation and perhaps adjusted Brenda's culpability from nearly complete, to some lesser fraction.

I needed to find Marcus and take a statement from him. I had enough to arrest him on PC if I could identify him. I needed to visit an Apple Valley car dealership. Jill had thought it might be the Chrysler dealership so I decided to start there. I collected trainee detective Paul Arens and headed off to Apple Valley Dodge.

Arens and I were greeted at an open desk just inside the door by a well dressed, athletically built, late twenties, black man with a very thick neck. I asked him, in the best non-conspiratorial tone of voice I could muster, if we could speak with the manager, and he directed me to a glass enclosed car-dealership-type office. I told the manager that I was looking for a black man, possibly named Marcus who was in his late twenties, early thirties, athletically built, that may have played football for the U of M. I left out the part about the thick neck and tried not to nod toward the black man who'd just escorted us to the office, since it seemed like that would be cheating. The manager unconsciously singled him out for me anyway, looking at the black man over his specs, and through the glass. After a long sigh, he said he did have an employee named Marcus who fit my description and played ball for the U. He added that this employee was his top salesman for the past two months and he did not want him arrested from the showroom floor. I told the sales manager that I could talk to him in the adjoining Parts Department and that I was not certain whether or not I would be arresting him.

Meeting Marcus was made somewhat awkward since the manager was now introducing us to the man who'd introduced us earlier to him, but we got past that. The sales manager escorted us to a small office in the Parts Department and left us alone. I asked Marcus if he knew why I might want to talk with him, and he said no. I asked him what he did Saturday night, and he said that he went to the Mall of America with a friend where he met a couple girls whose names he did not remember, one was blond, the other brunette, whom he escorted back to their hotel, where he kissed one of them goodnight before he left.

In my experience of interviewing criminal suspects, I learned that people, even guilty ones, want to tell the truth. Marcus had told me the truth. I suspected he did all the things he mentioned. I also suspected he left out some of the things he'd done with the two girls he'd met. I told Marcus that I was going to place him under arrest and take a complete statement from him at the police department. Though my partner, Arens, was a large, athletically built officer, I was thankful that Marcus did not choose to rumble since he had retained his football, weightlifter physique, and I had let what little physique I might have had eighteen years ago, atrophy—just a bit.

After my first reading of Marcus' rights per Miranda, he said this situation sounded pretty serious and thought he better contact an attorney before talking with me. I tried to contact the public defender's office for him since he said he didn't have much money, but it was after hours, and I received only voice-mail. (I wondered how little money the other car salesmen at the dealership made since Marcus was salesman of the month for two months running.) I invited Marcus to find an attorney in the Yellow Pages, but he said he wanted to clear this matter up as soon as possible and finally agreed to talk with me without legal representation.

In our post-Miranda interview, I learned that Marcus struggled with deception. I couldn't tell how practiced he was in the art, but quickly realized that he was, for the most part, a very simple, honest man. He managed to maintain fairly good eye contact until he lied—at which point he looked either straight up at the ceiling, or somewhere else, where his glance could rotate 180 degrees away from mine. He might as well have thrown a red bandanna into the air with the words "I'm lying now!" embroidered on it.

He started the interview telling of his childhood and his subsequent football scholarship to the U of M. He said his father never allowed him to drink or smoke when he lived at home, and that he never disobeyed his father on these orders because he believed these habits would affect his athletic potential.

Following his college football years, the glory days faded, and Marcus was arrested in Minneapolis for burglary. After a short stint in the County Workhouse he was released. He changed his name from Mike to Marcus and tried on a few professions until he stumbled on to car sales. He was good at this. His apparent simple, straightforward approach, along with his clean-cut look, his sculpted physique, and glory-days past, all played into his appeal. It was the twenty-fifth of July and Marcus had already sold twenty-one vehicles that month. No wonder his boss wanted him back at work.

Marcus said he and a fellow salesman, Robby, had met at the Mall to watch a boxing match at the American Sports Bar. At about 11:00 PM he met a couple girls on the dance floor but didn't remember their names. I asked him if their names might have been Brenda and Jill and he said they were, but didn't recall which was the blond and which brunette—so I told him. He'd already consumed about eight beers and had a pretty good buzz on by the time he met the girls. Daddy's rules no longer applied.

He liked the brunette, Jill, and the two of them smooched on the dance floor for a while before closing. He never bought either of the girls any drinks, but Brenda had brought a couple drinks over to him and Jill on the dance floor. He made an attempt to find his buddy Robby in hopes of setting him up with Brenda but could not find him. Over the course of the evening, he thought he'd seen both girls drink about two beers and one large "kamikaze" shot. He denied ever altering their drinks with any kind of drug and I believed him. He admitted he was attracted to Jill and wasn't averse to getting to know her intimately. He wasn't really attracted to Brenda, but she seemed nice enough. The three of them left the bar arm-in-arm with Marcus in the middle. As they approached the exit, Brenda asked him where his car was, and as he started to tell her, Jill interrupted and said he wasn't going to his car. He was coming back to their hotel room. A Bloomington cop working security at the bars noticed the big black man leave the area with the two white girls. He said they were laughing and stumbling a little, as happy drunks considering romance so often do.

They were next seen by the security guard at the Country Inn Suites who said that by the time they walked into the hotel parking lot, the black man was pretty much carrying the blond chick, and the brunette was walking out in front of them looking a little pissed. There was a group of hotel employees sitting on the curb taking a smoke break when the black man tried to bum a smoke for the blond chick. One of the men offered him a smoke but asked that Marcus give him one of his girlfriends in exchange. The guard said the black man had to hold the blond back, as she wanted to fight this stranger who was joking with Marcus.

Marcus said that when they got in the hotel room he and Jill had a beer and started listening to music. Brenda took her clothes off down to her panties and T-shirt and lay face down on her bed, passed out. Marcus covered Brenda with a comforter, and turned his attention back to Jill. He lay on Jill's bed and took off all his clothes while Jill took off her top. They kissed and "rubbed on each other." He unzipped her pants and put his fingers in her, but when he tried to take it further she said no. She touched him as well and he became very aroused, but each time he tried to get a little closer she stopped him. He finally became frustrated and got off the bed. Jill seemed to fall asleep almost instantly so he got into bed with Brenda. He initially denied ever touching Brenda—again looking at the ceiling as he spoke, but later admitted the eventual contact.

He said that although no words were spoken between him and Brenda, he understood that she wanted to have sex with him, and so he mounted her and had intercourse. The intercourse lasted about fifteen to twenty minutes until he ejaculated in her vagina.

I asked him if he'd had anal intercourse with her also, and he said he didn't think so.

I asked him if he'd noticed that Brenda was having her period, and he said he had no idea.

I asked him if, after thinking about it, he thought he'd made a mistake having sex with Brenda without asking her when she was extremely intoxicated, possibly even unconscious, and he said, "Probably, but I mean...it didn't seem like anything was wrong..."

I'd hoped this case would be charged and that our suspect would be found guilty, but such was not the case. Marcus took the stand and testified that Brenda had pulled him down onto her and that he had interpreted her action to be an invitation. Brenda could not deny this, since she'd already testified that she had no memory of the sexual contact.

Jill's husband and Tom listened intently to Marcus' testimony as he recounted his thoughts, intentions, and actions the night he met their wives. He readily admitted his interest in a sexual relationship with Jill, and that she had given him every indication that she shared this interest. His eventual sex with Brenda was more of a release of pent-up sexual tension than the result of any meaningful relationship or even attraction.

As difficult as this was for Tom and Brenda to hear, they managed to salvage their relationship. Tom confided in me later that he was leaning toward divorce when he had a sort of spiritual awakening, and he was able to let the blame part go and concentrated instead on love, forgiveness, and healing.

Tom and Brenda's hopes and hearts sank, and my weeks of work disintegrated like the shiny mirage on the distant highway, when the jury announced its not-guilty verdict. Throughout the investigation and the months prior to trial, careers and families needed to be managed and relationships maintained. The facade of control and unity had to be restored for their children, and any lapses in concentration at work had to be rationalized away as something else. Tom and Brenda told their friends who knew about the case that the jury was flawed. Marcus told his friends that, luckily for him, the jury saw through the lies of these women who cried rape to safeguard their marriages. His boss gladly put Marcus back to work on the showroom floor, and his dealership sales were back on track.

The dogwatch officers would shake their heads and roll their eyes as dispatch put out another report of an intoxicated victim who believed she was drugged and raped. A SARS nurse and a detective would be paged from their beds and would respond in darkness to the hospital where their beer-breathed victim would recount what little she remembered of the incident.

The jury, men and women like us, clearly understood the game and culture of the bar-room-romance. They assume that as adults we know the effects of alcohol and understand that the process of getting from the bar to the bedroom is usually a cooperative effort. Understanding why these women exposed themselves to such an expected outcome is a matter of speculation. It was probably the product of a multiplicity of idiosyncratic personal characteristics and issues including the quality of their current spousal relationships.

Oftentimes there are no clear explanations for why adults do what we do when we know better. Perhaps whatever seduction we're seeking in the dark is worth whatever pain and sacrifice we encounter in its eventual discovery. Or perhaps the darkness shields our insecurities and sensibilities to the point where we just don't care.

Skin Deep

When put to the question, most folks vehemently deny owning any measure of racial prejudice, believing the wearers of that label to be among the most contemptible. I believe these denials are more a recitation of political correctness than reality, since racial prejudice in some form probably germinated unconsciously in our youth and evolved as we matured.

With a black man occupying the highest office in government one might wonder if racism is finally a thing of the past. But racial prejudice may be more prevalent today than it was in the civil rights movement of the 1960s. Issues ranging from immigration and gang violence to allegations of a broken, unfair criminal justice system that convicts and imprisons a disproportionate number of black and Hispanic offenders, revive the debate.

I define racial prejudice more loosely than textbooks, maintaining that if one makes assumptions or changes the way one acts, speaks, or even thinks, while in the presence of a person of another race—there are some racial issues. If we truly considered one another equal we would not carry these additional burdensome divisive preconceptions.

A study done in Ireland by the University of Ulster (June 2002) found that Catholic and Protestant children in Ireland had developed religious prejudices as early as age three. They didn't arrive at these conclusions alone from inside a glass bottle. I don't recall exactly when my own lessons began, but I can follow some events in a general way that led to my conception of race. My first memory was linked to my father's job as a railway postal clerk. He rode the Milwaukee Road train from the depot in downtown Minneapolis to Kansas City, and returned several days later for a couple days off before repeating the journey.

In the early sixties, my mother drove my brother and me, who were toddlers at the time, to the railroad depot to pick up my father. Since my mother suffered from freeway-a-phobia, we traveled on residential streets through north Minneapolis, specifically Plymouth Avenue, which was one of few areas at the time populated almost exclusively by blacks. My mother made no effort to hide her fear of traveling through this neighborhood at night. Upon nearing Plymouth Avenue her panicked voice ordered us to lock all doors and close the windows, regardless of the weather; we had no air conditioning.

My brother and I sat bolt upright in our seats and stared wide-eyed over the door to see the source of our mother's alarm. We watched the street come alive during those hot summer nights. Young black men with huge Afros walked the streets and boulevards with their friends, talking, hailing friends down the block, and laughing. My mother stared straight ahead at the road, too frightened to chance eye contact. The men and women we saw here had their own walk and their own talk. Their speech was their own, foreign and intimidating to us in our suburban naiveté. Cadillacs were abundant, old and new, stock and custom. Drivers stopped to chat casually on the road, side by side with another car,

unconcerned with any traffic held captive behind them. My
mother gasped, exasperated, but afraid to appear annoyed as
she waited for them to move. Finally, they did, and my
mother continued on her way. She would say, "This used to be
a good neighborhood," and sigh with relief, like a hostage
released, as we escaped the neighborhood, traveling from
Penn Avenue to Highway 55 where we cruised unobstructed
into downtown Minneapolis.

The trains looked enormous to us as we stared up at the
hissing steel behemoths from inside the depot. We assumed our
father probably had a lot more to do with the actual operation
of the train than simply sorting the mail—which is all he actually did. It all seemed bigger than life to us as "three-footers."

The sixties were a tough time for race relations and the
small strides made by civil rights advocates were canceled out
in the public eye by racial violence, the blame for which was
always disputed.

When my older brother Bobby and I were seven and six
respectively, my parents took us to Theodore Wirth swimming
beach. I think the tiny lake is a darker shade of murky brown
these days but then, as now, if it was hot enough, people swam
in it. Bordering the majestic golf course of the same name on
the Near North Side, the beach was frequented by more and
more black families. As Bobby and I burned our tender feet on
the asphalt parking lot, we heard a commotion up by the con-
cession stand. Commotion was exciting, and we scurried past
our parents seeking the source. We saw a black man with his
back to us, leaning forward from a multi-colored, woven, fold-
out lawn chair. He drank from a beer can within a paper bag as
two black boys about my brother's and my age fist-fought
reluctantly with one another. The younger boy pleaded with
his father through swollen, bloodied lips, "No more, Daddy.

It hurts—No more!"

The older brother cried as he swung half-heartedly at his little brother's face. "I don't wanna fight no more, Daddy."

His father's response was loud and deliberate. "You gonna be fightin' the white man all your life. You need to be tougher. Keep hittin' him—You stop, I'll beat you myself."

The smaller boy had blood smeared from his nose to his mouth, obscuring the origin. I stood dumbstruck, my feet locked in place ten feet from where they continued swinging their loose fists at each other, exhausted. Their father stared at me, defiantly self-righteous. My mother caught up to us, grabbed my hand, and pulled me toward the beach.

Like the picture on our nineteen-inch Zenith, resting comfortably in our living room on its wrought-iron TV stand, I perceived things for that moment in black and white only.

"Did you see that?" I asked my brother. He nodded his head yes. We'd had plenty of fights between us that resulted in a few bloody noses and such, but never at the behest of our parents. We were spanked for fighting, and I always thought the punishment sensible in a nonsensical kind of violence-begetting-violence quandary. My brother and I were both string beans at this age, as were the black boys who were fighting, but I knew they would be tougher than we. As a result of their father's *training*, they would be tougher and meaner. They would know how to take a punch and keep fighting. Their father was trying to prepare them, better than he had been, to fight back. We couldn't possibly train for this type of toughness, living outside of their experience, and our empathy only went so far. Five minutes after witnessing the fight we were jumping jubilantly in the cool, murky, lake water. I looked for the brothers on our way back through the lot, but all that remained was a discarded beer can.

The public school system was attempting to change the tides of racial tension, indoctrinating the youth in the rallying cries of the late sixties and early seventies—peace, love, and equality.

The Youngbloods sang, "Come on people now, smile on your brother. Everybody get together, try to love one another right now."

For the most part, the musicians and teachers were preaching to the choir. We thought racial prejudice ridiculous, and confined our thoughts to the promise of a better, more equal, future society. There were only a handful of blacks in the Robbinsdale Public School System at the time, and they were celebrities among the student body for the most part, simply because they were black. I don't recall ever hearing a racial epithet directed at them from other students. Len Daniels, who graduated two years before me, was captain of the gymnastics team, Homecoming King—and black.

In my group of friends a black boy from Ethiopia, Solomon Walter, was a near-constant companion. He played on the soccer team and was a very good student. We called him Solly. I would later use his name as a generalized term (not always complimentary) for black.

At the University of Minnesota, it seemed most of the black students I met were visitors from Africa rather than American blacks. Again, I never noticed any animosity between races at college.

Upon becoming a Bloomington police officer in 1982, things changed. With a population of 85,000, approximately eighty-five percent of which was white, a discrepancy in the number of blacks committing crimes within the city became readily apparent. I noticed that the voicing of racial epithets by officers, though uncommon, was seen as a semi-acceptable practice by a small group of mostly old-timers. That it wasn't completely acceptable was apparent from the need to whisper the word "nigger." I never witnessed an officer call a black man a nigger to his face, but rather referred to him as such when talking about him out of his presence with other officers. This was believed to be a safe practice, since officers were loath to snitch on each other for anything, let alone what was considered by this group to be a very minor, if not humorous, social faux pas. An occasional white victim of a crime committed by a black suspect would "feel the officer out" by referring to the suspect as a "spook" or "colored" and if he or she sensed encouragement, or at least no resistance, would easily slip the descriptor of nigger into the conversation, usually in a hushed, look-both-ways-before-you-say-it tone.

With the birth of the Affirmative Action program, black officers were starting to be hired in much greater numbers in the Twin Cities area, especially within the Minneapolis and St. Paul Police Departments. Of the approximately twenty-five students in my Skills class, only the four minority students (one Hispanic male, three white females) were actively recruited. Naturally, many prospective white officer candidates were passed by to recruit black and Hispanic officers, much to the whites' chagrin. Our department had no black officers when I started and remained exclusively white until 1996. Upon hiring the first minority officers, the department seemed to become hypersensitive regarding race. Memos were circulated throughout the city that cautioned employees against any word or deed that could be deemed discriminatory.

At this point I found myself whispering the word "black" to other officers when referring to a black person. This seemed ridiculous but necessary. Referring to someone by race had become politically incorrect. Even vehicle registrations and driver's license records did not specify race. They documented full name, height, weight, date of birth, hair and eye color, but not race—which would have been very handy to know from time to time. Discussion of someone's race was to be avoided if possible, and descriptions should include race only if absolutely necessary.

Racial trends that were difficult to accept became apparent to me both as a rookie officer and later as a detective. Generally speaking, there were crimes that white perps tended to commit, like burglary and auto theft, and crimes that black perps tended to commit, like robbery. Both races seemed to beat up their wives and children with similar zeal, but did so in different ways.

As a child abuse detective I noticed that white abusers used theirs hands, belts, or whatever was handy to inflict "discipline," whereas many blacks tended toward the more traditional switches (thin flexible tree limbs) or extension cords. I was called to one of the elementary schools in the city regarding three black brothers who complained of discomfort sitting in their chairs. When the teacher asked them if they were hurt, they lifted their shirts to show marks on their lower backs that were clearly raised and abraded loops caused by being whipped with an extension cord. As I prepared to take the children to a shelter, their mother arrived at the school to bring them home. Her dark narrowed eyes telegraphed her defiance before she started venting through clenched teeth. She confirmed, without remorse, that the marks on her children were the result of a "whoopin'" she'd given them for their misbehavior at school the previous day. She said her children "…were niggers and needed to be whooped like niggers," that white people's "time outs" were not effective with her children. This mother's response to me was by no means typical of a black mother. She was the exception. Her method of discipline and her rationalization for it was an example of a failure to break a destructive cycle.

Along with my child protection partners, I examined count-less white children with hand marks and belt marks on their backs, buttocks, and thighs. The parents' typical rationalization was that this type of punishment had kept *them* on the straight and narrow, so why not their children?

At the time of this writing there are about a dozen black and Hispanic officers on our 120-officer department, but there remains a real willingness to hire qualified candidates of any race, and minorities are encouraged to apply. Attitudes of black officers (like whites) vary by personality and life experience. They range from the belief that everything that happens in their career is the result of racial prejudice, to the belief that they alone direct their destiny. I spoke to a couple black offi-cers on our department about their experience as minority officers. Malcolm told me that the pressure for a black officer to perform within a predominantly white department is mul-tiplied considerably when under the microscope of the major-ity. There is a cumulative toll taken when pejorative comments, expressions, and whispers are tallied day by day. Another officer, Greg, said he considered racism within our department to be uncommon but not completely absent. He said he has overheard officers out of sight, but within earshot, make racial slurs, usually as a joke, and has heard officers refer to black suspects as niggers. He said all the black officers have had similar experiences.

This was painful for him, much more so than I would have imagined—painful, hurtful, embarrassing, and an obvi-ous source of antipathy. For some reason I had thought Greg would have written off the offensive officer—maybe have told him what he thought of his comment and dropped it at that. But this was not the case. The feeling of being included, by virtue of skin color, in a racially derogatory descriptor went much deeper than that. He said he could forgive the offending officer for his comments, but probably wouldn't forget that he'd made them.

While on the topic of racial discrimination and prejudice, I voiced my opinion about the much debated racial profiling of black drivers and criminal suspects. I told Greg that I thought it ridiculous that blacks in Minneapolis were complaining about being stopped for traffic offenses more than whites, and of being sought out and questioned as suspects in criminal matters more often than whites. It seemed logical to me that if the description of a robbery suspect or other such crime included the racial designation of *black*, and was broadcast to squad cars as such—that they would stop and question suspects fitting that description. As for the stopping of more blacks than whites for traffic offenses, I questioned whether officers would discriminate by race which cars they would pull over to issue a speeding ticket. Oftentimes on dogwatch, the race of a traffic-stopped driver couldn't be determined until the officer approached the driver's window.

Greg smiled magnanimously and shook his head, citing my time off the street as reason for my ignorance. He agreed that officers needed to look for a black hoodlum if that was the description given by a victim, but he disputed my cavalier dismissal of racial profiling, purporting instead that the practice was quite common. He used himself as an example, recalling two instances when he'd been stopped while on his way home from work. According to Greg, the officers stopping him had no probable cause to pull him over. He said he identified himself as a cop to the officers who stopped him, and asked them why he'd been stopped. In both instances, he considered the officer's hurried explanation contrived and unsatisfactory.

One of our more aggressive patrol officers conceded to me that stopping beater-cars on dogwatch occupied by young "homeys" in gang wear gave the officer a better than average chance of getting a warrant or drug arrest from one or more of the occupants.

I think back to the sixties when our high school teachers, our church leaders, and some of our parents attempted to prepare us for a future of racial equality. I remember thinking as a high-schooler how ridiculous the current bigots appeared. They were laughable. The Archie Bunkers of the day were dinosaurs whose bigotry was fodder for comedy. He and his ilk would not be replaced by others like them. I truly believed that racial equality was a lock for the baby-boomer generation, once we came to political maturity and replaced those currently directing the nation. It astounds me that, from that soil, the seeds of acceptance were somehow choked out by stronger weeds of fear and misunderstanding in a society that seems to be taking a giant step backward rather than forward.

I believe fear has always been, and remains today, the impetus that propels simple misunderstanding to prejudice. It's the anchor that prevents an empathetic awareness from surfacing—fear of the unknown, of diversity, of change, and fear of losing something or giving something up.

The prevalence of criminal gangs has had a horrendous impact on race relations. The image of young men of any race with sagged, baggie pants, exposed boxers, and myriad tattoos flaunting gang affiliations elicit the desired reaction. The gang appearance, coupled with media stories of gang violence, has the aggregating effect on law-abiding citizens of evoking fear. This fear sometimes expands beyond the gang.

When I see a black man, whom do I see? Do I see the father at the beach ordering his sons to continue fighting, the boys' loose fists heavy with conflict, their tears mixing with blood? Do I see a sixties montage of race riots, of Martin Luther King standing at a podium starting his "I have a dream..." speech? Do I see O.J. Simpson being acquitted; the movie stars, professional athletes, and musicians? Or do I simply see the man standing before me as he is?

Greg said I could never understand what it was like to be black in our society, and I know he's right. He invited my family and me to his all-black Baptist church in Minneapolis, saying that it would be an interesting experience for me, that I'd enjoy the music, fellowship, and the service. He said the pastor would ask my family to stand and introduce ourselves as the congregation welcomed us with applause and invited us to return. I said thanks, but no thanks. The thought of being the only white people in a large room filled exclusively with blacks didn't appeal to me. Why? —It would be uncomfortable. I told Greg that he was used to being a minority, but I wasn't, and I felt no desire to experience it.

Greg laughed at my chicken-hearted excuse and left me to consider how I was going to get from here to there without moving. I considered what he said, and thought that dropping all the politically correct rhetoric would be a good place to start. There is nothing wrong with including a man's race in his description if there is reason for it. And there is nothing wrong with arresting and tagging black drivers if stops and tags will be meted out randomly among all offenders.

It seems that rather than confronting the big elephant in the room, we pretend there are no racial problems, or at least none that we are willing to talk about. We chant slogans, have marches, and retire that most offensive word, *nigger*, replacing it with a one-letter acronym where all nasty words, like the F-word, end up. Of course until everybody considers its retirement mandatory, the word will still be used. The shunning of the word is microcosmic of the greater problem of racism, and avoiding the word and the problem, or assigning an initial to it, only creates a circuitous road to an inevitable dead end.

Finally, I resigned myself to the fact that real change needs to start with people like me taking up offers from people like Greg. Until then we will remain standing on different sides of the fence, posturing by daylight to tear down the fence we fortify by night.

The Secret

As a neophyte sex crimes investigator I studied old case files of sex orgies that occurred in our city before I was hired. The reports read like science fiction since the actors in these scenes truly seemed like aliens from another planet. Like a Rembrandt painting, these files, along with the accompanying photographs, evoked a dark, mysterious foreboding. Sex orgies were usually not criminal as long as the participants were consenting adults. In fact, the very idea of an orgy brought to mind a kind of cheesy casserole of sweaty men and women wearing only their cathartic expressions as they writhed and grunted in collective ecstasy. These precious moments were usually memorialized with photographs taken by the participants, as they lay resplendent in their creatively entangled positions. Snapshots such as these were often recovered in search warrants allowing investigators—in weaker moments—to fantasize about occupying the bologna position in the ménage à trois sandwich. But this vision of victimless pleasure changed drastically when you substituted some of the participants with children.

Rembrandt's depictions of children, though often nude and vulnerable, were always the precious object of love—never of deception or sexual depravity—and you can tell the difference on a child's face.

As I consider it now, Mike Rodman appeared far too apathetic for the circumstances. The revelation of the found Polaroid photographs, graphically illustrated beyond a shadow of a doubt that his housemate, Curtis Oldman, had been sexually abusing the children of the family they were living with. I went in the basement, where the sexual assaults were alleged to have occurred over the past two years, and directed the crime techs to seize the bedding, underwear, lotion, the red-plaid sleeping bag, and the contents of Curtis's safe where the photographs had been found by Cher, the boys' mother.

Mike Rodman continued to sit on the couch in the living room, looking down pensively at the old brown shag carpeting that enveloped his puffy, pale bare feet. The search of the five-bedroom home took hours to complete. The place was huge. It housed the owners, Bill and Cher Itie, along with their five children and the two interlopers, Mike and Curtis. The children were composed of two separate camps. The three oldest boys were from Cher's first marriage, and they slept downstairs in a bedroom adjacent to Curtis's. The two toddlers, fathered by Bill Itie, slept upstairs in a room next to their parents, with Mike's room also upstairs and down the hall.

Cher had become suspicious lately, as well she should have. Having your five children live in a house with two convicted, registered sex offenders was suspicious enough, but allowing them to sleep in the same beds as the sex offenders was downright moronic. Her phoning the police in an outrage gave some credence to her claim that she was unaware of the sexual contact between Curtis and her eldest boys.

Of the two subsequent allegations, the first involved sexual contact by Mike and Curtis with the three boys. The second allegation claimed child endangerment by the parents. Both cases cast an agonizing weight upon the children that pressured them into denial. And though these mystifying cases were separate, there was a confluence of time, place, characters, and circumstance.

Mike Rodman and Curtis Oldman met in the St. Peter, Minnesota Sexual Offenders' Program. They were both convicted of sexual assaults with child victims. Both were pedophiles whose preferred sexual partners ranged from pre-pubescent boys to adult men. Mike appeased the directors and completed the program. As a result, he was granted early release, while Curtis struggled with some of the staff and was forced to serve out his entire sentence. Once Curtis was released, he sought out his old friend, Mike, and the two decided to move in together and share living expenses. A romantic relationship developed between the two, but was short-lived. Mike would later tell me, stuttering through rolling tears, that his feelings for Curtis were deeply felt, while Curtis's were based solely on lust. While the romantic split was emotionally taxing on Mike, it had little effect on Curtis, as the two continued to live together in what was now a platonic relationship.

Money became a scarcity for them, and the two were evicted from several rental properties. Mike had a steady job in a greenhouse nursery while Curtis tried to stake his claim in the construction business. He partnered up with his old friend, Bill Itie, whom Curtis knew from the reservation near Curtis's hometown of Babbitt, in northern Minnesota. Curtis would later tell me that as a young teen, Itie had forced him to perform oral sex on him. Itie had his own construction business now, and was married to Cher, one of the few women Curtis was attracted to.

Another eviction forced the two into living out of their car until Bill Itie invited them to live with him and his family in Bloomington—until they could get back on their feet. Curtis jumped at the chance, while Mike was more ambivalent.

Seasons came and went. Curtis lost his job with Itie as a result of apathy, boredom, and laziness, but it didn't matter. A pattern had developed, a symbiotic relationship between Curtis and the Ities. Curtis played with the three older boys in the basement, which gave Bill and Cher some time with the two toddlers. Time was precious and there was far too little of it.

Curtis came into some money as a result of a lawsuit, and he and Mike left the house in Bloomington and started to build a new house. They stayed in a Bloomington hotel while the house was under construction.

Curtis looked tiny walking in front of me from the jail cell to the interview room. I considered myself small at 5'11", 170 pounds, and I towered over him. Having seen the pictures of him kneeling behind the nine, eleven, and twelve-year-old boys, penetrating them from behind, he looked bigger than them, probably because his genitals were just that much more developed, but the boys were nearly his equal in stature. His criminal history detailed him at 5'4" 125 pounds. The word "dangerous" was juxtaposed beside the physical stats, completing the irony. We turned into the interview room and he sat in the chair facing the hidden video camera. I got my first real look at his face, and I was once again shocked.

"What happened to your face?" I asked, as my prisoner looked back at me from the interview chair, with two grotesquely swollen black eyes.

He shielded his eyes with his hand as if guarding them from the sun. "Nothing. I had a bad dream."

"What happened, Curtis? You didn't have those when you came in." After hearing all the officers saying they wanted a piece of this guy, I was almost sorry I'd asked. The interview room we occupied was both video- and audio-taped. If he would have said that a jailer beat the shit out of him, my case could have been in jeopardy.

"Nothin'," his voice quivered as though he might cry, "I had a bad dream. It was all white and then I woke up, and..."

"Curtis, did you do this to yourself?" I asked, leading him down the preferred path.

He paused and brought his hand down to his thigh. "Yeah, I did it the day I got arrested."

Two days ago. I remembered the jail officer mentioning that Curtis was feigning all manner of illness claiming heart murmurs and dangerous anaphylactic reactions. I didn't know if the injured eyes were a ploy to get to the hospital and out of jail or what?

"What did you do?" I asked, more curious than compassionate.

"I just punched myself—-I was just so pissed."

Relieved, I sat in the chair opposite him, strategically placed so as not to block the hidden camera. "Curtis, I'm Detective Greelis, and I'm the lead investigator on this case. Before we talk, I need to read you the Miranda Warning. 'You have the right to remain silent...'"

He looked back at me from pained, sober, raccoon eyes, taking it in.

"...Do you understand these rights as I've read them to you?"

"Yeah," he answered.

"Having those rights in mind, are you willing to talk to me at this time?"

He looked back at me confused, and said the word most despised by any and all detectives—the "L" word. I had assumed he would lawyer-up since a conviction in this case had the potential to send him back to prison for life.

"I can't really afford a lawyer."

"Like I said, if you can't afford one, one will be appointed for you without cost."

He took a long, cleansing breath and like a rat in a cage, looked from one bare white wall to the other. "You know, I really need a cigarette. I can't be expected to give up everything in one day."

"Well, like every other office in Minnesota, this is a no-smoking building. I'm afraid if you lit one up, the sprinklers would probably start up."

"They wouldn't," he said, confidently, but with shaky hands.

I looked at his hands. He noticed my glance and rubbed his hands together.

"Sorry," I lied.

He looked down at his bare feet. "I just really need a ciga-rette. If you give me a cigarette I'll tell you everything."

It sounded like a script from a bad fifties movie, but I didn't dwell on that. Pivoting toward the door I turned back to him, "I'll be right back."

I watched each of the three boys as they struggled through their forensic interviews at Cornerhouse. Interviewers at Cornerhouse specialize in child victims of sex abuse. There are no better-qualified interviewers in the nation, and their final determination of whether or not sex abuse occurred was often-times the deciding element that convinced the jury of the sus-pect's guilt. The Itie children taxed their every talent, their every strategy and tactic, since leading questions or suggestions could not be used by the interviewers to help the children talk about what was often the most difficult subject to broach.

Without exception, the children minimized the sexual contact. Bobby said he was only penetrated once—the time depicted in the Polaroid with Curtis kneeling over him. Fat chance. The pictures were about a year old. Their mother could age the photographs by her children's growth. Without the Polaroid photographs, there was no case. There was no physical evidence, no realization that Curtis had been anally penetrating the three boys in the family he had lived with for the last two years; the three boys whose father, Bill Itie, had grown up with him. How precious those photographs must have been to Curtis that he would save them in his fire safe, knowing their discovery would catapult him from freedom into the quagmire of the criminal courts, and then finally deposit him into the infinite quicksand of the penal system. How long could it have continued had their mother not found the photos? Curtis had told the boys that he would no longer be interested in them—sexually—once they reached puberty. Perhaps Bobby, the oldest, would have told, out of spite, once it ended for him while it continued with his younger brothers.

Gordie said the most without ever speaking. He indicated his answers by pointing to the line drawings the interviewer provided and demonstrating with the anatomically correct dolls. He answered direct questions in silence, with head nods. Like a mute, he communicated that he and his brothers had been anally penetrated approximately two or three times a week for the last two years. Oral sex was an occasional option, but secondary to Curtis' overwhelming preference for anal intercourse. Gordie denied any sexual contact with Mike, but I would later learn that it was Mike whom Gordie slept with on a nightly basis, and it was Mike who touched him sexually all these nights. Unlike Curtis's lust for anal sex, Mike preferred oral sex, and he preferred Gordie to the other boys. Gordie loved Mike the way children love adults who show compassion and *seem* to care for them. Gordie did not give up Mike during the interview.

Finally, Colton, the youngest at nine, said he was fondled by Curtis, and admitted taking the Polaroid photographs at Curtis' request, but insisted that he was never penetrated. He looked down as he spoke and, like his brothers, he never smiled—this was not easy to talk about. There was a trust being violated. A trust of someone they had known, befriended, and confided in as a guardian for years. They were breaking a covenant, the result of which would have further reaching consequences than they could have ever imagined.

Since the faces in the photos were either strategically turned from the camera or cropped, I had to re-interview Colton at the police department to put faces to the nude bodies. There were twelve pictures. I numbered them 1 through 12 and we examined them one at a time in detail. Colton sat next to me in the interview room on the only other metal office chair in the room. I turned over the first picture that depicted two nude, kneeling, pre-pubescent boys in the act of anal intercourse.

"Do you remember taking this one?" I asked.

He squirmed in his seat, experimenting with different positions, searching for that elusive comfort zone found only through continuous contortion. "Ah, I think that's Bobby on the bottom and Curtis on top."

"Do you remember taking this one?" I repeated.

Still squirming, "Ah, well, I took all of them, but I guess, I'm not sure."

I looked closely at the photo. "It just looks to me like two boys, cause there's no hair on either of their butts and if you look at this one," I pulled another from the pile, "...you can tell that this guy's an adult cause he's got hair—are you with me?"

"Yeah, I guess." He studied the photo, still squirming, and I wondered how he could focus on any detail while in this state of perpetual motion. "I don't know," he finally conceded.

We went through about four or five more pictures. He described the room the pictures were taken in, the red-plaid sleeping bag they were on, and the actors, which other than the first picture, depicted only Bobby and Curtis. On the tenth picture he once again picked out Bobby as one of the actors and then paused. Like the first photo, the lack of pubic hair on the actors suggested both were boys.

"I guess the other one is me," he finally said.

Rather than confront him on why he'd denied any anal penetration in his earlier interview at Cornerhouse, I made a written note, documenting the actors as I had on all the others. "Okay," I said, matter-of-factly, as I flipped the photo over and went on to the next.

When we finished with the stack, we returned to the first. He stared at it for a long time then looked at my face somewhere below my eyes. "I guess that one is the same as number ten."

I shook my head putting the two together. "Did Curtis tell you guys to do that?"

"Ah, yeah, probably. Or Bobby might have just said, 'I think I'll do it with Colton now.'"

"Did Curtis do that to you too?" I asked.

He looked at the floor, hoping to evaporate into it. "Yeah."

"Did that hurt?" I asked.

"Not really," he said nonchalantly, as he finally slipped out of his chair onto the floor.

"Why not?"

He jumped back on his chair, unfazed, and continued squirming. "Curtis always used lotion."

None of the boys, not even Colton, ever pointed the finger at Mike. He was different. Whether he truly cared for the children or whether he was that much more conniving than Curtis, I don't know. The boys seemed to believe that he represented some stabilizing factor in their lives. He helped them with their homework and told them that he loved them. The sex was, according to him, a by-product of that, different than Curtis, who was unpretentious in his unmitigated lust.

I set the phone back on its cradle and thought about what I was going to tell the boys' mother. Both the county attorney and the assigned Hennepin County Child Protection worker wanted the visitation order changed so the parents could have no contact with their children until after court. The Ities had no idea that the County would be pushing for permanent placement and termination of their parental rights.

"I'm afraid I'm going to have to place a hold on your children," I said, trying my best to sound confident and resolute.

Her face crumbled and her hand came to her mouth. "What?" she shouted, bouncing to her feet, her attitude changing in an instant from cooperative to defiant, "No, you're not going to take my children. You are not going to take my children!"

"It's not just my decision," I said. "The county attorney and Child Protection agree that, until we can resolve this, the children should be in shelter."

"No" she shouted, wailing through her hand, "Are you serious? Take my babies? My three-year-old, Anna, has never been away from me for a single night. How is that going to work? Are you going to rip her out of my arms? Why? Why would you do this?"

"I'd be lying if I told you that your judgment didn't have a lot to do with it. The County people haven't seen you interact with your children. They're just reading reports that document you knowing of two housemates' status as sex offenders and of you allowing them to sleep with at least one of them. However you read that, it brings your judgment into question—whether or not you can adequately protect them."

"Oh my God!" She shook her head in disbelief. "And I told them to trust the police, that everything would be okay. Bobby told me that Curtis told them that they would be taken away from us if they told the truth. What lesson have they learned? What lesson have you taught them?"

Taking children from parents, who a day earlier called the police to ensure the safety of their children, seemed somehow incongruous. The three-year-old daughter screamed, "No, I want Mommie," as an officer prophetically pulled her gently from her wailing mother's arms. Gordie lay on the sofa by his father, surreptitiously attempting to pull a ragged fleece blanket over him so he might go unnoticed and left behind. His father rubbed his back and told him it would be okay.

For five children in choral anguish, the crying ended mercifully quickly after the police van pulled away from the house. The female officers worked their maternal magic on the frantic children and tried to assuage their pain and their fears, talking about the new toys, friends, and games they would find at St. Joseph's Children's Shelter. They assured them, and believed their assurances to be true, when they told the children that their stay in the shelter was only temporary, and that they would soon be reunited with Mom and Dad.

I had ambivalent feelings about these parents who obviously loved and bonded well with their children. Their judgment in allowing their children to live with two registered sex offenders, let alone their tacit permission that the children be allowed to *sleep* with them, was unforgivable. Everyone who learned the details of the case recited the same line as if it were scripted, "I can't believe they allowed them to sleep with two convicted sex offenders."

With five children and a relationship plagued with frequent separations, their mom, Cher, who suffered from a panic disorder as a result of sexual abuse, was relieved when Curtis offered to entertain the three older boys downstairs until bed time. Their basement bedrooms were side by side, and Curtis enjoyed playing Nintendo and goofing around with them. She would find them asleep the next morning as a group, sharing either Curtis's bed or with Curtis sharing theirs. It seemed innocent enough to her. At least that was her perception.

I frantically searched the police department for my buddy, Bish, who was the last of the chronic smoking detectives. I finally caught up with him returning contentedly from one of his many afternoon smoke-breaks. I told him about my suspect's plea for a smoke and what it might mean to my case. Silently gauging quitting time with his next mandatory nicotine fix, he somehow found peace, and offered up his pack for the cause. I returned to the interview room with the smokes.

True to his word, once he lit up, Curtis started to talk. "Did you arrest Mike yet?"

"No," I answered without explanation. Of course I suspected Mike as well, since, like Curtis, he was also a convicted pedophile, and what pedophile could resist the tantalizing smorgasbord laid out for him at the Ities' house? Unfortunately, I had no evidence at the time to arrest Mike. He was not depicted in any of the photographs, and the children hadn't implicated him in their statements.

He shrugged his shoulders. "They had to know," Curtis said, as he took a long pull from his cigarette, allowing the long flaccid, feather-light ash to fall on the thigh of his faded black Levis.

"Who?" I asked.

"Cher and Bill."

"Why do you say that?"

He flicked the ash from his leg with his pinky. "Well, she knew me and Mike were sex offenders. She'd put them in pajamas at bedtime and find them in bed with me the next morning either naked or in their underwear."

I shook my head in acknowledgement. The transfer of blame onto someone other than himself made Curtis feel somehow less culpable. So far he'd pointed the finger at Mike and the children's parents.

"There was usually a bottle of lotion laying around too. She *should* have known if she didn't."

"Was this an every-night thing, or how often was it happening?

"At times it was every night," Curtis said, shaking his head in admission. "I was so attracted to Bobby, so turned on, he was my main focus. I just, kinda went to the other two when Bobby wasn't interested—which became more and more toward the end."

"What do you mean?"

"Lately they'd rather do it with each other than with me. I'd usually have to pay them or promise them something."

"What changed?"

"I think Bobby just started getting older, maybe thought of himself as homosexual or something, I don't know. I told him what we do don't make us homosexual, but..."

I looked at the notes I'd been taking and saw that our interview, though clearly a court-worthy confession, was scattered. "Curtis, I'd like you to start from the beginning and tell me how this whole thing got started. Take me from there to the Polaroids."

Curtis took a long drag from his cigarette and signaled his willingness to complete the story as he exhaled. He started with his meeting with Mike in St. Peter and their getting together after being released. He took me through the circumstances leading up to their moving in with the Ities and subsequently moving from the Ities' to the hotel while Curtis's house was being built.

"That's when it really got started," Curtis said.

"When you moved out?" I asked, confused.

"Yeah," Curtis said, eager to explain. "Mike and me got this paper route and we asked the three boys if they wanted to stay with us on weekends and help us deliver papers. Of course they wanted to. It was something to do."

"How did the sexual contact begin?" I asked, wanting to fill in the gaps.

Curtis paused for a minute, either recalling or creating the answer. "I think Bobby and I were clowning around on the bed one night and he started touching me. Yeah, he touched me first."

This sounded implausible, but it wouldn't matter for charging purposes who touched whom first, only that the touching occurred. I invited him to continue. He went on to say that the sexual touching started as a game, but once started became more than that to Curtis. Like a child intrigued with the magic of matches, Curtis's fire, once lit, could not be extinguished. He had fallen back into the pit of secrecy, deceit, and his forte—masterful manipulation. Bobby told his brothers about the secret, and eventually they all had a turn with Curtis, sometimes alone, sometimes as a group. He explained the rules of keeping this exciting part of their lives from their parents and anyone else who might find out.

Curtis said that Bobby quickly became his favorite, and that Gordie started spending more time in Mike's room. According to Curtis, Mike warned him about the incendiary sexual relationships with the children, but they both knew it was too late. He said the sex continued until their house was built. Once finished, they moved into their new place, and the substantial distance from the Ities' home limited the boys' visits until the house mysteriously burned down, sending Curtis and Mike back to the Ities'. Once there, the sex resumed and took on a life of its own, becoming the cohesive element that tied the boys together.

"The thing I can't figure out was how you kept the guys from telling? You're doing this nearly every night for three years! You must have threatened them."

"No, I never threatened them," he retorted as if offended. "That wouldn't have worked."

"Presents?" I asked, knowing this to be true from the boys' interviews.

"Yeah, I gave 'em stuff, Nintendo games, treats…"

I shook my head, still unable to fathom it. Three years in the same house with the parents right upstairs. "Did you ever tell them what would happen if you got caught?"

"Yeah," he said, stuffing the cigarette butt into an empty Pepsi can. "I told them that some people looked at the secret—that's what we called it, 'the secret' as a crime, and if anyone ever found out, that Mike and I would go to prison for the rest of our lives—and they liked us. They didn't want that to happen."

"Did you tell them that they'd get in trouble too?"

He held out the last cigarette I scrounged for him and signaled for a light. I leaned into him as I extended the lighter. Not wanting to be this close, I inadvertently allowed my thumb to slip off the striated cylinder that activated the flame, and barely lit the tip of the cigarette.

"Sorry."

He pulled hard from the filter, producing a tiny ember that traveled quickly to the enveloping paper.

"Thanks."

"Yeah," I said, and returned to my question, "The kids—did you tell them they would get in trouble?"

"No."

"I don't get it," I said, frustrated and sickened by this tiny man's smug satisfaction with the con he'd played on these children.

"Well," he offered," I did tell them if they ever told the secret, they'd be taken away from their mom and dad and never see them again."

Colton's dark eyes followed the trail of the photographs with magnetic intensity, while humiliation lurked behind them, subduing their brightness. I stuffed the pictures back into the manila envelope signaling a closed chapter in the interview and turned back to face him directly.

"What did Curtis say would happen if any of you told your mom and dad about what was going on?"

Colton continued to stare trance-like at the manila envelope resting on my notebook.

"Colton?"

"Um, I guess he said, like he would go to prison forever and we would get taken away from our parents." His eyes finally met and penetrated my eyes. "That's not going to happen, is it?"

I called Mike Rodman at the nursery where he worked. His whispered replies signaled his reluctance to come to the Police Department to give his statement, but he agreed nonetheless. It had been two days since Curtis' arrest, and Mike had to have known that Curtis, or the boys, or both, would have incriminated him.

When he arrived the following morning he wore a beaten expression of acquiescence, the same expression he'd worn that first night when we arrested Curtis—when he stared at his feet from his slouching position on the couch. The only way I could get Mike charged was by his own confession. There was no physical evidence tying him to the sexual abuse of the children, and only the one very weak allegation by Colton that Mike *may* have touched him once on his privates, over his pajamas with his hands. All Mike had to do was either lawyer-up or tell me he didn't do it—and he would walk.

We started talking about the case as though he was simply one of several uninvolved witnesses who never imagined the atrocities being committed by the little animal in the basement. There was no love lost at this point between the two. I asked Mike to fill me in on the history between him and Curtis, and their relationship, which I already knew. I next asked him about the sleeping arrangements at the Itie house and the frequency of Gordie spending the night in his bed. Mike stated that there was not room for all the children to sleep in the one basement bed, so oftentimes when he returned home from work at night he found Gordie already asleep in his bed. Not having the heart to awaken him, he simply moved him over and slept beside him. I nodded my head, wearing a fraudulent expression of unassuming understanding.

I'd finally arrived at the part in the interview where I would accuse him of a crime and gauge his reaction, and the intensity of his denial. I mentioned an incident Curtis had divulged about Mike and Gordie in the hotel room, and another about one of the children seeing Mike performing oral sex on Gordie in the shower. Gordie had denied involvement in both of these instances, so realistically, I had no victim. Mike too, denied any sexual contact in the hotel, stating that someone might have seen Gordie sitting on his lap and misinterpreted the scene. He admitted taking a shower with Gordie, which surprised me, since it was blatantly inappropriate. While he admitted sharing the shower, he denied any inappropriate touching while they showered. Though his voice remained quiet and calm, he was sweating profusely, and he would not make eye contact with me. I decided to come back to these later.

I had thought a lot about this interview since I considered this a significant case and, though Curtis's goose was well-cooked, Mike Rodman could get up and walk away from me and legally keep walking. I didn't want that to happen. I didn't think any deep philosophical debate or moral chastisement would elicit a confession. It needed to be simpler. It seemed to me that the outcome of a pedophile, sleeping with a child of the age and sex the pedophile preferred, was obvious. I needed to word my question and gear my accusation toward that obvious ineluctable, irrefutable truth.

"Mike, I know what happened between you and Gordie, and I want to give you a scenario to demonstrate what I'm trying to say. I'm trying to make this easy for both of us. Is that okay?"

Mike folded his arms in front of his chest. "Sure, that's fine, but nothing happened."

"Okay, I want to show how it would be natural for you to have sexual contact with Gordie—more than natural—unavoidable."

"But like I—"

"Let me finish my scenario and then you can say whatever you want. Okay?"

He nodded his head, acquiescing.

"Thanks. Okay, I'm going to give you a scenario now: I'm a heterosexual, single, male adult, sleeping alone in my bed at night. I'm awakened by someone opening my bedroom door. Through my door walks one of the Victoria's Secret underwear models. I know she's a Victoria's Secret model because they send me their catalogue three times a week in hopes that I have a girlfriend who could use a few new pairs of undies." I paused. "Are you with me?"

Mike nodded his head and managed a short charity smile.

"Needless to say, this girl is beautiful. She smiles at me when she enters the room and without saying anything she takes off her clothes—the same ones she wears in the catalogue—and drops them at her feet. Then she pads over to the bed, lifts the covers, and gets into the bed with me. She moves close to me on the bed and I feel the warmth of her soft skin. Guess what, Mike?"

"What?"

"I am sexually aroused. I can't help it. I'm a man; she's a woman. She may have just fulfilled a long-standing fantasy, but whether she did or not, guess what? I want to have sex with her in the worst way." I paused. "Are you still with me?"

"Yeah," he said succinctly, still wrapped in his own arms.

"That's my scenario. Now you've told me that you're a pedophile, and we both agree that you will always be a pedophile. You really have no choice in that; what you have a choice in is, whether or not to act on your urges, right?"

"Yeah, I suppose," he said, trying to sound bored.

"Okay, so you're a male, adult pedophile who prefers young prepubescent boys as sex partners. When you get home from work there is a handsome young boy whom you like very much—"

"Whom I love," he interrupted.

"—whom you love, laying in your bed. You get into bed with him and your skin touches his."

"No—" he started to object, but I rolled over him, knowing I could not afford to lose the momentum.

"It's all over, and it's not your fault, unless you want to say that moving into this particular house was your fault, 'cause once you did that, this outcome was inevitable. You can't stop yourself from being sexually aroused by this boy any more than I could with the Victoria's Secret model. Am I right?"

"Yes," he said, without hesitation.

His agreement took me back a moment, but I knew I needed to keep the ball rolling. "What happened after that was not your fault. It wasn't Gordie's fault. It wasn't anybody's fault. It was just fate." I stopped to take a breath. "Would you agree with that?"

"Yes."

"Okay," I said, trying to mask my satisfaction. "Let's finish this, Mike. I know what happened. The boys have all been interviewed—Gordie has been interviewed and, let's face it, if there is one honest, good kid left in the world, it's Gordie. He didn't want to get you in trouble, but he was conflicted since he is such a good boy, he finally felt the need to tell the truth."

Mike allowed his head to fall forward, his chin bouncing off his chest as he saw his hope fade away. Having accepted his fate, he went on to confirm for me how he had been touching Gordie when he was sitting on his lap, and how he had indeed been having oral sex with Gordie in the shower. He said he had engaged in oral sex with Gordie dozens of times, too many to remember. Most of the contact took place in his bed when he returned home from work, with Gordie's parents fifteen feet away from him in their bedroom.

I was always surprised by how much insight could be gained from a perp who gave a full, true statement like Curtis had. He had poured his heart out to me for some reason, maybe expiation, but I doubt it. I don't think he understood the concept of guilt the way most people do. When I put him back in his cell, after his confession, he thanked me for listening to him without passing judgment. He said, "I appreciate what you did. I can tell by they way they look at me that most of the cops around here just want to beat the shit out of me." Like any experienced investigator, I had learned to mask any judgment I might have made about a suspect.

The rules in children's lives are supposed to be simpler than adult's. Children can even change the rules of their games to fit the circumstances. There are rules that fit a baseball game for nine players that do not apply to a game with only four. When unavoidable things happen in a street game of kick-the-can, like a car driving through the game, you call a "do over" which allows the kicker to start again without penalty.

It seemed the only fix for this family was a "do over." Innocence, however, once lost cannot be renewed. No erasure, no forgetting, no putting it behind you. This ship had sailed. There would be therapy, and there would be attempts made to *deal* with it, but there could be no starting over.

While other boys and girls pondered the cliché, parental platitudes of limitless potential in direct relation to effort, Gordie, Bobby, and Colton obsessed on the intrigue, excitement, and physical pleasures their bodies had known. Their consciences formed a protective shield of ambivalence, but they could not name or combat the opposing emotions. They knew of nothing more exhilarating, inviting, and mysterious than the sexual adventures they'd shared. They knew this wonderment, as they'd experienced it, filled gaps in their lives, but these intangible moments only created larger, more expansive gaps. They understood that something was missing, and the necessity of secrecy confirmed it. They knew this missing link had something to do with the connection between the pleasures of the body and those of the heart and soul. Whether or not they succeeded in finding that connection, the secret would be there for them, and that was enough to mitigate anything—at least for the time it took to experience it. Then it was gone—worthless, reduced to a shameful memory.

Split apart and devastated, this family was falling, not
through the cracks but into a chasm, descending in perpetual
motion down a well of misery that was built three years ago by
two men, a gentle manipulator and a tiny man aptly described
in his criminal history as: 5' 4", 125 pounds—dangerous.

The Yin, the Yang, and George

Most sex crimes I'd investigated tended to follow a common pattern: a vulnerable victim as a result of alcohol, mental illness, or age, and a suspect driven by lust to be sexually satisfied. The lust freight train was usually stoked with alcohol or other chemicals that lessened the suspect's inhibitions, blurred his judgment, and dissolved his morals—but had no effect on the speeding train.

I had always been told by various sex-crimes professionals that sex offenders were driven more by their need to dominate than any true sexual desire. But in my experience, it seemed that these two desires, sexual satisfaction and domination, seldom crossed in cases that didn't involve sexual sadism. The majority of sex cases I had investigated were "date rapes" that involved men driven by their desire for sexual satisfaction who were not the least bit interested in domination, though they might use it as a last resort. They were far more likely to use psychological pressure, drugs, or alcohol to subdue their prey than any forceful physical assault. But there was another type of sex crime I'd never investigated.

I'd seen the all-too-common comedy sketches involving shiny black leather-clad duos spanking and stroking one another, and all their pain-inducing instruments of sexual pleasure, but I never once had a case dropped on my desk involving a dominant/submissive relationship.

On a freezing November afternoon in 1999, a frantic woman, dressed only in her nightgown, stumbled into an Amoco gas station pleading to use the phone. Most of the early winter's snowfall had melted, leaving only the dirty remnants of piles left by the snowplows. It was much too cold this day, even for a disturbed woman, to be dressed so scantily. She was crying and difficult to understand, but she managed to tell the suddenly-attentive station attendant that she'd been raped. The attendant called the police department and told the dispatcher that a twenty-year-old drunk chick had stumbled into his station in her nightie, claiming to have been raped.

The first responding officer on the scene handled the call properly and transported the victim to Fairview Southdale Hospital for a sex assault exam. What information he could gather, he relayed to my boss, who then accompanied me to the reported crime scene. The victim lived with her mother in an upscale townhouse in West Bloomington. The sexual assault was alleged to have occurred in the victim's bedroom, where the suspect was last seen passed out on the victim's bed.

Patrol officers beat us to the victim's townhouse and found George still passed out on the bed. They awoke him, slapped on the handcuffs, and told him he was under arrest for Criminal Sexual Conduct. Strangely enough, he looked at them like they were crazy and told them he couldn't be arrested for Criminal Sexual Conduct, because he had a contract. Now the police officers looked back at George like *he* was crazy, and the two stood momentarily dumfounded, wondering who was the bigger nutcase.

One of the uniformed officers at the scene accompanied us into the victim's townhouse so we wouldn't appear to the neighbors as burglars dressed in cheap sport-coat disguises. The townhouse was clean and well furnished, but unkempt, with books, newspapers, and magazines strewn about. The morning dishes were stacked still dirty in the kitchen sink, and a few articles of clothing were left hanging over the backs of chairs.

On a coffee table in the living room I noticed a three-page document labeled only as "Contract." Not being a "number-cruncher" I rarely took interest in such items but gave it a spirited cursory scan. I quickly discerned that this contract had nothing to do with number crunching or any kind of numbers for that matter. It involved another realm altogether. It spelled out that two individuals, a man named George, and a woman, Christine, were entering into a legal contract. It documented that George would henceforth be referred to as the Dominant, or "Dom" for short, and that Christine would be referred to as the Submissive or "Sub."

The Sub, as one might expect, was to be at the beck and call of the Dom in all matters. Direct eye contact with the Dom, or any other male for that matter, was strictly forbidden without the Dom's permission. Strict obedience was expected in all matters, and last, but certainly not least, the Sub was expected to be willing and available at all times to perform, or submit to, any sexual desire of the Dom. Any disobedience would be punished as spelled out in the contract—which specified spankings as the preferred method of discipline.

Also spelled out in the contract was a three-step process by which the Sub could *cool* the sexual contact or punishment. If the Sub wanted to tone down the physical punishment she would utter the code word "yellow." If she wanted to temporarily stop a punishment or sexual encounter she would say the word "unicorn." And finally, if she wanted to end the relationship completely she could do so with two words, "black unicorn." Though lacking in allegory and literary significance, the words signaled the Dom that he must stop whatever action he was taking, leave the dwelling he was sharing with the Sub at the time, and not return or contact her ever again. This was to be the Sub's insurance policy against being forced into anything she was not prepared for, or willing to sustain. This contract was signed and dated by George and Christine.

Christine had told the reporting officer that she and George had been willing participants in a sexual relationship for a couple months, but that George was starting to take it too far. Earlier that day while in her bathroom, George had threatened to kill both himself and her, not necessarily in that order, with a knife. According to Christine, he had held the knife to her throat and her belly. He'd also given her instructions on how long to wait before calling the police should he stab himself and not die quickly enough. I found the knife, a butcher type with a six-inch blade and a wooden handle, along with a nearly empty bottle of E&J Brandy in her bathroom.

After finishing on the main floor, my boss and I moved upstairs to the bedrooms. On the victim's bedroom nightstand lay a vibrator and some lubricant. We took these items, along with a notebook we found in the victim's bedroom outlining the preferred sexual devices and restraints needed for a quiet evening of discrete bondage. Stuck within the pages of this notebook was a photograph of a man I assumed to be George. To say he was frighteningly hideous would be cruel and politically incorrect, but…the photo was really an 8 x 11 representation of his face as he squished his head into a copy machine. He looked like Charles Manson's twin, with the same long, dark-brown, frazzled hair, a goatee, and fierce, piercing, dark-brown eyes. He was sticking his tongue out—not in a silly way, but in a fiendish, dead-serious expression of pure malice.

This was not going the typical route of a *normal* sex crime investigation, and I could already see problems in getting the case charged, the most significant being the signed contract that allowed the suspect any sexual contact he desired, any time he desired it. You say, "Black Unicorn," I say, "Red Herring." The second problem was the fact that the two of them had apparently enjoyed their respective roles in the dominant/submissive realm and had an established history.

If there was any good news from an investigative standpoint, it was that only two people were involved. There would be no extensive driving to distant witness locales, because there were no witnesses. There was a victim and a suspect—period. As per proper investigative procedure, I interviewed the victim first.

I have a bad habit of making instant judgments based solely on appearances. I know this practice to be unfair, un-Christian, and basically unfriendly, but I can't stop myself. A skinny guy with a high voice is a femme, a fat guy is lazy, and a well-dressed, handsome man with a soft voice is gay. A guy with well-coiffed hair is arrogant, a guy with unkempt hair is a slob, and a poorly dressed man with balding hair and a pocket protector is a dorky egghead. I have a similar list for women, but you get the idea.

Christine met me at the police department to give me a statement in a room situated not twenty feet from her alleged rapist/contract partner, George, who lay relaxing on a cot in the pit we affectionately call our jail. Christine wore dark jeans and a light sweater. She was slender with thin features and long, dark-brown hair that enveloped her pale but very attractive face. She leaned forward in her chair and chewed her gum quickly, telegraphing her anxiety. I tried not to telegraph the first ten judgments I'd made about her before I'd asked my first question.

After rambling through the casual rapport-building small-talk, I asked her to tell me how she met George. She said she met him on an Internet site called "maskedintruder.com," a site, she explained, where couples meet and enact sexual scenarios with one another. After chatting briefly with George on the net, she agreed to meet him that same night at the Lincoln Del restaurant in Bloomington.

They talked briefly in the restaurant parking lot about scenarios before going in for a drink.

"So we went inside, got a drink, and just kept talking. Then he changed seats and started coming on to me, feeling me."

I asked her if they discussed the safety code-words at all, and she explained the significance of the three words I'd already read about in the contract adding, "We left before it closed, and I got in my car. He got into the passenger side of my car and started kissing me, and he said that, you know, that he would have the trailer to do the scenario, like a kidnap-masked-intruder scenario if—"

"So, basically a rape scenario?" I asked.

"No," she said, "I don't know if it was a rape scenario. Masked intruder. I don't know that it was a rape in my mind, but I suppose you could consider it that."

I watched her face change as she spoke, and it struck me that her present expression of befuddled shell shock was probably a quality that George found endearing, or at least consistent with his unspecified qualifications for a Sub.

She said she walked into his trailer later that same night as per their plan, and George jumped out of the darkness wearing a mask over his face. "He had me strip, and he had me dance a little, and then he got me on the bed. He put handcuffs—he had sex with me, and then he got in front of me and had me suck him. Then he called it off. He unclipped my cuffs and that was over."

"You never said the safe words?" I asked.

"No," she said.

I couldn't help but wonder how differently I would be reacting if I were her father. What would I say to her when I was done pulling all my remaining hair out? Where would a father begin? Before my obligatory lecture, I invited her to finish her story.

She went on to tell me that George had asked her to contact him by e-mail if she wanted to see him again, so the following day she invited him to her house. He told her he was looking for a "submissive" and thought she could fill the bill. She'd had a previous submissive relationship a few months ago, another instance of Internet matchmaking magic.

She agreed to a trial relationship. "So he came over, and we talked, and then, it must have been the next day, he gave me this list of things to do, like make your bed, clean your bathroom, exercise every day—that I was supposed to follow."

"Mm-hmm," I muttered, biting my lip.

"Okay," she said. "I don't clean my room, this is cool, I have somebody guiding me, right?"

"Mm-hmm," I muttered, my lip now bleeding as I considered my luck in fathering only boys. Christine, it seemed, had allowed herself to become like an institutionalized prisoner, desiring the control she had become accustomed to and felt she needed.

"...and calling me a good girl that I was doing my work. I wasn't being lazy. And then I came home one day from work...and I went into my room to call him like I was supposed to do, and he's sitting in my chair. And there's something called "present." It's where you sort of kneel in front of him. And I kneeled in front of him and he started yelling at me—that he read my journal about all the guys that I slept with—all these different guys... Now, I've been celibate almost up until a year ago for twelve years because I wasn't in touch with my sexuality. I think that this is probably why this happened so explosively."

"Why had you chosen to be celibate for so long?"

"Because I got sick, and I was put on medication, and I was diagnosed as manic-depressive, and it just—I was working through my head stuff...relationships were part of it."

The black leather lampshade was finally lifted as her mental illness was brought to light. I figured she was off her meds or needed new ones—stronger ones, the kind that make you sleep all day, or make you want to be celibate again.

Much to her and her mother's dismay, George soon became a fixture in their house. Little did they know, George had recently left a note with his wife of seven years that read, "I will be gone. I hope you'll be happy. No matter what others try to tell you, it's your fault."

Christine and her mother soon discovered his food in their refrigerator, and his junk in their garage. Next, he was pressuring Christine to sign the contract and spying on her at the Caribou Coffee shop where she worked. George finally read the contract to her, rather than allowing her to read it. "I was scared and intimidated, and I signed it."

The next thing she knew, George was showing up at her work and chastising her in front of her co-workers for talking with a male employee. He also told this male co-worker to stay away from his woman.

After two months of George and the contract, public humiliation and loss of personal freedom got old fast, and Christine decided she'd had enough. She came home with the clear intention of ending the relationship, changing the locks on the doors, and telling George to take a hike. She walked into her house and quickly turned around and locked the door behind her. When she turned back to the hallway, George was walking toward her with a folded belt hanging from his hand. She confidently tossed down her trump, and said, "black unicorn," but she might as well have said, "beat me black and blue," since the secret code-word had no effect on George. Instead of stopping in his tracks, setting down the belt, and leaving her house as per contract, he threw her up against the wall and started slapping the shit out of her. He then dragged her into the bathroom and handed her a butcher knife that lay on the sink.

"He kept trying to get me to stab him. Then he took the knife and held it to my throat, and then he said that he wouldn't hurt me, and then he put the knife down and smoked a couple cigarettes, still blathering about going to go to hell because suicide's a sin. That he's tried to kill himself before, that he's really going to do it this time. That if I call the cops before he's dead, like if he stabs himself in the stomach, I'm supposed to just lay—sit there and let him bleed until a half-hour passed, and if I didn't, and he lived, he was going to come get me."

After a couple hours of pin the butcher knife on the jackass, George told Christine to strip. Christine said she thought having sex was the only way to get him to leave so she resigned herself to just do it, and get it over with. George left the knife in the bathroom and grabbed Christine by her wrist.

"He took me upstairs...made me lay down on the bed spread-eagle, and he got on top of me...He said he wanted to have my baby...and I didn't—I've had an abortion...if I did get pregnant I wouldn't abort it again. I would have the baby. I started crying, saying I couldn't kill a baby, and I got pretty hysterical."

George took Christine back downstairs and offered her the phone, asking her if she wanted to call 911. She grabbed the phone and started to call, so he snatched the phone out of her hand and hung it up.

"He said, 'You're a cold bitch. I knew you'd do that' Then he brought me back upstairs, had me lick his asshole, licked mine, made me say how much I liked that, then he went back on the bed, and I think that's probably when he—when he took my ass. I—or had anal sex."

"Mm-hmm," I said.

"And then he made me get into different positions, like off the side of the bed, so he could continue, and then he made me suck him again, and he fell asleep while I was doing it— started snoring."

His falling asleep was the good news. The bad news, according to Christine, was that while George was spreading pollen from flower to flower, he'd ejaculated in her vagina. This horrified Christine since the thought of having George's baby, and the reconsideration of abortion, was very frightening to her. I had to agree with her on this one. I thought the gene pool might be too messed up even for Freud to straighten out.

Of course George's dozing off while Christine continued with her contractual obligations gave her the opportunity to get away from him.

"So I just sat at the end of the bed watching the clock for a full minute." Christine then ran to three neighbor's houses in an attempt to call the police but found no one home. She then piled into her car and drove to the Amoco Gas station where the friendly attendant directed her to the phone—and the Tic Tacs.

As our interview came to a close, I felt I had to give her the fatherly talk—if not the mallet. I explained to her that meeting a stranger over the Internet, and agreeing to hook up with him in an unfamiliar location for the purpose of having sex, was akin to sleeping with your head under a rusty guillotine. I told her there are sexual sadists who would take great pleasure in torturing and killing her in really painful ways. I told her I had pictures if she didn't believe me.

"Yeah, I guess," she said, noncommittal.

I wouldn't have showed the pictures to her anyway. I'm afraid she might have liked them.

Prior to speaking with George, who wasn't going anywhere soon, I spoke by phone with his wife of seven years. She said her relationship with George was punctuated with frequent physical abuse to their children. She currently had an Order for Protection against him. She said he'd tried to kill himself when he learned of the order, and would have died from the self-inflicted lacerations (with a butcher knife) had he been allowed to bleed out. I asked her if there had been any sexual abuse to her, and my question was answered unconsciously with a long, pained sigh, followed with the simple response, "Yes."

"Are you all right talking with me about this?"

"Yeah."

"What did the sexual abuse entail?"

She again sighed her reluctance into the mouthpiece, but finally answered, "It was forced anal sex."

"Was this a routine thing?"

"Yes," she answered, not offering any excuses or explanations.

"Would you consider that when this anal sex occurred that it was a sexual assault, or did you just go along with it because he was your husband, and you thought you had to?"

"Yes, yes," she said, answering both questions without comment.

"Would you ever resist him and just say, 'Absolutely not, we're not doin' this,' and he would do it anyway?"

"Yes."

"Okay. Did it seem to you like he had a penchant to dominate you and that's part of the reason why he forced this type of anal sex on you?"

"Yes."

"All right. I can't really think of anything else," I said, sensing her curt responses a signal to wrap it up. "Is there anything you want to add to what I've asked you?"

"No," she said, leaving it open, "—Just that his whole personality was that he needed to be in control."

"Thank you very much," I said, wondering how willing I'd have been to talk about my sex life on the phone with someone who said he was a cop. I was glad I'd talked to her. I'd had several cases where my suspect could not be intimate with his spouse. A substitution for intimacy was power—and domination a side effect. There could never be a real love relationship with this personality because the dominator thought of his partner only in terms of someone needing to be controlled.

I spoke to George later that same day. He had nothing else on his schedule, as he lay stretched out on the filthy bed, looking up at the ceiling in his dark, dingy cell at the Bloomington Police Department.

I can't help but look at someone a little differently when I know all the weird shit that person is into, and George was chairman of the Weird Shit Club. He appeared fairly comfortable for someone in custody for first-degree crim-sex.

He explained how he was a little bent over his wife getting a restraining order against him, denying him visitation of his kids, and could not understand why he'd been arrested. He said, "I was told she (Christine) was in the hospital. I never done nothing to her. Look at her body. The only things you will find on her body is a bruise on her butt. She likes to be spanked. I can prove that. We have a D/S contract...I would never harm her. The only thing I have ever done on a consensual basis is spanking and some mild, light bondage, and that's it. As I say, all that's documented. I covered my butt that way. I don't know why I'm here. I didn't break into the home. I didn't beat her up. I didn't threaten to hurt her that I know of. I don't like being in small places."

I told George my three concerns: that he'd entered her house without permission. That he'd threatened her with a knife, and finally that he'd forced non-consensual sex with her. George denied all three allegations again. He admitted being drunk and threatening to hurt himself, and even to cutting himself superficially, but not to either slapping or threatening Christine.

George admitted that he had sex with Christine on the day of his arrest, but stated he'd had sex with her every day since meeting her, and that she had never objected. George took me through the "safe words" and their meanings and assured me that Christine had never spoken any of the words yesterday or any day. He assured me that he had never forced sex on anyone in his life. I mentioned to him that both his wife Deb and Christine disagreed with him.

George was flabbergasted to the point of disbelief at his wife's disclosure to me of his forced sex with her. He said, "Seriously sir, can you look me in the face and tell me that my wife, Debra, stated that I forced sex on her?"

I looked into his eyes. "Yes. Why would I say that if she didn't?"

"I don't know sir. That is why you blew me away when you said it. Look at it this way, Deb is the kind of woman...I would have loved to smack her four or five times because she made me so damn mad, but she's the type of woman who would be like 'it's okay baby,'" he mimicked in a facetiously compassionate female voice, "'go back to sleep,' You see what

I'm saying? [After you fell asleep] she would take a baseball bat to your head. There is no way I would ever think of even imagining hurting her and then be stupid enough to go to sleep, okay?"

George went on to say that he had never used any force with Christine either.

I said, "Sometimes I think there is some force involved sexually by what happens."

"Meaning?" George said, understandably confused.

"Tell me about the order of the sexual contact once you got in the bedroom."

"Oh my God," George said, pulling his frazzled hair straight out to the sides where it stuck. "It's kind of fuzzy there. You know that I passed out."

"Skip that," I said, "and we will go to the last thing that happened after anal sex—according to her, it was oral sex. That's something that a lot of women wouldn't—"

"She does," he interjected. "That's what she wants. Either that, or she wants me to be her daddy."

"She was willing to do oral sex after...anal sex?"

"After any sex," he said, confidently. "She doesn't have no problem...when I leave she kisses my cock, and sucks it, okay—before I leave the house every day...I never had a shower there. I shower once I get home because her mom usually comes over at that time."

"And you have anal sex with her every day?"

"Pretty near every day," he said.

"Did you want to make her pregnant?" I asked, curious about his knowledge of biology.

He paused and looked curiously at the two-way mirror behind me. "We have discussed that. She is not happy with the fact of being pregnant because she might pass her schizophrenia onto the child, and she wouldn't want to do that."

Though George spoke like a man of limited education, he was not stupid. He had been down the road, and was cognizant of the implications involved in physically playing out his fantasies with live, human playmates. He was also aware of whom he was talking to, and what my motives were. I would not be *fooling* George, or unmasking him. He used so many masks; in fact, he might not even have known how to completely unmask himself. He had a mask for his fantasies, for each of his woman, for his children, for the administrator of the church where he worked as a custodian, and another for me. He was more than a chameleon, or an enigma, he was an anomaly, manipulative and intimidating, a choreographer of humiliation, an orchestrator of degradation.

Though this case varied from the typical sex case, it shared one thing—the vulnerable victim. George was the exception to my rule of suspects that just wanted to get off. George couldn't get off without dominating. He needed to dominate in all relationships but most of all, he needed to dominate women sexually.

He was released without ever being charged with a crime. His contract protected him from any allegations of abuse since all sex was consensual by contract, and talk of black unicorns was hearsay. He would most likely get back online and find another wounded woman who envisioned herself romantically as needing someone to guide her. Like Christine, she would be vulnerable. The empty spot in her soul, where confidence and self-esteem should have lived, invited users like George to take up residence and victimize her again and again and again.

Up North

A group of Bloomington cops started making what was to become an annual BWCA pilgrimage in the early 1990s and subsequently they became desperate enough for a stern-man to invite me to join them. I'd been to the Boundary Waters with a church group as a young teen and returned in college years with my girlfriend, so I knew what I was getting in to. You couldn't return from a Boundary Waters trip without a new *story*. Switching gears from rush-hour bumper-to-bumper traffic, to the view from your canoe of a glass lake with no one in sight, inspired such stories.

I am reminded of a story involving Seth, a first-timer to the area in October of 1999. Seth turned his Petzel headlamp backwards on his head while tramping his way to the plastic Forest Service toilet at night. These Forest Service "thrones" are basically outhouses without the houses. They allow for communing with nature while conducting business. They are positioned at the end of a path through the woods that originates at the campsite. Some of these paths to the head are longer than others. This "tail-light" effect was used in theory to thwart unruly bears and camping partners from sneaking up behind him while he was taking care of business. In addition to this strategic thought-provoking headlight tactic (he was, after all, a SWAT team member) he carried a .25 caliber Beretta with him on these trips, also for bear deterrence, but with the more practical effect of deterring us, his camping partners, from any shenanigans. I'm thinking that both the bears and us, his fellow campers, were fortunate not to have crossed paths with him on these nightly constitutionals.

If the bears only knew the preposterous precautions people used to confound them, they would probably take some sort of malicious pleasure in actually frightening us. We didn't see a single bear on that trip, but we did see a couple moose, and the whiteout blizzard we paddled into that left three inches of accumulated snow was definitely worthy of retelling.

Quixotic Minnesotans have always been drawn "up north" to the Boundary Waters Canoe Area Wilderness (BWCAW) for a taste of true wilderness camping. (I prefer the abbreviated BWCA since the W for wilderness was a later addition and seems redundant.) Thousands of trekkers, from around the country, come to this wilderness area every year, making the less adventurous, but otherwise able-bodied native Minnesotans, feel either a sense of duty to visit, or a sense of guilt for having passed up this near-wild heaven experience.

The lakes of the BWCA comprise a substantial percentage of the state's (underestimated) 10,000, and coupled with the towering pine forests make for extraordinary vistas during daylight, with the occasional candle-essence of Northern Lights at night.

For those who have never made the trip, the thousands of acres of wilderness appear on the map as a negative image of an archipelago with the many lakes attached by small tracts of land, peninsulas and islands. This wilderness area continues across the border into Canada's Quetico Wilderness Area. The land connecting the lakes serves as portages for canoeists to hike from one lake to the next. Trails have been cut out for portages by the forest service, but these paths are very rough with protruding boulders, felled trees, and roots, which act as obstacles for the canoe and pack-laden trekkers. These portages vary in length from fifteen rods (think of a rod as one canoe length) to three hundred rods and longer. The northern Minnesota forests remain wild with an abundance of native critters that include moose, bear, deer, wolves, and the usual assortment of rodents and birds.

Of this esoteric group of cops, Sam humbly assumed the leadership role. He had guided church groups through the area for years and progressed to racing canoes with fellow cop and BWCA devotee Ken. Sam was familiar enough with the lakes and surrounding area that he considered both compass and daylight to be superfluous extravagances for navigation. Jack took on the jobs of planning the meals, grocery shopping, and cooking. As time and technology progressed, most of the campers in our group began to replace heavier, old-fashioned camping gear with Kevlar canoes and other lightweight back-packing supplies to make the portages less arduous. They are arduous enough with the lightweight stuff.

In time, traditions took shape with our group that included staying in a dive motel the night we arrived in Ely so we could enjoy an evening in town and a decent early morning breakfast before heading out into the wild. The town of Ely, too, evolved, as the city became an entry hub to the BWCA. From very humble beginnings the town grew to include several upper-crust outfitters, outdoor clothing stores, art studios, and restaurants. There are a variety of national chain eateries, a few bars, churches, a high school, and a community college.

On a 2002 autumn night-before-excursion jaunt into town, we stopped for a beer at one of the bars and found the establishment to be mostly empty. There was a twenty-some-thing townie-chick playing pool by herself, a couple stragglers on stools at the bar, and a table full of mixed-company thirty-somethings with several partially consumed pitchers of beer on their table. I noticed an abundance of debarked, lacquered, nat-ural pine furniture in the joint, and a jukebox on the floor that was conspicuously silent. A lone, bearded man in a black Harley T-shirt appeared bored behind the bar where he sat on a stool. As our group of six entered the bar, the occupants turned to look at us, and we at them in that inadvertent way people do that sort of thing. After a couple of friendly head-nods thrown back and forth between groups, we moseyed into the joint.

Like children at a candy counter, we huddled in front of the jukebox, filling it with quarters and poking in our classic rock selections. The lone townie chick playing pool approached us with cue in hand and told us we looked like a group of "swampies," which she explained was the term used by Ely folk to describe a group of out-of-towners up for a trip through the BWCA. Apparently we had that look, which I assumed most strangers in this town must have during the temperate months of the year. This girl was slim and attractive, with shoulder length dark-brown hair and an unassuming friendly air one might expect from a gregarious small-towner. Figuring her for a local, since she was calling us swampies, I asked her what she did in this town. She explained that she was not a native, but rather a expatriate from civilization, having grown up in the Twin Cities, but then having fallen on unspecified bad times, she moved up to the great northern wilderness.

"But what do you do up here?" I asked. "It seems like it's

all tourist or food service. What else is there?"

"I'm a massage therapist," she eagerly replied. "I got my training in the Cities and then moved up here."

"Is there a lot of call for that up here?" I asked.

She took a big pull off her beer, draining it, and said. "Well, I've had to work a couple other jobs, but now that I'm up here I'm never going back."

"I don't blame you," I said, returning my attention to the jukebox.

"Hey," she said, sizing up our group of six. "I could give you guys a group deal on massages if you're interested."

We turned back to hear the rest of her pitch.

She lowered her voice and leaned into us. "Forty bucks a piece and I'll finish you off with a hand-job."

The hand-job part caught us off-guard. After all, this was Ely with all its pristine, untouched, virginal wilderness. Somehow a hand-job and the solicitation of it in this bar with all the natural pine furniture just didn't fit—or did it? And what about our sworn duty as law enforcement officers to uphold the law? Well, we were on vacation, out of our jurisdiction, and other than damaging our sensitive sensibilities, this seemed to be a victimless crime.

Being of sound back muscles, and bearing gold bands on left annular fingers, we all mumbled our ambivalence at her offer and turned back to the jukebox.

She paused, presumably reconsidering for a moment, and then leaned into us again whispering, "I was just kidding about the hand-job." She forced a smile.

We smiled back as if we believed her, or better yet, that we knew she'd been kidding all along. But of course she hadn't been, and if we'd have taken her up on her original offer, we'd have been standing in line in the parking lot next to her Ford Escort station wagon with the back seat folded down as she worked over all our muscle groups, toning, kneading, and rubbing.

The next morning we stopped at one of the town eateries and had a professionally prepared breakfast of eggs, bacon, sausage, and toast before dropping our canoes into Gabro Lake and paddling away from our trucks in the parking lot. One of the more recent traditions we had all agreed upon was to paddle in as far as possible on the first day, set up a base camp, and then paddle out on day-trips for the remaining days. This way we would not have to break camp and repack more than once.

With the eggs, bacon, sausage, and toast making its way through my alimentary canal, we paddled for about four hours before looking for a camp site. We floated into Bald Eagle Lake, which didn't strike us at the time as a perfect destination, but we needed to stop. The sun seemed to be making its arching decent with reckless abandon. We paddled all the way around this lake, and looked at every campsite, but found none worthy of our needs and expectations. We paddled off this lake and into an adjoining bay that happened to have a campsite there out of the waves. Having a group of six, we needed a fairly large site, one that could support three tents, with enough frontage to land and launch our canoes. This site was a good fit. We wearily dragged our packed canoes up on shore and started unpacking.

With a minimum, or perhaps an average amount of bitching, we set up camp. It was getting late so Jack had to do his cooking in the dark, which was not uncommon for our first night. We passed around a bottle of root beer schnapps, for medicinal purposes only, and felt the warmth of the alcohol chase the cold from our systems.

After dinner and the dishes, we made a nice fire and someone brought up the story of Zach getting a fishing lure stuck in the back of his head. This story was a perennial favorite, and one that was told at least twice on each trip, once in the truck on the way up and then once more around the campfire. This one, and all the stories of capsizing our canoes with us and our packs in them, made for the best retelling. Nearly all of us had gone over the gunwales at some point or another. We took our trips off-season, in September or October, so tipping over in the middle of a lake was a dangerous prospect, with hypothermia a very real possibility. We had all survived these mishaps, so they were now grist for the mill, and after a few more gulps of schnapps the stories took on a new twist or two that made them even more interesting—like *faction,* a few shreds of truth thrown into a pot of bullshit and mixed around. The theme of these adventurous mishaps leaned toward, "Whatever doesn't kill us makes us stronger"—but I don't think Nietzsche ever capsized into a freezing cold lake in the middle of nowhere, hours from medical attention and warmth.

So anyway, Zach, the only *non-cop* of the group, has this lure embedded in his scalp. A bad cast gone awry, or whatever. The prong part is stuck in the scalp but not exposed. A debate ensues over whether or not to attempt to push the lure out through the scalp so the prong can then be cut off with a Leatherman wire cutter, or to just yank it out from whence it came. Zach asks his trusted brother, Ken, to do it. "Just yank it," he says. Ken assures him that if he yanks it quickly, it won't really hurt that much. Of course the only anesthetic available is schnapps. Like an old western with the doctor poised to remove the embedded bullet with a pliers, Zach takes a gulp of booze and grits his teeth. Ken turns back to the group who at present is completely captivated by the impending surgery. The extraction takes only a second with a blurred movement of Ken's arm. Zach screams bloody murder as Ken yanks the lure backwards from his brother's head, taking a gravel-sized wad of scalp with it. Ken turns with the lure, smiling, and proudly displays the trophy of scalp to the rest of the group who was silent as death a moment before but who is now roaring with laughter. Zach is not laughing as his head bleeds freely from the pink spot on his scalp. Zach has more schnapps and holds a rag over his pocked scalp. His head stops bleeding by the sixteenth retelling of the story.

We move on to the stories of capsizing.

In the morning we decided to break tradition and move on to another campsite. With ample bitching, we collapsed our tents, stuffed our stuff into stuff sacks that were too small to fit it all, and then placed all that stuff into Duluth packs that were bulging with their overstuffed contents. The weather seemed agreeable from our position of cover in the bay, but we were protected and couldn't really get a good view of the lake from our vantage point. We'd have to get out of the bay and onto the lake proper to get an accurate reading.

My partner Rob launched our canoe first, and we treaded nonchalantly with our paddles as we waited for the others who were giving our campsite a once-over before leaving. We drifted ahead a bit as we chatted, waiting for the others to launch. As we floated out of the bay, we entered the rather large Bald Eagle Lake, and like soldiers caught sloughing and ordered to attention, we were instantly brought out of our lethargy. It became immediately apparent to us that conditions negated paddling on this lake. The surrounding bay had been protecting us from the windstorm.

"Holy shit!" Rob called from the bow.

The wind was too strong and the massive whitecap waves far too forceful for us to control our canoe. As we realized this, it was already too late. We were in it and there was no turning back. The act of attempting to turn in any direction would certainly force our canoe to capsize. I was paddling a Winona

Minnesota II, which I consider one of, if not, *the* most stable tripping canoe on the market, and I was certain we would capsize. I turned back and saw that all the other canoes had followed behind us and were frantically involved in the impossible task of keeping their canoes upright. It was already too late to warn them. We were all in this for keeps. The thought crossed my mind that I was glad we had all worn our life jackets. They would keep us afloat anyway while we were getting smashed against the boulders and sheer cliffs that made up the adjacent shoreline. I also thought about how we were going to collect our packs after we capsized, and whether or not it would be necessary to make any water rescues. Such rescues would be very complicated in the whitecaps, with the boulders and rock walls that the waves were pushing us toward.

"We're going under!" Rob shouted from the bow as our canoe tumbled down into the trough of an enormous wave that crashed over the bow, soaking Rob. It appeared and felt like our canoe was pitching down toward the bottom of the lake and it may very well have been. Our canoe shot down and bounced back up with the next wave. We were paddling into the waves at a slight angle, which was our best bet for staying upright. The shore was about thirty feet away and the waves were viciously pushing us toward it. I shouted for Rob to just paddle as hard as he could. We were going to have to continue on our present heading, since there was a bay we could turn into about a hundred yards in front of us on our present course. It was our only chance, but the powerful crushing pressure of the waves pushed us closer to the rocks with each cresting whitecap.

My corrective strokes to keep us on course were having little effect in changing our canoe's direction. It felt like the shoreline had a magnetic connection with our canoe that drew us inexorably closer with each massive wave that rushed against the canoe. I pushed my paddle down into the black water beside me and against the gunwale, in an attempt to rudder us, and I felt certain that my paddle would snap against the tremendous pressure of the waves. It was all I could do to hold it steady in proper position. My wife had given me the $150 carbon fiber paddle as a birthday present. It was an ultra-light-weight Zaveral with a bent shaft. I was waiting for it to break, imagining how I was going to paddle and control the canoe from the stern, with just the jagged shaft.

I shot a glance behind me and got a glimpse of the others in our group fighting the waves. I saw no one in the water yet. Ken was fighting the waves alone from his solo canoe. I assumed he would be the first to go. For open water, the waves seemed loud, washing over one another and crashing into and around our canoe. I heard muted shouts behind me but couldn't make out the words or the source. Rob paddled on valiantly, occasionally letting out a yelp as our bow pitched down into another seemingly bottomless pit. The bay was near enough that I had ambitions to make it there now. I yelled for Rob to give it everything he had—and he did. We entered the bay, and the waves, like birds shot in flight, ended their fury and subsided almost instantly. Rob and I sagged forward on our seats. We landed our canoe on a long flat lava flow rock, and climbed the top of the cliff overlooking Bald Eagle Lake. From our perch we could see the other canoes, paddlers bent forward in strenuous travail, paddling for all they were worth toward the entrance of the bay. The waves played with the canoes like a cat with an injured mouse, pushing them back and forth at their whim.

Amazingly, we all made it into the bay, even Ken in his solo. One by one as they entered the bay, the paddlers collapsed exhausted, soaked and astounded that they had avoided capsizing. The weather and water conditions during our past capsizing episodes hadn't been anywhere near as bad as these. That's what had made the stories all the more humorous—we were usually in calm water and just lost our balance. We laughed now, giddy and elated that we were upright and wearing semi-dry socks. Zach took a swig from his water bottle and blurted, "I was scared shitless, but I knew we'd be alright cause I had Sam in the back steering us—"

"Really?" I said, surprised at his confidence.

"Well let me finish," he said. "So I turned my head and shouted back to him asking if we were going to be okay, and he screams back to me in this panicked voice I've never heard before, 'Just keep paddling!' Now I'm really scared, and I'm paddling like a motherfucker!"

We laughed and someone produced the schnapps. Everyone took a pull as it made it around the circle. One by one we told of our close calls and our plan for getting the canoes and packs to shore after having capsized into the drink. We realized how lucky we were. We had another swig of schnapps.

The rest of our paddle that afternoon was not without its challenges. All of the big lakes were windy that day and we had to keep toward shore to avoid getting in to the ominous whitecaps. The temptation to use the shortest as-the-crow-flies heading got us into trouble more than once, but nothing like what we experienced that morning on Bald Eagle.

We came out of the BWCA at night for the second year in a row. Saying that Sam could paddle out in pitch black darkness was not an exaggeration, though I'm not a proponent of the practice. He got us out without even straining his orienteering or paddling skills. It's nice to have him along, even when he's not guiding us. We drove from our take-out spot back into Ely. The Twins baseball team was in the play-offs that year and we wanted to see the game and have a cold beer. The bar was almost full this time and some of us had to stand by the wall-mounted TVs to get a look at the game. The bartender, having seen enough paddlers to know, asked us if we'd just come out. I told him we had. He said, "You probably haven't heard then, there was three guys out on the Kawishiwi that they figure drowned a couple days ago."

"How'd they drown?" I asked.

"They figure they got into a current and they all went over. I guess none of them had their life jackets on."

"Oh, that's awful," I said. "Have they recovered the bodies yet?"

The bartender motioned with his head to a group of somber looking men at one of the tables. "Those fellas are with the rescue group that's here to find them. They got two of them out today. They go out again tomorrow morning. Tough job."

"Yeah."

I'd thought that maybe our ordeal on Bald Eagle might be our new best story of all time, but then it wasn't really very funny. Even if we embellished the story as we did with the others, it still wouldn't be. We had survived and, even if we'd have capsized, with our life jackets on I think we could have avoided the fate of those guys on the Kawishiwi. Maybe we'd save this story for another time. Maybe instead of our Bald Eagle story we'd tell the one about the lure in Zach's head a record three times next year. It seemed to get better with each telling anyway.

One Bureau

Henry holds a model F-14 jet fighter in each hand as he demonstrates a Himmelman dogfight maneuver to Jan, the new agent and final complement to our quad at the Minneapolis FBI Joint Terrorism Task Force. Somehow, Henry doesn't fit my perception of what the nation's top terrorism hunters should look like. With his desk-mounted computer acting as a miniature aircraft carrier lined with an anachronistic mix of mini-model naval planes, and his desk supporting disheveled piles of reports dating back to J. Edgar Hoover, he doesn't quite fit the FBI image. But Henry knows what he's talking about when he discusses naval aviation, since he was a naval aviator and instructor at Top Gun. He also knows what he's talking about when he discusses al-Qaeda, since he was the agent who figured out that Zacharias Moussoui was more than just a confused Islamic college kid who considered the landing part of flight school to be a superfluous detail. Sometimes Henry's acumen as an investigator and his accomplishments on "the big case" are overshadowed by the tragedy of 9-11 and the subsequent caustic letter to FBI director Mueller by Colleen Rowley.

Not only can Henry demonstrate various fighter plane maneuvers, he can tell you which pilots, in which wars, scored the most kills, where they flew, how many flights they logged and which planes they flew. He can also confidently recite the history of warfare from the time of the Roman Empire to the present—with as much detail as you require—without looking at notes or maps. You see, though he denies it, Henry has a photographic memory. He'll tell you that he couldn't memorize the Periodic Table of Elements for a million dollars, but of course it comes down to motivation.

Henry exudes a poised image of confidence, some might call it arrogance, but this is a facade to mask an inexplicable lack of self-esteem. At thirty-two years old, in his fifth year as an agent, Henry is a stocky (his mom bought him the husky jeans as a teen) 5' 8", with a permanent baby-face and a squared-away navy haircut. He admonished me daily on the positioning of my belt buckle, saying that my gig-line was FUBAR. It takes a while to see through the hubris to the very decent man and father within. When Henry starts his barrage of criticism and frustration with the "hundred-pound heads" (a term Henry said was born in the Navy to describe the engineers who designed the amazing aircraft) at FBI headquarters, I tell him he'll make an excellent history teacher some day—and he will.

While Jan is duly impressed with Henry's dogfight demo, she is not exactly ignorant of military aviation, since she herself was an officer in the Air Force prior to earning her doctorate in chemistry. Though it seems an unlikely route to the FBI, Jan's knowledge and skills will be highly sought-after once her probationary period has ended. The Weapons of Mass Destruction (WMD) Unit will want to utilize her expertise combating the terrorism epidemic that includes chemical/biological

WMD, and she will most likely be transferred to Headquarters. So far, the idea of multiple moves isn't that intimidating to her. As an attractive, single, thirty-three-year-old first-year agent, she has nothing holding her back.

That brings us to the third corner of the quad, and the agent who shares a common space on his desk with me. Like Jan, Pat is virtually a new agent. He graduated from the FBI Academy in Quantico in the class directly before Jan's. At thirty-five, Pat is at the terminus of allowable age for an agent. Prior to entering the FBI academy, he spent fifteen years in the Marines. Regardless of what he wears, as long as he keeps the haircut, he will always look like a "jarhead," an endearing descriptor to him. Like Henry and Jan, the haircut, the integrity, and the honor did not get left behind with the meticulously creased uniform.

Pat was the quintessential Marine, and he is the quintessential agent. A retired Force Recon Marine, he is familiar with the politics of the world in general and, in particular, global terrorism. He is sharp, physically fit—having boxed Golden Gloves in his youth—and, when wearing his suit, looks like a poster boy for the Bureau. Two weeks into his training period with Henry (Henry trains everyone in our quad), Pat is given a routine terrorism investigation that turns into one of the top cases in the nation. Pat is undaunted by the pressure, in fact he appears to thrive on it. He rarely seeks advice from Henry, and Henry rarely offers it.

I sit in the remaining corner of the quad, the lone Task Force member, a common flatfoot, surrounded by agents whose résumés all boast military experience and various accolades of merit. After twenty-three years with the same police department, I don't even have a résumé. From my corner of their world, the FBI hires quite well. You could drop a thousand dollar bill on the floor in my quad, or anywhere in the

FBI building for that matter, and walk away from it, with no worries of having it returned.

I caught Henry and Pat leaving for lunch one fall afternoon without humoring "the old guy" (me) with an invitation to join them. I asked them where they were going today, and they said they'd been invited to a special luncheon with Charles Lindberg, the only still-living Marine pictured in the first flag raising at Iwo Jima. (Raymond Jacobs disputed this, stating that he was one of the pictured flag-raisers also. As of this writing both have died, with Lindberg having passed prior to Jacobs.) Figuring I'd probably defer as usual and spend my lunch in the library, they invited me to come along—and I jumped at the chance.

There were probably fifteen FBI agents at the luncheon and several additional retired agents and miscellaneous others I was not familiar with. Some of the agents had brought their wives and children. The long foldout tables at the Richfield VFW were covered with paper tablecloths. I sat directly across the table from Charles Lindberg, hoping to absorb a portion of his uncompromising bravery through some kind of osmotic proximity. Lindberg wore an off-white, button-down shirt—only with snaps—and some old, brown dress pants that were pulled up with suspenders and fastened over his slight potbelly. The hero was still there, always there within, but dormant now with the passage of time and quieter days. As one of the few fighters who survived the brutal defensive by the Japanese, he was a living testament to the courage and sacrifice of the men who assaulted those fortified beaches. I imagined he must have told his story so many times in the last sixty years that he was not going to offer any unsolicited anecdotes—and he really didn't. But he was only too happy to answer questions and recount the iconic flag raising.

In an awkward moment of silence, one of the newer agents asked Lindberg if he would like to hear about the service records of the Marines seated around him. Lindberg said he would enjoy that. It was at that point that I realized I was the *only* person seated at the table who was not a Marine, except for Henry who was a Navy veteran. There had been a reason why Henry and Pat had not invited me, and now I wished I'd taken the hint. I wanted to be discarded in a corner of the room and covered with lime. The Marines seated around me gave a brief summary of their service record and as the circle closed in on me, I thought about what I would say. I could see that Henry was a little embarrassed when he offered that he was not a Marine, but had served in the Navy. Regardless of what I said, I knew I'd come off like a draft-dodger. I'm sure my complexion conveyed my discomfort when I said that I had not served in the military, but had been a police officer for the past twenty-four years. I thought I might get my ass "semper-fi'ed" out of the room, but they were civil. I ended up serving as the photographer at the end of the luncheon, you know, the guy that doesn't really need to be in the picture. I was glad to do it. I walked out of the luncheon ahead of the pack, but still clutching my autographed print of the flag raising.

The FBI likes to hire military types for a variety of reasons. First and foremost, these agents possess unwavering loyalty, patriotism, and integrity. Secondly, and almost as important, the FBI can screw with them unmercifully and they'll take it. They're used to it. And like their military service, the agents really have no choice. The Bureau rarely gives new agents their first pick of office location, rather they put them where they need them, and if they happen to be needed at the agent's first choice office, they will usually put them somewhere else. An agent who wants to work his way home will probably work harder and make fewer waves for the Bureau than one who's comfortable—at least that seems to be the Bureau's philosophy. Not only do new agents get pushed to a first office-site far from home, they will have to move from their first office to one of the top ten offices in the country three years after their date of hire, regardless of family circumstances. The rational for this is that the new agent will learn a variety of general skills in his first location, and will later specialize in the larger office. This makes sense in a cold, logical kind of way, but plays hell on a family.

Prospective agents know these things prior to entering the Academy, and they still want to be agents. "Special Agent" has a nice ring to it. Pick up the phone sometime and say it once: "This is Special Agent (insert your name.) Can I help you?" There's a kind of James Bond, Ephraim Zimbalist Jr., dark, sneaky, grandiose kind of mystique about the title. Realistically, they're an "ass in a chair" like most law enforcement investigator types. Though the agents, as a group, are remarkably good shooters, there's very little clandestine sneaking around in the dark, shooting at bad guys. Henry would like me to believe that because he's an agent, the chicks can't keep their hands off him, but I'm not buying it.

There is, however, a natural elitism among agents as far as how they view themselves beside other law enforcement officers. Though they maintain a poker face in deference to me and the other local coppers on the task force, it's the little things they say in conversation that reveal their true hand. I overheard a thirteen-year agent relating a traffic stop he was involved in. He said he was speeding—but not too fast—when this *rookie cop* pulls him over and starts giving him a ration of shit. The agent "badges" the young officer and by some incongruence with the planetary alignment, this rookie copper is not impressed with the agent's "creds" and continues to rag on

him. How dare he? Doesn't this puny agent-wannabe understand he is in the presence of greatness? The agent begrudg-
ingly accepts the citation he no doubt talked himself into, and
will continue to bitch and moan about it for the remainder of
his career, if not his entire life.

While this elitism is probably a natural result of the agent's
training, most agents respect the fact that grunt cops have paid
their dues on the street and, in turn, have gained the experience to conduct the true "hands on" part of law enforcement
that is usually foreign to agents. As incomprehensible as it
might seem, there are a handful of agents who started their law
enforcement careers as local police officers only to quit their
local department to enter the FBI academy. Like splitting the
atom or constructing a skyscraper that won't collapse in the
wind, this phenomenon will probably always remain an enigma
to me. Notwithstanding their obvious difficulties with sound
reasoning, these one-time police officers make the best agents.

I noticed other minor differences between FBI agents and
regular local coppers. First and foremost, agents don't wear carpenter jeans, painter's pants, or any other fashionable jeans.
They wear straight-leg Levis or a similar plain alternate ("relaxed
fit" for those whose busy work schedule has kept them out of
the gym.) Politically, they are even further to the right than regular cops, bordering on reactionary. They are very patriotic and,
like a strong marriage partner, they tend to support the president for better or worse. Man for man they have far more post-
graduate degrees than regular coppers, typically in areas of law,
computers, foreign languages, accounting, and Middle Eastern
Studies. With this education comes more of a worldview than
the typical provincial view of the regular flatfoot. As mentioned
above, far more agents have military experience.

At times the agents seem to be blind to the greased pit
they are trapped in, drowning and floundering in the deluge of

bureaucratic paperwork. The FBI has, for all intents and purposes, become an intelligence-gathering agency. With their
hands tied behind their backs, and their feet tied to their hands
in what is commonly referred to as a standard hog-tie, the
Bureau is so bogged down by restrictions, bureaucratic non-
sense, and red tape that it takes an act of Congress to get anything done regardless of how minor or major the task. Like
most of the other Task Force officers, I was dumbfounded by
the hamstrung attachment to the seemingly infinite paper trail.
Agents are equally frustrated but seem to accept it rather than
fight it. There is no way to explain it other than to say that the
task of unfucking it will be monumental. Added to that are the
years of tradition, and the fear of retribution for suggesting the
obvious changes. There is a new computer program forthcoming for filing and following up reports that appears to be a step
in the right direction, but miles more of these steps will be
needed to simplify this convoluted paper maze.

To say the FBI tends to generate a vast redundancy of
paperwork is like saying that squirrels like to eat acorns—everybody knows it, the agents know it, their supervisors know it,
the director knows it, the president knows it, I suspect the
squirrels even know it.

Added to that is the micromanaging from the hundred-
pound heads in Washington who need to authorize nearly
everything the local offices initiate. The nation realized the
futility of this practice when Minneapolis agents were denied
their warrant for Moussoui's computer by headquarters. This
disastrous micromanagement was the impetus for Rowley to
write her scathing letter to FBI Director Robert Mueller, and
make the letter public. From what I've learned of Rowley's
motives, she was not at all concerned with the subsequent hero
status and accolades she received from the media. The letter
and her words, which would be quoted and paraphrased in

hundreds of newspapers and news magazines around the world, were an ingenuous response to the shame she felt for the incompetence of her business—the nation's security. The sad part of Rowley's heart-felt efforts to improve the Bureau is that her sacrifice was meaningless. Agents who know say that her letter, though shocking at the time, will be old news soon enough and that nothing will change. There is no changing the Bureau unless the hundred-pound heads at the top decide to make the changes, and you don't get to the top by talking change.

As if the Minneapolis Office didn't get enough attention from the Rowley letters, reports of agents taking souvenirs from the World Trade Center debris brought on additional scrutiny. This incident was blown way out of proportion by the media. Agents had been given permission to take chunks of discarded brick from the destroyed towers. A Minneapolis agent took a damaged Tiffany globe from the wreckage, brought it back to the FBI office in Minneapolis, and placed it on a desk as a memorial to the tragedy. I could understand the indignation if he'd have surreptitiously brought the globe home and put it up for bid on e-Bay, but that was not the case. That agent, and hundreds like him, worked tirelessly to restore some semblance of order to the portrait of chaos we saw every day on the news.

The agents that make up the three corners of my quad are not the exception. Most of the agents I've met are dedicated, patriotic, intelligent, hard-working men and women who believe that their job and their personal efforts matter. I had the privilege of partnering with an agent on a robbery-homicide that occurred in Bloomington. Like me, he did not investigate homicides everyday, but he stuck with this investigation for six years—until the perp stood before a judge who recited the jury's verdict of guilt. This agent's friendship, and his confidence that we would solve the case, even when the trail was starting to frost, fortified my resolve.

Agents are offered a flat percentage of overtime pay for working what amounts to about an extra two or three hours per day, or a ten-hour shift, and are not paid for lunch, call outs, or additional overtime. Most agents probably average eleven- or twelve-hour work days, and often come to the office on weekends to catch up. Of course a more streamlined reporting system and autonomous individual offices could save thousands of wasted hours of bureaucratic bullshit, but agents are not holding their breath for these changes to occur.

In the meantime, in between discussing politics, war, stupid reality shows, past romances, and debating the deity of Christ, Henry keeps churning out more paper. Pat keeps working his case, digging through garbage and reviewing surveillance logs, and Jan makes time for moving her belongings from Iowa to Minneapolis, and buying and outfitting her new home. Through it all, they temper their frustrations with the Bureau and do their jobs.

There is an administrative supervisor at the Minneapolis office who sends admin procedural notices out to all the agents. He heads each inter-office e-mail with the following salutation: "Greetings fellow terrified underlings..." Though this is hilarious to me, I'm afraid he may be hitting the hammer right on the heads of his fellow agents. There's a fear of being powerless, nameless, and impotent, an intimidated pawn in the hands of the hundred-pound heads to be moved about the board offensively, defensively, or sacrificed at times for the good of the Bureau. Whatever the news, this admin supervisor ends each message with the spirited semi-tongue-in-cheek rallying cry, "...one Bureau!"

Katrina and the Waves

Like everybody else at the time, I'd seen enough CNN; I wanted to experience the aftermath of Hurricane Katrina up close and personal. Unfortunately, when our police department decided to send a team of relief officers to New Orleans, my name never came up. It would be our SWAT team who would get the final nod. After all, they were a ready-made team with the equipment, the physical training, the special weapons, and tactics— basically, *the right stuff*.

We needed a twenty-man team to round out the Minnesota Strike Force, which would include teams from Ramsey County SO, Minneapolis PD, St. Paul PD and our team from Bloomington. A number of our current SWAT members were unable to make the two-week commitment, which opened the door for some old-timers. As a former SWAT team member, I and a couple other retired members were allowed to rejoin the team for this deployment.

Our convoy of squad cars and police trucks pulling travel trailers snaked southward toward the devastated south central states of Mississippi and Louisiana. We slept somewhere in northern Mississippi our first night and crossed the border into Louisiana the following afternoon. We stopped on the freeway bridge made famous on CNN and saw the substantial heaps of garbage left strewn about by Katrina's hostages.

Once in New Orleans, we pulled our trailers onto a vacant field of knee-high grass adjacent to a small decrepit elementary school the New Orleans Police Department (NOPD) had occupied. In Minnesota, this school would have either been a historic landmark or a condemned building awaiting demolition. The elementary school housed the only group of NOPD officers still working. An enormous mound of bagged garbage was stacked outside the school on what was once a basketball court. Collecting the garbage in New Orleans probably seemed as futile as bailing the flooded districts with buckets. Inside the school were more piles of garbage along with piles of donated and requisitioned food, clothing, and police equipment. We were told that we could use the two sets of restrooms in the school but that the water was not potable.

The middle of our field bore a huge "H" painted on the grass, and though it could have indicated the seventh circle of hell, it was actually a marker to signal helicopters of the helipad our field served as. As we started to pull our travel trailers onto the field a helicopter circled overhead, preparing to land. This was the first of many harbingers that placed us in what came to feel like an anachronistic episode of M*A*S*H. The teams from Minneapolis, St. Paul, and Ramsey County arrived the following morning and set up camp in the same field. With the arrival of these teams, the Minnesota Strike Force was born.

In my fifteen years away from the team, I'd forgotten the alternate culture of SWAT operators. As opposed to regular street officers, for which a full-sized pickup truck usually satisfied the "manly-man" requirement, the SWAT guys had their own traditions. These I learned included: a swollen lower lip which eventually spouted a geyser of flying chew spit, bulging T-shirts, albeit sometimes bulging in the wrong places, and a desire for action, adventure, physical challenge, or, in times of peace—beer. I began journaling my first night in camp.

We were soaked after setting up camp in the 95-degree, shadeless field. Sean and I decided we needed to do some beer recon. We pulled Sean's marked squad in front of a liquor store at about 2030 but found it closed. There were no other open businesses in sight. Most of the stores were deserted with broken glass and piles of scattered litter as evidence of the looters' final visit. Sean and I decided to meet the NOPD cops at the school and find out if they knew where we could score some beer. A heavy-set black cop who appeared to be off duty for the night asked us what was going on. We told him our story of woe, and he motioned for us to follow him back into the school. We probably walked past twenty cops, some apparently on duty, others just hanging out watching TV on the big screen and having a beer. The "big room," as it came to be known, had a dozen or so large folding tables and chairs for the cops to meet for briefings or just shoot the shit off duty. They lived here twenty-four-seven.

He meandered his way through the school hallways and finally opened a door to some kind of janitorial closet. This closet measured something like six-by-eight feet and was stacked floor to ceiling with cases of beer. He told us to take whatever we wanted, so we each grabbed a case and thanked him effusively. He closed the closet and asked us what we wanted for hard stuff. I told him we were fine with the beer. He looked a little disappointed, told us to suit ourselves.

It looked like they needed it more than we did, anyway. This
beer was obviously a requisitioned necessity.

The group of NOPD cops at the school was comprised of remnants of their SWAT team and was organized (a loose and generous offering of the word) into patrol units. We saw no regular
NOPD squads patrolling the streets until we'd been there
almost a week.

After watching the NOPD officers respond to calls, we
learned that their police department was, at best, a reactive
entity. Neither they nor the city's emergency management had
planned for the eventuality of a category five hurricane such as
Katrina. They had not foreseen a breach in the levee and they
were devastated by the incident to the point of surrender,
which was manifested in an expression of defeatist apathy they
all seemed to wear. They had no leadership during the debacle
since their police chief and mayor were holed up somewhere
awaiting the cavalry—which was not coming for a variety of
reasons. They had no homes or families to return to and hence
no motivation to stick it out and persevere. A great number of
their brother officers were AWOL and nobody seemed willing
or able to take the helm of this sinking ship that was once their
city. Anarchy was just beyond the horizon and the tide seemed
to be pushing them inexorably toward it.

Our presence was felt like one more straw on their beleaguered camel's back. Perhaps the last. But nobody gave us
enough attention to really measure the weight of our potential
value. Rather than utilizing our 100-man strike force to lift
some of their burden, they shooed us out of their hair and onto
patrol where our skills as SWAT operators were negated. There
was really nothing left to patrol. The city was abandoned. Most
of the stragglers had finally been evacuated or scared off by
sheriff's deputies from who-knows-where Texas, who, as one of

those Texan deputies told us, had been given orders to shoot at any shady subjects who appeared to be running *from* rather than *toward* them. The looters and burglars (if such a distinction can be made) and the scam artists had no one left to loot, burgle, or swindle. The city was gone. All that remained was a stinking muskeg of wrecked structure, rotting biologicals, and the resultant stink-cocktail that burned your lungs with each labored breath.

We'd traveled 1,200 miles for nothing! Sure, we would return to a rescue heroes' welcome, hugs and kisses from significant others, and accolades of a job well done, but we really had nothing to do. FEMA was paying the bill for us to patrol the abandoned city so money was not a concern. They would even pay the overtime for the cops back home filling in, in our absence. Had we been paying our own ticket we'd have turned our convoy north and headed straight back home post-haste. Instead, we would stay and make the best of a rotten situation.

In sticking with the M*A*S*H motif, the field we occupied quickly became a tent-city of cops, Camp Victory, as it came to be called. The Stars and Stripes flew proudly above our camp. Camouflaged Humvees, carrying uniformed soldiers to and from various assignments, were common. An assortment of helicopters, Chinooks, Blackhawks, and a variety of others, private and military, shared the skies with the olive-drab behemoth C-130s. Camo-clad army reservists manned checkpoints throughout the city, allowing only emergency and relief workers into the restricted areas.

As we await our 1800 hours patrol shift a few guys start making their way toward the jury-rigged showers— hoses positioned overhead in the elementary school's court- yard—to rinse away the day's sweat and dust that have formed a thin, sticky film on our bodies. The cold water offers momentary respite from the heat and humidity but, like standing in front of an air conditioning vent, the effects are short-lived. As we walk back to camp the sweat leaks from our pores and the magnet-like dust finds us, reviving the film.

We split up into patrol teams with two or three SWAT members in each vehicle, two vehicles to a team. Our team, patrolling in an unmarked Ford Explorer with the word POLICE duct-taped to the rear glass, consisted of the team commander, Gary, a new guy, Jess, and an old guy, me. Gary was a little preoccupied with issues that continued to spin out of his control due to the inept and lackluster performance of the NOPD administration. Jess was the opposite, acting as the ADHD version of the Energizer Bunny. More than a *regular* new guy, he had energy that wouldn't—*couldn't* stop. Then there was me, an obvious candidate for No-Doze. From this eclectic pool, our team was formed.

Once in the squad, I directed the air conditioning vent to my chest, which was covered in three layers; a T-shirt, followed by body armor, and finally another T-shirt to cover the vest. While the fashion of *layering* is effective for a Minnesota ski trip, the practice is asinine in Louisiana. The effect of this layering is probably akin to wearing three or four sweatshirts. The AC has almost no effect other than intensifying one's desire to cool off. None of the NOPD guys wore body armor. They suppressed their bewilderment at our insistence on adhering to safety procedures. The NOPD had given up on procedure in general, and while I didn't blame them for chucking their vests—I was very willing to lose mine—they appeared to have let it all go. One officer told me that most of the department's officers were in a state of flux. (A large percentage of patrol officers—no one knew what this percentage was, possibly as many as one quarter of the department—had disappeared following the hurricane.) In the first week of our deployment, the only place we saw NOPD squads was downtown at Harrah's where FEMA was providing a free lunch. The squads could not be found on the streets.

I get flagged down early in my shift by a 30-something B/M/A with a female. He tells me he's not heard from his uncle and can't get into his uncle's house to check on him. He says there is a foul smell and we assume his uncle is rotting inside. We follow him to his uncle's house, which is only blocks away. Jess takes a halogen tool to the front door and we are set straight in our tracks by an overwhelming stench that is a combination of feces, wet moldy furniture, food gone bad in the reefer, etc. We can hardly breathe. There's a couple inches of stagnant black water on the floor. We search with flashlights and find no stiffs. The house was a pit before the hurricane.

I tell the nephew that his uncle's house is a "garbage house." Shit piled on shit. I tell him that his uncle was not on top of the piles of shit we checked, but that I could not tell what was under the flooded furniture and filth. I ask if his uncle has a girlfriend. He looks at me over his sunglasses and smiles. "A girlfriend—I don't think so." Then I make the connection with all the gay porn among the piles of shit and I get the drift. I advise him to check with the boyfriend. He thanks us and we leave.

The sad state of the city was beyond vanquished. There was a visible water-line on all structures demarcating the flood at its highest point. Most of the houses had hand-drawn quadrants, like a tic-tac-toe sketch, beside the front door, documenting the date the house was checked, who checked it, the number of inhabitants encountered, and the number dead. Very few people appeared to have perished within their homes.

With the prevalence of rotted, looted, moldy structures would come a time of demolition and construction of biblical proportions—think of the Noah's Ark story. The bill for this will be astronomical. President Bush had already promised Federal aid to the tune of $30-some billion to rebuild the city and that amount would be revised—how ever much it was, it wouldn't be enough.

With the proposed rebuilding came the very appropriate argument of whether rebuilding a city below sea level was such a prudent endeavor. Unlike the souvenir globe of Atlantis, New Orleans had not fared well when turned upside down and shaken with water. If the city was not rebuilt, where would its former inhabitants live? Where were they now, and how many of them would have the means and the desire to return? These questions are probably unanswerable. They formed a stew for the media to stir, and a source of debate for New Orleans' politicians in the forthcoming years.

The physical damage was only one aspect of the disaster; the looting and threats of violence left a more permanent stain that would wear longer than the hurricane's visible damage. Residents experienced anarchy for the first time. They saw a significant segment of society adopt a combined Machiavellian-Darwinian philosophy that allowed for survival of the sleaziest, and left nearly every retail business, and many of the more affluent houses, looted. The tragedy had become an opportunity for a few to prey on the many weak or absent. Painted warnings such as "Looters will be shot on sight" were common on the front doors of businesses and residences.

I sit on a picnic table under a tarp at our field. The tarp is for shade rather than rain. The heat index is over

100 degrees again and there is nowhere other than the air-conditioned trailers to escape it. The trailers have become claustrophobic and we are tired of sitting in them and reading. My upper bunk bed is too small to get comfortable in, and there is too much equipment in the trailers to make them usable for anything other than sleep.

Many of the NOPD officers were looking for work elsewhere, and who could blame them? Their pay was pathetic, the work conditions miserable—even on a good day—and the crime rate was spiraling out of control. The hiring standards of the NOPD varied drastically from those in Minnesota. An applicant need only have graduated high school, passed a civil service exam, and have no *serious* felony arrests on his or her criminal record. The pay was also substantially less than a Minnesota metro officer earns.

We understood that they were traumatized beyond words by the events following Katrina. Many officers had simply abandoned their jobs, two had killed themselves, and one was seriously injured by a gunshot wound to the head by an unknown shooter. Of the officers who stuck around after the hurricane, many doubted they'd be paid, and if so, they had no idea when they'd see a paycheck. Meanwhile, they were living in the elementary school, sleeping on mattresses scattered on the floor, showering under a hose, and sharing four restrooms with about a hundred and fifty officers. They called their loved ones on cell phones daily, scratched another X on the calendar, and then awoke the following day to a city that looked and smelled just as bad as it did the day before—or worse!

The NOPD cop babysitting us on patrol got bored around 1300 hours and asked us if we wanted to see the breach in the levee. Of course we did; sightseeing was our most favored pastime and the breach needed to be captured on film for the folks back home. We followed him to the site in the 9th district. This place was still partially under water, so we had to park and walk a circuitous path to keep our feet dry. He showed us the spot on the levee where a 200-yard section of steel-reinforced cement had peeled over. He pointed to a barge about 400 yards from the breach sitting flatly on about five houses like a duck on her nest. He told us the current theory had the barge crashing through the levee and landing where it was presently beached. No one knew if there had been anyone in the houses.

While photographing the breach and the barge from every imaginable angle, I noticed our guide was wearing $300 Oakley SWAT shoes. I liked these shoes. I commented on them, and he became passively defensive saying he didn't have any shoes after the flood, and could have taken several pair but took only one.

We ran into some guys from CNN snooping around the barge and chatted with them for a while. They were surprised to hear that we were from Minnesota. Next on the list was Fats Domino's childhood house...

FEMA came to our rescue the day after our arrival. They set up their massive trailers on a huge vacant athletic field. There were trailers that housed showers and others that offered free laundry services and medical care. Best of all were the hot lunches and dinners served daily. They were a great option to the military MREs (meals ready to eat) that were our planned sustenance. The FEMA folks were well organized, friendly, and very well received.

There's a young woman doctor at the FEMA camp who treats cops and rescue workers for whatever ails them. (I can picture her expression as her sympathy wanes; "Your what hurts?") Nels and Jimmy have gotten to be regular customers since she is pretty, young, friendly, and rumored to be wearing black thong undies. This was apparently confirmed by a number of prospective clients. She should run for her life!

We learned some things about the South on our adventure, and while I never visited New Orleans on one of its better days, I can say that on its worst day it has all the appeal of a third-world country. The real estate was of course worthless, the clean-up incalculable, and the prognosis for a fix was very bad. Grits are offered on breakfast menus as a substitute for hash browns but of course no one in our party consumed a single grit that I am aware of, so I can make no comparison. The thought of trading a hash brown for grit, or anything else, is almost unthinkable.

The heat we bitch about for a couple weeks a year in Minnesota is even more uncomfortable in Louisiana, lasting all summer long and then bleeding into the spring and fall. Whether their heat is actually worse than ours or not, it provided for a fluid source of bitching. Like poison ivy, it gets under your skin and gets worse before it gets better, enveloping you in custodial misery. There's an expectation that it has to cool off tomorrow—and then it doesn't—again. Add body armor to your uniform and you are instantly soaked. We felt like sausage simmering in a pan of gumbo, and contrary to our professional appearance in Minnesota, in New Orleans we were starting to look like a poster for *The "Wrong" Stuff.*

There were packs of dogs, pets turned feral, which would not approach us despite our good intentions and our baby talk solicitations to call them to us. They looked at us like we might be hunting them for food. And like many of the absent homeowners, they had lost faith in humanity. We left large bags of donated dog food for them on the sidewalk when we saw them in the area.

Of the differing varieties of trees, magnolias are probably beautiful when absent ornaments such as speed boats and lawn chairs. Generally speaking, streets in New Orleans, even on their best day, are in horrendous shape compared with Minnesota roads. Impoverished areas in New Orleans are probably similar to impoverished areas in Minneapolis and St. Paul but they seem to take up a much greater portion of the real estate in New Orleans.

There remained areas of the city without power and water, and these districts were off limits to all but law enforcement and rescue workers. Complete darkness within a big city seems anomalous, like being out on a deserted country road in the middle of nowhere, but with a barely discernable skyline breaking up the blackness. Perhaps on a cloudless full-moon night, one could make out the houses from the street, but that was it. We wore night-vision goggles, which were incredibly helpful, turning the pitch-black darkness into an ethereal green, but visible, netherworld. We stopped all the vehicles we saw in these areas, of which there were few. One pick-up, whose taillights we spotted in front of us, sped up when we turned on him and initiated our emergency lights. We chased him down a rutted, bumpy two-way road at speeds of up to 90 mph. He finally ran out of road and within seconds had three Glock-wielding SWAT operators ordering him at high volume to remain still. He told us he was working for the pumping company and had just gotten off work. He said a group of gang-bangers had shot at him in an attempt to car-jack him the night before. He thought we might be them since we were driving an unmarked SUV with lights but no siren. Later that night, we ran into a couple mopes who'd stolen a semi-truck and trailer, and had gotten it stuck while trying to back it into one of their yards. Backing it into the muck in daylight would have been a tricky enough operation. NOPD whisked them off to God-knows-where. The same two mopes showed up the following night in the same area and were rearrested. We wondered if the NOPD guys had simply driven them down the road, given them the *what for,* and then kicked them loose; after all, they didn't really have anywhere close by to take them.

We followed a group of NOPD squads code three, into one of the more affluent districts, on a call of possible loot- ers. We located three teenage boys preparing to leave the area in a vehicle, and we detained them. One of the boys said they were working for his father who was reclaiming valuables for the absent owners. We called the boy's father and requested he come to the scene. Prior to his arrival, one of the younger NOPD SWAT guys stepped out from the group and unloaded what looked to be a .22 caliber pistol with a sound-suppresser. I'd never seen a cop with a silenced pistol. After tucking the pistol into the front of his SWAT camos he told Mike, a member of our team, that these boys were lucky our Bloomington team was here, implying that he would have used more dramatic enforcement measures had we not been there to witness it. I believe his comment was more posturing than reality, and as I watched this offi- cer later on, I noticed he was not representative of the NOPD in general, but rather more of a showboat.

The Ramsey County SWAT team rigged up a drive-in movie the- ater at their end of the camp, projecting a DVD movie onto the side of one of their RVs. While watching Johnny Depp swash- buckling through *Pirates of the Caribbean*, an NOPD officer, cradling a perspiring Budweiser, lamented about the sad state of his department. He said it was going to be a long time before the police department got straightened out. The citizens not only distrusted the cops, they feared them. There could be no semblance of community-involved policing when the community was afraid to call the police. (The beating of the elderly black schoolteacher two weeks after we'd left gave credence to this fear.) The NOPD cop said the department would need to screen its candidates more closely; they would have to increase the educational requirements and pay them commensurate with other law enforcement officers. But even with these changes, it would be years before the problem officers were weeded out or replaced through attrition. Either way, he was leaving. He'd had enough. He'd tested with Phoenix PD and thought his chances of getting hired were pretty good. We talked to several other officers who were looking to move on as well. The city of Minneapolis had fifty-some homicides at the time of Katrina, and we thought that number was bad. New Orleans had 240 at the time of this writing—that they . *knew* of.

We worked a night shift last night and had a record four flat tires among the patrol vehicles. We have no more spares that have not been plugged. Some have been plugged several times. Most of us have gotten practice fixing punctured tires for the first time. The culprits are screws and roofing nails that litter the roads. There's no way to avoid them. FEMA set up a tire repair station just north of downtown and after suffering a late-night flat on patrol, we decided to give them a try. It was so dark in this area, the station had no lights, that we drove past it twice before finding it. Jess shined his flashlight on a cardboard sign that read, "Tire repair. Yes, we're open." There were two black men laying on cardboard scraps in the parking lot. A boom box was playing Penthouse forum. (I didn't know there was an audio version—really.) We woke the men, and they got down to fixing the tire—in the dark. Jess shined his flashlight on another sign by the station door. "No loitering, No selling crack, No selling cats. The facts."

On the brighter side, in the short two-week span we were there, we saw signs of the slightest recoveries. The water at our school supposedly became drinkable but I never had the guts to try it. Toward the end of our second week, we noticed the freeway bridge, made famous on CNN, had been cleared, along with most of the trees obstructing road traffic. Much of the residential flooding had either receded or was pumped out—just in time for another nasty bitch.

We fled Camp Victory and Hurricane Rita in a serpentine convoy pulling our trailers and supplies to McComb, Mississippi, about one hundred fifty miles north of New Orleans. The people we met there made "Minnesota Nice" seem like "Minnesota-Fair-Weather-Friendly." There is something to be said for southern hospitality. We waited out Rita's torrents for three days before turning around.

We arrived back at Camp Victory the day after Hurricane Rita visited her wrath upon the city. Thanks to Rita, New Orleans had taken a giant step backwards, as the recently receded districts were flooded again. NOPD squads had now taken to the streets and the governor had opened up most of the unflooded districts and invited those residents to return home.

On the night of our last shift we drove through the downtown area. Though we couldn't find a road sign for Bourbon Street, since they had all fallen victim to souvenir hunters, people had no trouble locating it. The bars had finally opened their doors, and music could be heard as we passed from the street. Bourbon Street was lined with cars, and for the first time, these cars had no emergency lights. People on the street waved to us and offered a thumbs-up as we drove past them.

Meanwhile, dust containing dried feces, dead animals (and people), and rotten food was raised with each car as residents returned to the city to survey their damage. On a humid day this dust was still palpable as it entered our lungs.

Though our time here was not utilized as productively as it could have been, it had not been totally wasted. Our squads' presence on the street was very much appreciated by the returning citizens, and the NOPD SWAT officers we temporarily replaced were finally offered substantial respite to evaluate their own damage and connect with loved ones.

The city of New Orleans will survive. Like the flood Noah witnessed, the aftermath offered a new beginning. Right or wrong, New Orleans would be rebuilt. While some of the long-time residents said the hurricane was the best thing to ever happen to the place, others said it should be allowed to wash into the gulf—cut the map off at Mississippi.

> *As I sit here now at a picnic table in our camp, bored, and inviting heat stroke, I'm reminded of all the pre-trip bitching about who was chosen to go and who wasn't. (If they only knew what they were missing.) Some of the rank and file thought the decision should have been made like most decisions in police work—by seniority. They had a point, but what I didn't realize until I got here was that the team dynamic (of the SWAT team) more than anything else determined our success. When things didn't go as planned, and they rarely did, it was this spirit of sticking together that kept us from falling into an abysmal pit of despondency and revolt. As it was, there was hardly a murmur of mutiny.*

When we arrived back in Minnesota I kissed the ground. Luckily it had just rained and there were no dogs in sight. As I write this, on November 1, 2005, I'm sitting outside on a bench in downtown Minneapolis wearing a light coat and a baseball cap. It's about fifty degrees and I feel like I'm in heaven. The birch trees surrounding my bench in Cancer Survivor Park struggle against the breeze to hold their remaining leaves, which glisten with a magnificent mixture of gold and yellow. The sun shines through them, producing a translucence that makes them look more like an abstract painting, and when the breeze moves them, they reflect upon one another fluttering like a million chips of mica suspended from heaven.

I'm sure there's probably something really nice to look at back in New Orleans now, but as I sit here in the shade of the majestic birch, I can't think of what it might be.

Growing Up at Fourteen

I was about fourteen when had my first fight and probably didn't get into another until I was wearing the uniform, making arrests and getting between others who wouldn't stop swinging. In that first instance, a kid on the bus had challenged me to fight him the following day when the bus dropped us off. "I know I can take you," he said, balling up his fist in front of my face. I thought it was gracious of him to schedule this event one day ahead of time, rather than just going at it without warning. We weren't really enemies or anything; in fact, our older brothers were good friends. For some reason he was just itching to prove that he could take me. Of course, I couldn't refuse his challenge without being labeled a coward for the rest of my life. At least that's how it seemed at the time.

I thought about the impending fight from the moment he challenged me until the following day when we stood face to face. I didn't know anything about fighting. Aside from the daily, mostly bloodless skirmishes with my older brother, I'd never been in a fight. Though my challenger and I were almost identical in physique, I thought my chances were pretty good, since I had followed my older brothers into sports, while he had followed his brothers under the cars in their garage. I had no idea what it meant to be tough.

The next day when we stepped off the bus, he turned to me and instantly put up his dukes like a boxer. I had an *Oh shit*, moment, thinking that he might actually know how to fight. The fact that he knew the fighting stance demonstrated a significant advantage over me. He took a swing at me and, as I ducked, I rushed in and tackled him to the ground. I managed to overpower him, and while sitting on his torso, punched straight down into his yap of crooked teeth, which simultaneously cut my hand and filled his mouth with blood, most of which was his. This was an ambivalent moment for me since I really didn't want to hurt him, yet I definitely didn't want to lose the fight and get hurt in the process. Luckily, this one punch was all it took. Hoping for a "yes" response, and pressing with bravado from my position of power on his chest, I asked if he'd had enough. Fighting back the tears and embarrassment of having to fight them back, he said uncle and we were done. Fortunately, he never demanded a rematch.

There were a lot of these types of fights when I was in junior high and high school. Growing up in Robbinsdale, Minnesota, home of professional wrestling pioneers Vern Gagne and Larry "The Axe" Hennig, fighting was almost a hobby for some. (Jesse "The Body" Ventura, in nearby Minneapolis, would come along later.) In my Robbinsdale graduating class of 1976 alone were: The Axe's son, Kurt "Mr. Perfect" Hennig (I always thought his moniker should have been, "The Hatchet"), "Ravishing Rick Ruud," Dean "Brady Boone" Peters, and Tom "Z-Man" Zenk. The next year's class produced John Nord, "The Barbarian," and Steve "Nikita Koloff" Simpson. The above were all very successful, nationally known, professional wrestlers.

Fights in high school were almost a daily occurrence, and some of them got pretty rough, resulting in hospital time. These were boys, coming of age, out to prove their manhood, but of course they were still boys, and as the adage goes, boys will be boys. But what about the girls? A catfight was nearly nonexistent, and when it happened, it usually proved to be more snarl than bite. But like a lot of things these days, the old days are just that—old, antiquated, and obsolete.

The number of visitors to the Mall of America exceeded everyone's expectations. Saturday afternoons get so busy that Bloomington police officers have to direct traffic, and there are days when the ramps fill up completely and we are forced to direct the cars in a circular pattern around the behemoth. Walking through the Mall on any given day, one sees a wide array of shoppers scampering helter skelter, their scattered conversations evaporating with the widening of distance and space.

For two fourteen-year-old girls, on Cinco de Mayo, the Mall offered a place to shop, meet friends, and offer themselves as bait for girl-chasing boys, of which there was never a shortage. Besides, this was a rare excursion to the Mall sans mom and dad. This independence added to their excitement since they realized, without saying so, that they were growing up. They were dwelling in that dubious space between dependent child and young woman. An almost prideful confidence indwelled the two girls as they tested their navigation skills through the big mall.

These particular girls had just finished their shopping. Now they teased one another about the cute boys they saw as they passed the food court, stifling their laughter at times and laughing loudly at others. As they turned from the food court into a quiet walkway enveloped by stores, one of the girls, Rita, stopped in her tracks. Approaching her dead ahead was her sworn enemy, who saw her as well and locked glares with her. The enemy, Monique, turned to her accompanying girlfriend and whispered something to her. The girlfriend obeyed and stepped aside as the enemies continued toward one another. These were the kind of enemies who had promised battle upon their next contact, so they each braced for what was sure to come, their skin tingling with the quick rush of adrenaline. Retreat was not an option either could live with tomorrow, so they suppressed any sign of fear with the veneer of prideful self-confidence. A closer look would have exposed a frantic dread, but there would not be time for that.

These girls were very small. Neither of them weighed more than 115 pounds. Their bold threats sent via *My Space* now seemed like the cowardly taunts of children, yet here they stood, face to face, with no words spoken and none solicited. Their respective girlfriends stood back, a little confused and uncomfortable, wondering what their role should be and how that role might change should their friend start to lose.

The combatants dropped their purses ceremoniously in front of them and walked slowly toward one another. They had tunnel vision at that point and could see nothing outside the aura of their adversary. Like a cat pursuing its prey, they'd taken on the characteristics of predators, stalking one another, with a watchful eye for the first aggressive movement. Finally, Monique swung wildly at Rita's head, connecting with her left temple. Reeling from the pain, Rita responded with a haymaker of her own, and the two came together grabbing and rabbit punching. At first glance, they appeared like two children playing, but the intensity, the loud breaths, and grunted exhalations quickly cleared up any misgivings about their relationship. These were enemies.

Monique now held the other in a headlock, while Rita squeezed her combatant's mid-section in a bear hug. Suddenly

Monique noticed a gratuitous flow of blood onto her blue jeans and her white athletic shoes. She released her grip on Rita's head, and examined herself looking frantically for the source of blood loss.

Monique noticed her forearm, halfway between her wrist and elbow, was sliced deeply, for about four inches. She saw the meat of her muscle and sliced tendons like a raw split chicken, on either side of the gash. Her blood spurted from the wound as she screamed, "She cut me! I'm cut! I'm cut!" If that wasn't enough, to her horror she watched as her T-shirt changed color rapidly from the pretty mustard yellow she had proudly put on after her shower to a bright wet burgundy-red. This was the wound that poured freely onto her shoes. Monique lifted her soaked T-shirt, stunned to see a gaping wound from under her left breast disappearing around her side. "My God, I'm going to die! She cut me! I'm going to die." She looked for her friend who was now sitting on Rita's abdomen, pinning her to the floor. "Call my mom! I want my mom!"

Three women approached Monique and surveyed her injuries. The youngest of the three told Monique that she was a nurse and she was going to help her. "You need to sit down," she said. Monique just stood there in shock, looking back at her. The nurse repeated it more loudly, and a passing shopper told the nurse to calm down. The nurse looked back at the shopper like the moron she truly was, and dismissed her just as quickly. She asked her friend to offer up her outer shirt as a tourniquet, and the friend produced it. The nurse guided Monique onto the floor and gently laid her down on her back. She applied the tourniquet at the elbow and got an apron from a passing restaurant worker. She asked her other friend to get some belts from gawkers to tighten the dressing she had applied to the girl's chest wound.

A Mall security officer arrived and noticed Monique lying on the floor. She appeared well tended so he surveyed the scene further and saw a young girl sitting atop another girl, Rita, who was struggling to get away. He was in over his head and he knew it, but he had to do something, so he ordered the girl atop Rita to get off of her. When she offered resistance he forcibly removed her, and as he did so, Rita hopped up and started to walk away quickly. In the confusion of the moment no one stopped her. The nurse who tended to the injured girl noticed Monique's girlfriend, holding her cell phone to her face. She ordered her in no uncertain terms to hang up and dial 911, RIGHT NOW! The girl complied without reply or hesitation.

The police arrived within minutes, having been alerted by Mall security prior to the 911 call. The first officer asked the supine, still-hysterical Monique, what had happened. She said she was cut during a fight, that she didn't know what cut her, but that the girl who cut her was a fourteen-year-old Hispanic girl named Rita, five feet tall, about one hundred pounds. The officer stifled the irony of broadcasting a child suspect smaller than his youngest daughter, and put the description out to the other cars.

However far-fetched this story seems, it really did happen at the Mall of America on May 5, 2007, and though the actors were real, they seemed to be more stereotype than actual flesh and blood. It could have passed as a modern remake of *West Side Story*. Though the girls denied gang membership, they both admitted to knowing friends and family in gangs, and each had an affiliation to a rival gang. Each of the girls could name the other girl's gang affiliation. The stabber, Rita, was an Hispanic *Blood*; the stabbee, Monique, was a black *Bogus Boy*. The fact that this happened at the Mall of America propelled the story to the national news, with CNN reporting the assault the following day.

Regardless of their denials, this incident was all about gangs. As if to layer the irony, Monique later told me that she had been assaulted a year ago by a group of Bloods, also black, at Martin Luther King Park in Minneapolis. After being assaulted, she started making disparaging remarks about the Bloods on her *My Space* site, which was picked up by other girls, like the slasher, Rita—a Blood. The two started communicating via *My Space*, and threats were made that could not be back-peddled from at a later date when the two ultimately met. This meeting could have been at one of their respective schools, on the street or at a social event. It happened instead at the Mall.

The weapon used was a utility knife blade. Just the blade, wrapped in tissue paper. This weapon was easy to discard and difficult for police to recover. "What blade?" This suspect was too naive to play that card. She was crying when I interviewed her about an hour after the stabbing.

Rita had almost made it home free. After walking away from the crowd at the Mall and the large pool of blood marking the fight scene, she had called her mother. She was truthful with her, having told her that she had gotten into a fight and had cut the other girl with a blade. Her mother advised her to try to make it home. She hurried through the Mall, knowing she stuck out, since her pants, shirt, and shoes were spotted with blood. Rita walked to the restroom and washed the sticky fresh blood of her victim down the drain. She realized as she washed that there was a lot of blood. As she continued to rub her hands together under the warm water she noticed that the blood would not go away. She was bleeding as well. She had cut her own hand, as knife fighters often do, during the scuffle. Other than the minor, self-induced laceration, she had done pretty well. No one had seen the knife. She wrapped her small, lacer-ated index finger in tissue and fled the restroom.

Of course, the smart thing to tell me during our interview would have been that she was invoking her Miranda right not to talk to the friendly policeman, but Rita must not have known this. Instead she nodded, yes, to my question, "...Having these rights in mind are you willing to talk to me at this time?" She would probably never make this mistake of naiveté again.

Rita may have still been on the phone when she looked out from the underground transit area of the Mall of America. She could have seen some natural light from where the transit station parking ramp ended and exited to the city streets. She may have anticipated her successful escape with this glance toward the light of freedom. She walked from the parking ramp and transit area, and attempted to cross 24th Avenue, which would have put her off Mall property, but the traffic was too heavy as it often is on Saturday afternoons. She turned back from the street and headed to the sidewalk that ran parallel to 24th Avenue. As she did, an officer who had just finished his assignment of directing traffic into the Mall noticed her and matched her description with the one put over his radio just moments before. He stopped his personal vehicle, jumped out, and drew his weapon on her, ordering her to the ground. As he looked more closely at her, he could see her bloodstained clothing and shoes. She was the right one, after all. Soon Rita was surrounded by on- and off-duty cops. Minutes later, her hands were cuffed behind her back and she was seated in the back of a squad car.

Tears continued to roll down her cheeks and into the crevices her smile had formed over her short fourteen years. Rita was not smiling now as she wiped the tears away self-consciously before they could drip from her chin. When asked where she thought she had cut the other girl, she replied that she had cut her on the arm because she didn't want to hurt her too badly. She said she wasn't sure where she'd stashed the blade after the assault. She said she may have discarded it in a trash can outside of Bubba Gump's or perhaps in the restroom she washed up in. MOA security video would show her discarding something in the trash outside of Bubba Gump's.

Since Rita referred to her weapon only as a blade, I requested she sketch it for me. She proceeded to draw a near-scale diagram of a utility knife blade complete with the small indentations atop the blade that secured it to the actual utility knife. She said she got the blade from a friend, that the blade was still in the case, so she knew it was new and sharp. At my request she completed the drawing, encircling the blade in tissue that would protect her hand and make it appear to bystanders that she was simply holding a tissue rather than a weapon. Not one witness, including the victim, ever saw a weapon in her hand. If she hadn't admitted possession of it, the prosecution would have been challenged to prove it. We never recovered it, and the video simply showed her discarding some stained tissue.

Two fourteen-year-old girls with a combined weight of just over 200 pounds entered into what was almost a fight to the death at the Mall of America—*a place for fun in your life*—over gang representation. Two fourteen-year-old girls throwing down a challenge on *My Space* to see who was tougher, with no space to back down.

At my twenty-year high school reunion, in a moment of anger or bravado, someone bounced someone else over the buffet. The buffet and the table that supported it went crashing to the floor along with the unfortunate alumnus that was sent airborne. Everyone shook their heads, not really surprised, but having hoped that the "Boys will be boys" stage had finally ended. Not so.

The wrestlers at the reunion looked even larger in person than they did on TV. Their muscles bulged from every conceivable crevice, forcing them to wear what I presumed to be some stretchable fabric, like their wrestling outfits, that could double in size if necessary. Their necks were larger than the thighs of most other male attendees.

All but one of the four pro wrestlers I graduated with died in their early forties. One died in a car accident, while the other two died from what was reported to be "heart complications." Drug abuse in the form of cocaine, pain killers, GHB, and steroids were said to be factors in these tragic deaths. Suffice it to say, their lives were not all wine, roses, and baby oil. They knew the dangers of their profession, both the possibility of injury in the ring and the price for medicinally supplementing their bulges. To them, it was worth it.

When Monique was released from the hospital she was picked up in her family's long blue Cadillac. The media got wind of her release, and staged in the hospital parking lot in hopes of getting some video and a quick comment. Monique made it to the car without noticing the newsies, but as the Caddy moved past the mob of cameras, Monique realized that they were there for her. As the long car slowed down, Monique lowered her window and, donning large, movie-star sunglasses, she mugged her best Julia Roberts smile and waved as though surrounded by adoring fans and paparazzi. It seemed that she had finally achieved rock-star status. This vignette was played and replayed all day on both local and national news outlets.

Weeks later, my partner, Leigh, photographed Monique's scars, which wrapped around her torso like the stripes on a peppermint stick.

While I will admit to owning a certain degree of existential cynicism, I still like to think that anyone can change, and that everyone has a chance to succeed. I believe we all have choices, and that these choices, rather than circumstances or fate, determine our happiness and success—or lack thereof. With these choices come the inevitable mistakes which we can learn from or deny.

Rather than digging their heels into the gang culture, I like to imagine that these girls gleaned something positive from this experience. Unfortunately, I can't think *Disney* hard enough to dream up a happy ending to this, *West Side Story at the Mall of America*. Like most gang violence, this incident would most likely be followed up by a perpetual cycle of reprisals. There would be more blood, more media coverage, and more questions. The most bewildering question would be why young men and women would give their allegiance to a gang in the first place. Criminal gangs make no secret of their intentions. Unlike white-collar criminals, they don't hide behind the guise of any legitimate enterprise; there are no virtues or values. They are in the business of making money through whatever means necessary. Guns, drugs, sex, and violence are not only the commodities they deal in, but the central theme of their music and their lives. It's not much to aspire to, but it's easier than applying oneself in school and then working for a living.

Marching to the Beat of an Anarchist Drummer

Everyone wants to change humanity,
but no one wants to change himself.
Leo Tolstoy

A towering honey locust grows from the middle of the outdoor patio at the Seward Cafe in Minneapolis. Its voluminous canopy of tiny leaves provides dappled shade for the wobbly wooden picnic tables beneath. From our vantage point in the corner of the patio we sat drinking coffee, and swallowed with it, the realization that we could never fit in here as regulars. (Yes, we were the two antiseptic looking guys and the slender brunette, trying not to look like cops.)

The folks who frequent the Seward wear what the real Harley dudes and their ol' ladies used to wear in the seventies and eighties: work pants like mechanics wear, with a dark T-shirt, or an un-tucked, button-down shirt. This ensemble is often supplemented by a vest and a black leather belt bearing the usual accouterments: a carabineer for keys, a sheathed buck knife, and some tools hanging from another clip. The young men have chains on their wallets and long clumping dirty hair.

Their faces, like their ol' ladies' armpits and legs, are scraggly, unshaven. Like their Harley brethren before them, they have myriad tattoos; but rather than straddle noisy black hogs, they ride crappy old bicycles with bedrolls and camping gear strapped on. They laugh easily as they chain-smoke, drink coffee, and sample the Seward's mostly vegan menu.

I waited at least five minutes for the lone occupant of the Seward's unisex restroom to clear out. Once inside, I found myself in a claustrophobic cloud of pungent B.O. The wading pool I stood in suggested that the former occupant had used the sink as a mini bathtub. Hurried business preceded a swift return to the open air of the patio.

In addition to being a hangout for older hippies, younger goths, and artistic types of all ages, the Seward Cafe is one of several anarchist hotspots in Minneapolis.

They look at us, the interlopers, and we back at them. Then we leave. We walk past the bike rack and drive away in my brand-new black Chevy Malibu, my undercover cop car. There were twenty people at the restaurant and twenty bicycles in the bike rack. I think they made us. It doesn't really matter. The Republican National Convention (RNC) is still four weeks off. They don't know what we're up to. We don't even know ourselves.

Before the RNC decided to make St. Paul its Mecca I would have guessed that a "sleeping dragon" was a mixed martial arts move meant to put one's opponent to sleep—the hard way. I would have thought a "tranarchist" to be someone adept at driving a five-speed, and that "direct action" described the exhaustive practice of getting off the couch between movies to get another beer and re-snack.

The 1968 riots at the Democratic National Convention (DNC) in Chicago provided an unprecedented display of how out of control a modern-day political event could get—in America. Prior to that, there were many revolts of one kind or another, beginning with the American Revolution—an interesting thought. After the Vietnam War, political unrest slowed down enough to lull police into a happy place where they remained in blissful hibernation until the disastrous riots in Seattle at the 1999 World Trade Organization (WTO). In the wake of those riots, Attorney General Janet Reno pulled the proper political strings to ensure that law enforcement received the financial backing of the federal government to train and prepare for future high-profile conventions. As police prepared for pro-testers, protesters prepared for police. This situation made for a cat-and-mouse game, with both camps dedicated to the astute study of their opponent's strategies and tactics.

Police departments prepared differently for their assigned conventions. With the bruises from the WTO still healing, LA planned for trouble at their 2000 DNC. On June 19, 2000, their department experienced a "practice" riot to gauge their pre-paredness when the Lakers won their first NBA championship in twelve years. Falling short, and humiliated by live media coverage of the crowd setting fires, flipping squad cars, and looting local businesses, the LAPD ramped up training for the DNC. Their extra numbers and additional training paid off. Even with substantial setbacks including a court judgment allowing the protesters close proximity to the Staples Center, a free Rage Against the Machine concert, and the international anarchist convergence, "August Collective," held just days before the convention, the LAPD managed to keep some sem-blance of law and order.

New York brought out the numbers for their 2004 RNC as only they could do. With a virtual city of police officers in place, they had the ability to arrest and hold nearly every unruly protester they encountered. Their methods were quick and decisive. Over eighteen hundred protesters were arrested, many of whom were held until after the RNC concluded. Lawsuits abounded, but the city maintained that, if they took some liberties with the U.S. Constitution and the laws of the land, they did so to ensure that their city remained standing after the event, and that the Constitution, though temporarily amended, would be restored after the anarchist's attempt to have it replaced by something with more of a Socialist twist.

With more hotel space than Minneapolis and St. Paul combined, Bloomington became the default location for delegations coming to the 2008 RNC. Eleven Bloomington hotels were chosen to house sixteen delegations, while additional hotels catered to other RNC attendees and workers. It was rumored that Dick Cheney, Arnold Swartzenegger, and other less-popular delegates would book rooms at some of the more prestigious West Bloomington hotels.

A new intel unit was created within our Investigative Division and I was asked to postpone my retirement to lead it. Having the RNC come to town was a once-in-a-career opportunity. I was working as a narcotics investigator at the time, preparing to end my career after twenty-six years. I had some intel experience from a four-year stint with the FBI's Joint Terrorism Task Force, and thought this event was probably worth sticking around for. If nothing else, the RNC would provide a break from my usual duties of rummaging through drug dealers' garbage and executing search warrants at their typically filthy houses. My arm didn't need much twisting.

Having a full-time intelligence unit would have been optimal, but the drug and prostitution businesses didn't abate, so with my intel partners Leigh and Carl, I split time between narcotics and intel. During the RNC and for the months preceding it, Leigh and I posed as a couple—an odd couple no doubt, since I was nearly twenty years her senior. But it didn't seem to matter. Spending more time together that summer than we spent with our own families, we got to know one another very well. And though I drove her crazy from time to time, we made a good team.

A conglomeration of dedicated activists took the lead in opposing the RNC. They called themselves the RNC Welcoming Committee (RNCWC), and started planning their resistance a year before the event. Their ranks were filled by anarchists, anti-authoritarians, and anti-capitalists. Their agenda was: to "Crush the RNC," to stop it, as a way to demonstrate their opposition to the war, the two-party system, gentrification, capitalism, imperialism, racism, sexism, and other "isms" depending upon affinity group. The Welcoming Committee served as the umbrella organization under which any affiliated protest groups could crawl for tactical, strategic, and logistical assistance.

The Welcoming Committee sponsored training through various affinity groups, such as the National Lawyers Guild (NLG) and Citizens Against Police Brutality. These groups trained volunteers to be legal observers and videographers. Police sent informants to these, and other open classes, to learn what the training amounted to. Once trained, NLG volunteers were expected to wear the lime-green baseball caps that made them stand out in a crowd of protesters while they awaited the inevitable confrontations. When these confrontations arose, the observers' instructions were to make notes on actions taken by police and record the names and badge numbers of officers involved. Videographers typically left their video cameras in the "off" position during confrontations with police, while protesters surreptitiously pelted the officers with rocks, garbage, excrement, and urine squirted from Super Soakers. When the police finally had enough, and brought out the tear gas and hickory sticks, the cameras started rolling and continued to roll until the last mope was piled into the last police transport. The videographers then turned their cameras off and offered up their video to any of countless sympathetic media outlets covering the event. (A movie, *Terrorizing Dissent,* released by Glass Bead Collective, et al., was made after the RNC using a compilation of these types of clips.)

Peaceful protesters, whose numbers dominated the marches, were conspicuously absent from media coverage. Instead, video of police utilizing their cornucopia of riot gear made for a more interesting, if not myopic, view of the cops' coup de grace. This denouement was usually served up to TV viewers as a vignette showcasing some beefy, helmeted cop growling an incoherent string of expletives behind a foggy face shield while dealing out a gratuitous thumping. This made for good family fun on the six and ten o'clock news.

The Welcoming Committee utilized other service groups as well. StreetMedics, a band of volunteers with varying degrees of medical training, provided street-level first aid and could be picked out of a crowd by the red crosses adorning their backpacks, usually two crossed strips of red tape. The medics assisted protesters who suffered the ill effects of tear gas or pepper spray; basically they turned the victims' faces into the wind or flushed their eyes with water. While we watched most of the conscientious medics busy themselves offering sunscreen and bottled water to overheated marchers, an intel unit we'd partnered with discovered a small group within the group who acted as scouts for the Welcoming Committee. They carried 800 mega-hertz radios and advised the anarchist tacticians where various groups of police were stationed.

The Welcoming Committee also sponsored Sex Awareness Training and Direct Action One and Two. (This was a two-day course, with day one covering such mundane fundamentals as

Making Effective Blockades Using Only Your Body. Day two might cover more creative endeavors such as "Unarresting" Techniques, or Theory and Methods of Flinging Excrement.)

Though the Welcoming Committee claimed sponsorship of the resistance, their sway over other local affinity groups seemed more ephemeral at times. Peaceful protest groups were wary of aligning with them. Their cautiousness became apparent when the Welcoming Committee invited groups to "Adopt a Sector" within St. Paul to protest from, and few if any local affinity groups signed up. It was the out-of-state anarchists (and our intel unit) who answered their call.

The Internet served as the communications medium that guided everyone, at least at some level, on how the cat-and-mouse game would be played. The Welcoming Committee had to get their message out to a national audience of demonstrators because they needed big numbers to accomplish their published three-tiered plan. In order of importance, Tier One had the protesters encircle the Xcel Center in St. Paul where the convention was held. If enough protesters arrived, there would be an inner and outer perimeter of protesters. Tier Two focused on interference and impedance of delegates in order to thwart their arrival and participation at the convention. The final tier utilized protesters to blockade the bridges that connect Minneapolis with St. Paul. To accomplish all three tiers, they needed thousands of protesters, more than they could possibly muster from Minnesota alone.

Some 40,000 protesters showed up for the Seattle WTO, and St. Paul PD had to prepare for just as many, if not more. The federal government provided fifty million dollars for security. Thirty-five hundred cops worked the event in some fashion. Twelve hundred of these were trained as Mobile Field Force (MFF) officers and outfitted in "turtle gear." Their training prepared them in all aspects of riot control. Most police administrators agreed that too many well-trained officers and too many days spent training were better than an overwhelming force of protesters testing an untrained, undermanned police contingent.

The intel officers' job was to let the Mobile Field Force know what to expect. Again, nearly all information available to the protesters was made available to the police via the Internet. The Welcoming Committee expected the police to infiltrate their ranks in an attempt to gain more intimate intel, the secret stuff, unavailable on the Internet. One particular attempt by the FBI to place a fringe criminal source in a position to move within the inner circle of activists backfired when this individual chose to remain "unattached." After parting ways with the agents he decided to share his story of intrigue with the Welcoming Committee, who published the saga, along with the names of the agents, in the *City Pages* newspaper, *Indymedia*, and sundry radical media outlets. But this deterred neither the FBI nor any other law enforcement agency, each of which understood the adage: *When at first you don't succeed...*

Our intel unit entered the game late and so was at a disadvantage to send in undercovers. Our chief had overcommitted our department by promising St. Paul PD, who hosted the event, that our department could lead the South Division Mobile Field Force and provide nearly a third of the officers needed to supplement its ranks. This commitment meant employing the majority of both our Patrol Division and Investigative Division as Mobile Field Force officers. No vacation or time off was permitted officers during the RNC, and if a patrol officer were to call in sick during the convention, we would be at a disadvantage to complete our city's normal patrol contingent. Our department was responsible for leading the South Division of the Twin Cities, which included officers from our department along with cops from Burnsville, Edina, Plymouth, Minnetonka, Eden Prairie, Richfield, and Eagan, as well as Scott County and Dakota County, for a total of 153 cops.

In early April, Bloomington Police Commander Bergey was informed by St. Paul Command Staff that our intel unit needed to coordinate with their department's intel unit. A weighty pause preceded Bergey's reply since, at the time of that meeting, our department had no intel unit; hence, Bergey's panicked request that I put off my retirement and begin the seminal process of organizing a plan. By the time we were on line, the various affinity groups had vouching requirements (established group members had to vouch for new recruits) to keep the cops out.

Through the process of gathering intel, I learned a lot about anarchism and the psychology of protesting. I learned that one couldn't really generalize about protesters any more than one can generalize about cops, teachers, or librarians. Some anarchists profess a strong, almost venomous, desire to pick a fight with the cops, while others favor more peaceful methods. For some reason, the vast majority seemed to prefer venom to virtue.

About a month before the RNC, my partner Leigh and I visited an open informational meeting at the Northfield Public Library with a panel of protesters who planned on resisting the RNC. The purpose of the meeting was to allow panel members the chance to say a little about their groups and their protest strategy. These leaders were also passively attempting to recruit audience members into their ranks. With two prestigious colleges, Carleton and St. Olaf, the city of Northfield was ripe for the picking of student activists. Our purpose in attending was to learn if any of the groups, most notably the Welcoming Committee, was advocating violent resistance.

In addition to the two spokespersons from the Welcoming Committee, the panel included representatives from Vets For

Peace (VFP), The Coalition to March on the RNC, Peace Island, and a supporter of one-time Republican candidate Ron Paul, who was planning a "parallel" convention in Minneapolis during the RNC.

I arrived late, as the VFP guy was wrapping up his spiel on his group's plan for a peaceful march just prior to the RNC. I climbed over a chair and sat beside Leigh, who was looking somewhat out of place, since the audience appeared to mostly consist of the over-seventy set mixed in with a few college kids wearing black T-shirts. From my seat in the back row I noticed what I assumed was another undercover cop—who I was not familiar with—sitting two seats away from me, looking mostly at his feet and probably feeling as out of place as we did.

Scanning the members of the panel I came upon a face that I instantly recognized, and just as quickly realized that my status as an anonymous, everyday unaffiliated audience member could come to an abrupt end with disparaging finality if this panel member chose to *out* me. She was none other than my ex-FBI office mate, Colleen Rowley, who was on the panel to talk about her group, Peace Island. In a traditional undercover move that is both ridiculous and kind of futile in a small room such as this, I scooted down in my chair using the skeletally thin woman seated in front of me for concealment. I whispered my apprehension to Leigh, who received it with her usual equanimity; but I decided to play it out. I had a feeling that the panel members knew that Leigh, the gentleman two seats away, and I were police; but no one confronted us—yet. (I later learned that the gentleman seated two seats from me hailed from the ranks of Emergency Medical Service (EMS) rather than police, but shared our purpose in attending.)

My uneasiness climaxed near the end of the meeting when an audience member asked the panel what they would do if they found a police undercover in the audience at this meeting. Rowley fielded this question, beginning her response, "Well, I had a friend at the FBI who..." But she went on to talk about another agent who, like she, backpacked his way from the FBI to Peacenikville. I don't know how she could have missed me—a June bug behind a gnat; perhaps she'd forgotten me, or maybe she still possessed some measure of loyalty to law enforcement that prevented her from humiliating me. Either way, I was grateful and will try to send a dollar to the Peace Island picnic fund.

I was encouraged by most panel members who, like Rowley and the Vet for Peace, espoused only nonviolent demonstrations and protest. One of the Welcoming Committee members, however, had a different agenda. His casual delivery belied an obvious contempt for law enforcement; his arrogance was transparent beneath the polished veneer of articulate presentation. He told the would-be protesters in the audience that they should never trust the police, that the police would be committing most of the violence and would not be giving nonviolent protesters any kind of free pass. He cautioned them, that even though they might be peaceful protesters, they should respect other protesters who, "might be acting out, using *other* tactics." He said that "we" don't want the police differentiating between protest groups, referring to some groups as *good* and others as *bad*. It was an issue of solidarity and everyone knows that solidarity is a *good* thing. His comments seemed to make other panel members tacitly uncomfortable, but no one objected or offered a different opinion.

Now their allegiance to the Welcoming Committee would be tested from the dark closet of solidarity where motives and virtues hung in opposite corners, and the first group to seek light outside the closet would be labeled a pariah. This young man wanted to unite all the affinity groups against law enforcement, knowing that the police had no qualms with peaceful protesters. He wanted a polarized "us-against-them" convention. His comments were enlightening.

As a citizen of a country born of protest, I appreciate the legacy of our First Amendment rights, especially those that address free speech and *peaceful* assembly. I respect those who invoke these rights and I give them credit for dedicating their time to political issues rather than chasing one another around in an intoxicated, hormonally charged bliss—like I did at their age. But I wondered how they got from where they started, to standing clad with ominous black bandannas, carrying signs, and chanting.

The reasons for resisting, and the wisdom behind those reasons, varied considerably among the protesters we met. From the signs they carried and the slogans chanted, the war in Iraq and the prospect of intervention in Iran seemed the prominent issues among the protesters. But judging from rally speeches, eavesdropped conversations at radical bookstores, and everything in between, most funneled their discontent onto the president.

Not that our president or our country is without fault, but I wondered if these protesters had really done their homework to separate fact from fiction, and fault from simple misadventure, bad intel, or forgivable mistake. I give historians like Howard Zinn, an anarchist favorite, credit for his study of U.S. history. In his book, *A People's History Of The United States*, Zinn, a Socialist, gives his scholarly opinion of why the U.S. really entered and fought the wars we did. He crushes many of the feel-good myths of our country's history and gives instead a more realistic view based on his research. Some of the lessons, like those of Abe Lincoln's true feelings about racial equality, can be disheartening; but the truth, once simmered, is better soup than a quick, happy recipe mixed with unsavory misinformation. I think a well-informed protester is less zealous and more introspective than a single-issue ignoramus who just wants to throw a brick at something.

Aside from the usual skullduggery, much of our intel, including the identities of some of the Welcoming Committee's inner circle, was gained through sharing information with intel units from St. Paul PD, the FBI, and the Ramsey County Sheriff's Office. (After the RNC, the Welcoming Committee's inner circle, dubbed the "RNC Eight," were indicted for their plans to incite riots at the RNC.) These leaders were both the most learned and the most contentious of the protesters. They could argue socialism and democracy all day and back up their positions with snippets of historical intrigue and current government policy. Their website, www.nornc.org was well constructed and well written. At the same time, these leaders seemed to drool subconsciously as they conspired to set in motion a replay of the 1999 WTO riots in Seattle.

I found it incongruous that learned adults advocated violence, mayhem, and destruction of property as catalysts for political and societal *reform*. A passion for change shouldn't cancel out logic, perspective, or integrity. And one's conscience allows only so much equivocation when considering the basics of *right* and *wrong*. I respect disagreement and debate on any issue when a basis of understanding exists prior to discussion, but this *zero-to-brick-throwing* mentality, prevalent among the anarchists, did not favor their cause.

I understand that there can be a time for violence, *"a time for bricks, turn, turn, turn..."* The American Revolution was such a time, as was the U.S. entry into WWII, but the decision to employ violence should be the result of an exhaustive analysis of alternatives followed by a consensus to do so as a last resort. I found no evidence of such analysis or consensus among the affinity groups. The inner circle of the Welcoming Committee made the decision for everyone. Anarchy turned oligarchy.

Most cops begin their careers in their early twenties and, like the young protesters, they are still poking their toes in the cold, riddled, waters of politics to see how the system works and how they might fit in. Young cops are under some pressure to think conservatively like most, but not all, of the veteran cops who for many reasons tend to prop themselves up on the right side with their night sticks. Part of this conservative tendency is due to the daily, firsthand look at perceived abuses of some of the more liberal-born, social service programs. Our view, like that of a drug-court judge, is admittedly narrow; since we see only the abuses, we have little contact with people who thrive as a result of legitimate inclusion in the various programs. So as the young officer looks through his helmeted mask into the angry eyes of the young protester confronting him, the cerebral barrier between them is thin, mainly facade. Most of the separation is a result of simple choices and circumstance rather than any sort of rigorous ideological study.

Fortunately, few protesters are willing to actually throw a brick. Protesters divide the zealousness of their protest participation into color-coded zones. A Green-Zone protester was one who planned to march or demonstrate within the law and had no intention of stepping over the line. A Yellow-Zone protester was a fence sitter, waiting to see if the pendulum swung favorably toward civil disobedience. With proper motivation, or a more subtle application of peer pressure, he might be convinced to join in the fray. A Red-Zoner planned to participate in civil disobedience or a direct action, which he or she knew might result in his or her arrest. These protesters had the phone number of the National Lawyers Guild, or Cold Snap Legal

Collective, on their forearms, and wore adult diapers when locked into a human sleeping-dragon barricade.

Black Bloc protesters were usually true-believer anarchists or other anti-authoritarian anti-capitalist demonstrators. They often wore black bandannas or masks to cover their faces during protests. Many were looking to throw a brick and start a fight. If none came their way, they were willing to provoke one. They trained in guerrilla riot-inciting techniques, including mixed martial arts and advanced brick-throwing techniques not normally seen during civil disobedience. They tried at all costs not to be arrested since they wanted to protest tomorrow as well. One way to accomplish this was to lead the Yellow-Zoners off the fence and into the fray. Once the fence sitters started pitching bricks, the anarchists melted into the crowds. Their aim was to turn the tides of peaceful protest into all-out riot. A perverted sense of ethics seemed a prerequisite to play this role, but they convinced themselves that achieving their agenda was worth any means necessary.

The fun part of working intel, or any cop job for that matter, is to screw with the bad guys without them knowing it. Not in a malicious way—but with tactics that backed your unwitting suspect closer and closer to the precipice. I'm sure the same phenomenon applies for the bad guys. It may even be one of those universal truths we don't like to talk about. It's like hiding your dog's bitter antibiotic pill inside a treat. Disappointment accompanies the epiphanous aftertaste but, by then, it's too late.

The anarchists expected law enforcement to infiltrate their ranks, and they had vouching precautions to prevent this, but the police did it anyway. As the convention drew nearer and the Welcoming Committee's recruitment continued to wane, the vouching process became lax and finally disintegrated, since they couldn't risk scaring off *any* potential protesters.

Rather than sending in cops—who typically look, dress, smell, act, and talk like cops—we sent in sources who were younger, better looking, and willing to work, either for dismissal of drug charges or simply for money.

One might think that all the good guys—the cops—would work together to achieve this goal, but such was not the case. Politics and egos tended to get in the way. We saw this happen. Most guilty in this endeavor was a certain law enforcement administrator who wanted to be the overall, end-all boss of the cop element of the RNC. He wanted the credit for saving St. Paul from the sky that was, according to him, falling fast. As Chicken Little of the law enforcement community, he took great pleasure in his (rumored) off-the-record leaks to the media about the grave state of affairs in the upcoming RNC. (As much as it pains me to admit, some of his worries about the sky falling were substantiated.) In addition to airing his concerns, he tended not to play well with other cop-types who did not work for him—like our intel unit.

Little had a longtime, reliable undercover in the Welcoming Committee who was getting him good intel. When he learned that our intel unit had inserted a source into the group as well, he became adamant that we remove him; adamant enough that he followed our intel unit back to Bloomington from a surveillance in Minneapolis, and performed a traffic stop on the truck I was driving. Though he was also in an undercover car, I recognized him and pulled my truck into a commercial parking lot just off the freeway. When cops talk to one another in vehicles, they position their cars, driver's door to driver's door, and speak out the windows. This positioning is the result of both years of tradition and years of performing this maneuver as patrol officers. But when I pulled around to talk to Little, he continued in a circle, guiding his car around behind me determined to execute a routine traffic stop on my vehicle. Denying him the pleasure of chasing us around in circles until we were all dizzy, I stopped and allowed him to position his car behind mine. After all, we were all cops here, and we were in my city. He wasn't even in his county. He had no jurisdiction in Bloomington. As he approached the passenger side of my truck, Leigh reluctantly lowered her window. Expecting obsequiousness, or at least acquiescence, he was disappointed to find that Leigh and I staunchly defended our position and strategy. Though I had a good working relationship with Little's intel commander, there had been some miscommunication between agencies, and Little overreacted like a spoiled child.

While most cops live by that "brotherhood in blue" thing, and rightfully so, it seemed more than a Little possible that our source in the Welcoming Committee was in danger of being ratted out. We took him out of the group before that happened, but the ill will did Little to foster that one-for-all and all-for-one, solidarity team-building thing.

Since we lost our undercover within the group, we decided to answer the Welcoming Committee's website solicitation to "Adopt a Sector" of St. Paul to protest from. The Welcoming Committee divided the downtown area of St. Paul into seven sectors and published a strategy of "3S's"—Swarm, Seize and Stay. This strategy proposed that protesters swarm into a valued area like a busy intersection, take control of it, and refuse to give it up.

Our intel unit made up an affinity group, gave it an appropriately provocative name, and got to work. We followed the Welcoming Committee's directions for claiming a sector and wrote our anti-capitalist manifesto which was then published on the RNCWC's website and other local and national radical websites. These anarchists are sharp, though! Days after adopting our sector, the Welcoming Committee's website started lighting up, smelling a cop-rat. The pronouns "we" and "they" had been used in such a way within the manifesto that, at times, the "we" became temporarily estranged from the "they," which constitutes a major faux-pas within a solidarity movement. The comments were hilarious to me:

> "This looks shady in many ways. Does anyone know the people behind it? Be careful that this isn't cops trying to mess up the sector dynamic. And if I'm wrong, I apologize for the people who are about to get down in [this] sector."

> "But it's some scary shit if the FBI or NSA or any-one actually put this together. I mean that would have taken some fucking courage, and if this is bullshit, they really did some fucking research and are using major COINTELPRO style shit. I don't want to scream fire in a crowd, but imagine if there will be some agents mixed in with blocs? Or what if these people really show up on the day, and it's a set up or whatever...."

Though shrewdly smelling our rat, they were never able to fully flesh us out. And although our adopted sector ended up being the site of several confrontations, I like to believe that our adoption of it caused an ulcer, or at least a gassy stomach, to the anarchist strategists.

My boss, Commander Michael Bergey, and I went to the DNC in Denver on August 24th for an intel prelude to the RNC. The anarchist group, "Recreate '68," sponsored the resistance in Denver. We walked with the protesters and sometimes carried signs and chanted with them:

"Whose streets? Our streets! Whose war? Their war!"

"You're sexy, you're cute; take off that riot suit."

Again, we were the old guys wearing clean Ragstock clothes and smelling of a recent soaping. Two nuts in a jar of screws but, surprisingly, we never got burned.

The protesters were very astute at picking cops out of the crowd. Nextel Direct Connect push-to-talk phones and Oakley sunglasses were dead giveaways. Those "burned" detectives were photographed, surreptitiously or not, and their pictures were posted on radical media websites the following day, in effect ending their undercover protester careers. Like calling a police dispatcher after taking a little blue pill four hours ago, and having to report symptoms of blindness, deafness, dizziness, and an area suffering *unyielding rigidity*, getting burned was embarrassing.

Denver PD's Mobile Field Force boxed us in during one of the unauthorized protest marches in their city, and Bergey and I experienced the feeling of being at their whim. They could push us in any direction they wanted, using horses and sheer numbers of MFF officers with their long black sticks. We had code words to keep us from being gassed, smacked, and arrested, but we wanted to avoid using them at all costs, since uttering the code words in front of real protesters would get us burned. We managed to slip out of their dragnet before it came to that but, before we made our exit, we witnessed the difference between *effective* and *offensive* police conduct. While holding a line at Denver's Pepsi Center, a police supervisor sarcastically told the protesters within earshot that their presence at the DNC was paying for his next vacation and probably for Christmas as well. He wasn't making a joke, and he came across like a pompous ass. Rather than fostering respect, his words served to further polarize the protesters against the police. Nearly all the other police we encountered in Denver were disciplined and composed. We were mostly impressed by their professionalism and hoped we could match it.

Denver had 152 arrests at the DNC, and we came home with a couple of stupid tee shirts *(Party Organically)* and a feel for what it was like to march as protesters. We found that Steven Stills was seriously mistaken in his Buffalo Springfield anthem, "For What It's Worth," when he sang about the police having a field day with the thousand, street-marching protesters. Streets jammed with a thousand *angry* protesters do not make for a police field day. Trust me on this. The Mobile Field Force in St. Paul had their work cut out for them.

We found that a unifying theme among protesters was their blanket hatred for police. A twenty-something black anarchist at the Denver rally held a closed fist to the sky and led the chant, with due angst, "Fuck the pigs! Fuck the pigs!"

Police, like protesters, are not seen as individuals but rather as a symbol, a line of blue, with helmets, black metal armaments, and long, all-business riot sticks. The police objective, according to the protesters, was to uphold the status quo and trample the protesters' First Amendment rights. With such cavalier hatred chanted in their faces, many cops, not surprisingly, reciprocated the sentiment.

Having walked with the protesters and listened to their rhetoric, I found myself floating along with them, like a sailor who, with his shipmates, had abandoned ship and now awaited a slow death in an endless sea. It all seemed so futile, a game to be played out for posterity and then put away in a closet for some indefinite time until the time arose again to march and chant. Perhaps when the protests ended, they would resume their Anarchist (street rules) Bowling League. I don't know. What does an anarchist do in the off-season?

An anarchist on the informational panel in Northfield told the audience that nearly every anarchist she knew had a different definition of what it meant to be an anarchist. If you asked a random non-anarchist, say, a cop, for instance, what anarchy meant to him, his answer would probably mirror Webster's first definition: "a state of society without government or law." (He might not use those exact words, but rather an acceptable paraphrase with a possible expletive thrown in to make the statement more colloquially satisfying.) This definition, however, would not satisfy most of the anarchists we met. Webster's third definition seems to come closer to a unifying general belief of modern day anarchists: "a theory that regards the absence of all direct or coercive government as a political ideal and that proposes the cooperative and voluntary association of individuals and groups as the principal mode of organized society." Basically, a libertarian-socialist society.

In addition to scrambled political beliefs, the anarchists we came in contact with shared several other characteristics. Barring few exceptions, most ranged in age from twenty-to-thirty years old and appeared to eke out their existence through menial jobs. Most had some college under their belts, dug indy-rock, and ate a vegan diet, although we saw several eating a mixed diet of garbage-can cuisine. Many rode bicycles as their primary mode of transportation and seemed averse to razor blades for the purpose of shaving. And, judging from any position even slightly downwind, the ever-present sour stink of body odor suggested that many anarchists considered a monthly bath in the Seward's sink sufficient.

Though Webster's definition of anarchy is devoid of any propensity for violence, the anarchist protesters made up the most vocal, radical, volatile, and dangerously violent group of protesters represented at the RNC. Through the use of dedicated informants and undercover operatives, Chicken Little and his intel unit were able to conduct preemptive search warrants on several of the anarchists' dwellings and on their convergence space—a converted dance hall in St. Paul—just prior to the RNC. These searches yielded a gun, caltrops (bent nails used to flatten squad tires), bats and clubs, large rocks, buckets of human urine (for balloons and Super Soaker squirt guns), bolt cutters, shields, helmets, and the components for making sleeping-dragon barricades. Along with the seizures of these items, several leaders of the Welcoming Committee were arrested for the felony charge of conspiracy to riot.

Guns and incendiary devices such as Molotov cocktails are very uncommon tools for modern day protesters. Fortunately, the majority of today's demonstrators advocate peaceful protest and will only participate in a civil disobedience, such as a sit-in or blockade, when conducted in a nonviolent manner. Molotov cocktails, capable of starting fast and furious conflagrations, are seen by most protesters as well beyond the norm of acceptable protest behavior.

The FBI in Texas investigated an anarchist group called "The Austin Affinity Group" or "The Group" who, though lacking literary flair, planned on heating up the RNC with these bottled incendiaries. Two young men from The Group mixed up the Molotov cocktails seized in St. Paul using liquor bottles filled with two-parts gasoline and one-part motor oil; the oil was added to make the liquid stick to the surface it shatters upon. Tampons soaked in lighter fluid were used as wicks. The boys tested these devices and planned on using them to fire-bomb some police and Secret Service vehicles. One of the boys said it was "okay" with him if a cop burned along with the squads. After their arrests, one of the boys' fathers made the trip up from Texas to petition the judge to release his son based on the fact that his son was naive and really had no understanding of politics. A boy from Michigan was also mixing Molotovs; but the FBI caught up with him as well, and pinched him before he could light up the infrastructure within the Xcel, as he had planned to do. Like the Molotov slingers from Austin, the Michigan boy told an FBI source, "I will light one of those pigs on fire."

Having spent some time leading up to the RNC among the resistance culture, I was once again struck by the eagerness of young men to go to such extremes, including a willingness to take lives, for a cause they may not have completely understood. It seemed more joyride than an ingenuous principled act of ideological defiance.

The bicyclist group, Critical Mass, held a special ride on the Friday prior to the RNC kick-off. The ride represented the anniversary of the previous year's imbroglio when riders clashed with random drivers and the Minneapolis Police, resulting in the arrests of nineteen riders. Critical Mass riders consider bicycles rather than cars to be the preferred mode of transport for reasons of ecology, health benefits, and fewer traffic jams. In an effort to gain intel and help police avert a violent reprise of the previous year, Leigh and I decided to ride with the group. We knew little about the ride, other than that the group appeared to be leaderless, and lacked a prescheduled route. We figured we'd ride around downtown Minneapolis for an hour or so and hopefully pick up some decent scoop.

We met at Loring Park, straddling bikes scrounged from the police bicycle impound garage. Like the ugly, rheumy-eyed dog from the pound that nobody wanted, these were unclaimed bikes that would be auctioned off or given away. They were not in terrible shape, but neither were they modern, well cared for, or tuned up. A bike aficionado from our department lubed up the gears and checked the brakes. He probably saved our lives.

After some encouraging words from Minneapolis Police Chief Tim Dolan, we set off on the streets of downtown

Minneapolis with the Minneapolis Bike Cops as escorts. The beautiful late-August day was warm and sunny. Five hundred riders filled both lanes of traffic for about five or six city blocks. The bike cops made sure that cars sharing the roads yielded to us. Some of these drivers had to wait five minutes and longer for the entire group to pass. Forcing drivers to wait for us felt rude, but hurtling down the road and upshifting through red-light intersections empowered us as we took over the streets. Maybe there was something to this Critical Mass thing after all. I leaned over to Leigh who peddled beside me and whispered, "We're getting paid for this!"

Previous to this ride, neither Leigh nor I had ridden a bike for more than five minutes that summer. On this day, we rode nonstop for three-and-a-half hours, looping back and forth through Minneapolis and St. Paul. We witnessed some horrendous raspberry inducing, flesh-and-metal-tumbling falls, and cussed our way up mountainous Ramsey Hill in St. Paul.

At the end of the ride we found ourselves peddling in the dark, unescorted, on East Lake Street. Of the five hundred bikers who started the ride, six remained—including Leigh and me. As a marathon runner, Leigh probably could have ridden all night, but I was dying. Disco Steve, a gay rider wearing short shorts, provided the beat for the entire ride with a mega-bass boom box strapped to the back of his city bike. When he finally turned off at Lake and 34th Street, he left us ambivalent as we adjusted to the disquieting silence with only the sound of our chains, rhythmically encircling the gears, to keep us connected. We called it quits when a city bus nearly picked off Leigh at Nicollet and Lake. We looped into Dulono's Pizza on Lyndale, and called for Carl to pick us up. We were spent. There would be no skipping, dancing, or jumping for joy. We sat on a curb in the dark parking lot awaiting our ride. For reasons I still don't fully understand, Leigh would not speak to me or even look in my general direction. (This traditional shunning, usually reserved for insensitive spouses, may have been the direct result of my inane compulsion to *stick with it*, even in the dark, until Leigh was nearly flattened by the bus. My bad.)

Surprisingly, we both felt pretty good the following day, and Leigh resumed speaking, limiting her responses succinctly to monosyllabic replies, but speaking nonetheless. Though we had no odometer, bikers who ride a lot estimated that we peddled as far as fifty miles or so on our two-wheeled adventure.

There was no violence on this ride and only sporadic rudeness to random drivers we encountered. The goals of increased driver awareness of bicyclists, and the utilization of bicycles as an option to driving cars, are commendable. However, the rudeness and arrogance of the few riders who confronted police and arbitrarily frightened drivers canceled out any positive aspects the ride might have offered. Notwithstanding the cardiovascular benefits of our ride, we didn't really gain much intel. We saw some Critical Mass riders at the RNC protests the following week but they were not organized like the riders at the 2004 RNC in New York.

After spending the summer immersed in anarchism I started to wonder where the hard-core, vegan-eating, bike-riding, brick-throwing anarchists came from? Aside from the flawed, "no-hugs, no-baseball, no-prom" theories some philosophical cops offered, there were other equally spurious assumptions as to why they chose this off-road path rather than the one paved with smooth pedestrian conformity. One such theory is that they arose as outcasts from the ranks of the affluent, continuing a pattern of rebellious malcontent, having never tasted true hunger in any form, until embracing this extremist lifestyle. I'm not buying this one.

The antithetic theory has them growing up poor with no chance of the "American Dream." This theory proposes that whether anarchist or capitalist, a common ideology was less significant than their simple economic plight. Like a homeless man who breaks his last cigarette in half to share with his homeless brother, it's a form of solidarity that requires no title or political affiliation. There's an unconscious thought process that begins and ends with wants and needs that are not satisfied. Then, misery loves company, and shared discontent serves to form and solidify "the cause," whatever it is.

It has always been the poor and disenfranchised who have taken a stand against those who control and covet society's riches. Communism and Socialism sound pretty good when you can't feed your family, but less attractive when you've just finished paying off your med-school loans and begin to pocket the fruits of your labors.

Having done no serious research on the matter, I'd wager that the ranks of the anarchists are probably filled from an amalgam of American society like most other groups—barring The Young Republicans.

Not to be shown up by a political event, Hurricane Ike arrived in Galveston, Texas, as the delegates were deplaning in St. Paul. President Bush and Republican presidential candidate John McCain cancelled their appearances at the RNC, deferring their attention to the hurricane and its aftermath. This turn of events prompted a warning among intel units that the anarchists would throw all their eggs in the opening-day basket, since the possibility existed that this might be the only day of the convention.

We started the day at 0500 hours. St. Paul's intel unit had been working with the FBI on *The Austin Group*, who had parked a trailer full of helmets and shields with protruding screws in front of a residence in their city. We assisted St. Paul with surveillance on this house and other houses where suspected anarchists were storing weapons and barricading materials.

The first day of the RNC coincided with the largest march to oppose it—The Coalition to March on the RNC. Estimates of expected protesters ranged from five thousand to forty thousand. About ten thousand protesters showed up to march, compared to about fifteen hundred at Denver's big march. The Welcoming Committee held a press conference prior to the event, promising not to interfere with the peaceful Coalition to March protest. This promise turned out, not surprisingly, to be deceptive. We watched a group of mostly out-of state anarchists move throughout the downtown area, branching off from the main march, confronting and distracting the police on the streets, and then moving on.

Using his eagle-eye powers of observation, Carl managed to spot the as-yet-unarrested leader of the Welcoming Committee in downtown St. Paul that afternoon. With the help of a Ramsey County FIT team, they were able to take him into custody without incident.

One of the first *direct actions* of the day was discovered by a State Trooper who came upon a group of protesters laying across an entrance ramp to I-94. They were linked together in a sleeping-dragon barricade, which consists of a line of protesters utilizing their bodies, locked together at their arms with a chain enclosed in PVC piping. An electric saw and bolt-cutters are usually needed to separate the protesters from one another, and this dismantling can be time-consuming. The protesters wore diapers, in case this process took longer than their bladders could withstand. The diapers turned out to be a good idea since the troopers had no time to deal with the group. Rather than deploying the fire department to begin the process of cutting the protesters apart, the trooper set out some orange cones and closed off the ramp to traffic. This group of protesters lay baking in the street wearing mostly soggy diapers in the humid, ninety-degree sunshine for hours before the fire department came to their rescue. The group's strategy to divert emergency resources from the Xcel didn't turn out quite like they'd planned.

As if synchronized with the rising sun, it didn't take long for things to heat up. Different groups set off in different unauthorized directions, stretching the limits of the Mobile Field Forces. Ultimately there were about fifteen intersections with confrontations between protesters and MFF. Our intel group walked with the largest group of renegade protesters until we were blocked by a line of MFF.

A twenty-five-year-old woman approached us from another altercation, crying from the effects of a recent gassing. Her cheeks, like her eyes, were bright red and wet with tears. I asked her what happened, and she said she was just gassed indiscriminately as she stood in the crowd. I took a picture of her, documenting her misery, and advised her to stand with her face into the wind to neutralize the effects of the tear gas. We offered some verbal TLC and then left her there, sobbing face-first into the breeze.

As we waited for something to happen, the tires of a *Fox News* van parked across the street from us were slashed. A woman in her early twenties standing near me pointed across the street and said flatly, "That guy running there just slashed the tires on that *Fox News* van." As everyone within earshot looked across the street at the van, which started to sag onto its rims, a young man in the crowd admonished her, "Hey, you don't need to be a rat," to which she replied, "But I like *Fox News*." On the Anarchist list, "Ten Things We Really Hate," *Fox*

News is second only to "The Cops," (After that comes, Bush, Cheney, McCain, Condi, any other Republican, meat-eaters, conservative Democrats, and finally, oppression of any kind— *unless we're doing it!*)

There were many other instances of property damage, including bricks thrown through squad car windshields and the windows of retail stores.

Our intel unit was divided into three Field Intelligence (FIT) Teams, Leigh and I, Carl and Coz, and two retired cops, Dale and Joanne. We reported to the intel commander, Michael Bergey, who then reported to the Intel Operations Center (IOC). (With FBI involvement, an abundance of acronyms is a given. I had to ask an FBI partner what the TIC (Tactical Intel Center) the JIC (Joint Information Center) and the JOC (Joint Operations Center) stood for. Once learned, I requested they keep their TIC and their JIC out of my JOC if they wanted to get along.) We were supposed to keep one another in sight during the march, but this turned out to be wishful thinking, as this frenetic crowd moved like living waves, tumbling forward and back, then changing speed and direction like a capricious tropical storm.

Midway through the first day, a protester lobbed a brick though a large plate-glass window at Macy's while Carl and Coz were there taking a restroom break. As they emerged from the store, resplendent and renewed, a wily Macy's security employee fingered *them* for *the* brick-thrower. While they were being thrown up against the brick wall of the Macy's building, muttering code words that fell on the deaf ears of their diligent arrest officers, Commander Bergey was nabbing the actual brick thrower about a block away. Just prior to initiating the never pleasant, much maligned cavity search, their badges, guns, and police identifications were discovered by process of a thorough pat-down search. Though disappointed by the revelation that their arrestees were actually cops, the officers released them, as Bergey's successful arrest of the actual perp was broadcast over their radios.

Later that same afternoon, in a rare moment of all-togetherness, our group of undercover intel detectives were gassed in a way that left us temporarily blind and effusively snotty. Massive numbers of protesters and MFF faced off on the large flat field at Kellogg and Wabasha. We stood on the sidelines and watched the action unfold as officers mounted on horseback and bicycles formed a perimeter behind a skirmish line of standing MFF officers at least one hundred yards long. All the officers had donned gas masks at this point.

As the protesters taunted the MFF and lobbed garbage at them, the order was given to fire tear gas and smoke, depending on positioning of protesters and available escape routes. Different colors of smoke and gas were deployed, saturating the lower atmosphere in a toxic, stagnant, multicolored fog. I watched as a young protester picked up a canister of gas in an attempt to lob it back at police and was struck in the thigh by a less-lethal marking round. These rounds were used to both mark the subject shot with colored paint for later arrest and to temporarily immobilize him, since these projectiles are very potent. The young man went down hard like an animal shot on safari, and got back up slowly before limping back into the retreating crowd.

The tear gas followed the breeze and found us on the sidelines covered up with bandannas that were completely useless in warding off the effects of the gas. Like miniscule shards of burning glass, the gas forced our eyelids shut, saturating our cheeks with the overflow of tears. As I tried to focus my inflamed eyes on the field, the melee took on the appearance of an epic battle, what a skirmish must have looked like on a bigger field in Virginia with blue and gray soldiers facing off. Almost completely blind, I grabbed hold of Coz's sweatshirt as he led our retreat from the area.

One of the MFF commanders surveyed this field after the incident and told me weeks later that he was surprised to find such an abundance of projectiles (mostly discarded beverage bottles) strewn about the area the police had occupied. A subsequent viewing of a video of the altercation revealed a volley of these objects descending upon the line of MFF officers just after the order to deploy gas was given. Fortunately, no one was injured.

Monday went long. We worked sixteen hours and went home exhausted. Tuesday found the tempered Hurricane Ike moving on. Galveston had withstood the downgraded category-two hurricane, and the convention was back on.

The day's events started out slowly with a march planned for the afternoon leaving from Mears Park. After an uneventful hour or so of speeches, a disturbance on the northeast intersection adjacent to the park fired up the lethargic crowd. I later learned that an intel (FIT) team intercepted a young man who was hauling a backpack laden with bottled urine. While this young man was being handcuffed, a large group encircled the arresting officers and chanted, "Let him go! Let him go!" About thirty St. Paul Horse Patrol and Bike Patrol officers arrived to provide security for the arrest, but it quickly became clear that there were not nearly enough police for the crowd. The hundreds of protesters who had been attending the rally at the park swarmed the intersection and joined in taunting the police. Bike cops held their bicycles to their chests and used them as barriers to push the swarming throng of protesters back. The group was totally polarized against the police, like our friend at the informational meeting in Northfield had hoped it would be.

Our FIT team huddled quickly and agreed that if the situation started to go too far south, we would take the burn and assist the St. Paul MFF. For now we stood on the sidelines and chanted with the burgeoning crowd. A woman in front of us crowded a mounted rider, and was inadvertently brushed in the face by that horse's tail. Completely uninjured, she screamed like she'd been flogged with a bull-whip and let fly a litany of expletive-riddled insults toward the mounted officer, who wisely directed the rear end of her horse in the woman's general direction and ignored her. These horses could turn back on a dime, and two horses side by side could make the move simultaneously and squeeze a man to Jell-O with their huge, muscular hindquarters, if he tried to sneak between them. The mounted officers demonstrated this pincers move several times, inadvertently or not; but having seen it, no one attempted to penetrate their line.

A news crew climbed atop their van and starting filming, unobstructed from their improved vantage point, as another man and then a woman were arrested. (I later watched this footage on the news.) The crowd grew bigger, louder, and even more truculent with the additional arrests, but the mounties and bike cops, receiving no reinforcements, held their ground. It seemed like forever until the transport squad arrived and took the arrestees away. With them gone, the cops departed and the crowd dispersed.

Most people, including cops, are naturally cautious. From a survival standpoint, we consider the likelihood of injury and distance ourselves from circumstances and *things* that are likely to harm us. Bravery is really a matter of understanding that the risk of injury or death exists—and standing your ground. In the case of police (and soldiers and firefighters), bravery is mostly the manifestation of an unspoken promise to stand beside your partners come hell or high water. Other factors might include: training, a sense of duty, or a conviction in a specific mission deemed more important than one's personal safety. That understanding made the difference in this standoff where the police were uncharacteristically, hugely outnumbered and could have easily been overrun. These cops stood their ground and mitigated what bordered on all-out riot. The mettle and discipline of these thirty officers lay in stark contrast to the five hundred or so protesters, now a mob, who, for all appearances, just wanted blood.

In the days to come we were herded like sheep at the hands of the MFF who used horses, motorcycles, bicycles, gas, smoke bombs, and flash-bangs to corral our fellow protesters and us. Their strategy, tactics, and deployments were well planned and extremely effective in controlling us without harming us.

Of course there were cries of outrage from the innocent bystanders and press people who ended up being driven like farm animals with the rest of us. But most of the bystanders were asking for it with their presence at the protest scenes. The press people were hoping for a confrontation so they would have something to report. We saw them at all the protests, right there in the front lines awaiting controversy. I think some of them secretly considered pitching a brick themselves, at times, when confrontations went too long without action or resolution. We read their "woe is me" accounts in the *StarTribune* for days after the convention left town.

Typically, the confrontations began when protesters chose to veer off the approved, permitted route into an unauthorized area. The MFF then blocked their path, and the subsequent extended standoff would begin. These face-to-face confrontations tended to go on and on inexorably. Like curious children who've captured a frog and then surrounded it, anticipating its marvelous leap, everyone—protesters, bystanders, MFF, newsies, and FIT teamers—stood by awaiting for someone among the protesters to take that *next step* up the riot ladder. But this almost never happened—when people were watching.

Without exception, gas, smoke bombs, and flash-bangs were used after hours of confrontation and stalemate that would have extended well into the night. Nobody stopped the protesters or the press from leaving when the police donned their gas masks and ordered the crowds to disperse, hence my lack of pity.

In the end, we were left to wonder what had been accomplished by the anarchists, by the peaceful protesters, and by the police. Who had triumphed in our game of cat and mouse? Like a first-grade baseball game in which nobody was supposed to keep score, both sides always claimed victory. But nobody really wins at these things. The police kept the peace as best they could, and the protesters took some attention away from the RNC.

In order to achieve social change, which may or may not have been the goal of the anarchists, their message needed to transcend the chanting, marching, and violence—but it didn't.

The City of Bloomington and the delegates staying there were left mercifully unscathed. Hopefully, some of the protesters, and a few of the cops, grew to regret some of their actions and over-reactions during the convention. Some who should have, probably didn't. Eight hundred protesters were arrested; violence, possibly even mass casualties and a falling sky, may have been averted by Chicken Little and the FBI, whose separate investigations and search warrants yielded the gun, both caches of Molotov cocktails, and sundry tools of destruction.

Ultimately, and to no one's surprise, McCain was nominated the Republican candidate for the president of the United States. The following day, the serenity that St. Paul is known for returned to the downtown area as city workers took to the streets sweeping up glass and removing scattered refuse.

Back on the Seward Cafe's patio, the regulars, now clad in sweatshirts, sat under the umbrella of the giant honey locust, the edges of its tiny leaves now painted the yellow that would finally cover them before they fall. With this the anarchist off-season began.

Epilogue

Friends ask what writing this book meant to me and why I wrote it in the first place. I don't have a simple answer. I had the desire to write, like every writer—the itch that could only be scratched by writing. I also had a desire to record some of my more memorable experiences while they were still fresh in my mind. There is another side of life that cops and few others witness. Most of these stories include some glimpse into that other side. Choosing which experiences to write about was easy. They were the ones I couldn't forget even if I wanted to.

In the process of writing these stories I was forced to examine my own actions in fine detail, a procedure that was rarely flattering. I made my share of mistakes as a cop, and knew that I needed to record the bad with the good. The process is akin to watching yourself trip and fall, close up, in slow motion. Having said that, I thoroughly enjoyed writing these essays.

Readers should know that every cop has a bank of stories, similar to mine, but unique to them. Some cops enjoy sharing their stories, while others prefer to keep them private. A smaller percentage of this group push their on-the-job experiences to the fortress of their subconscious mind where they won't need to deal with these sometimes troubling memories. I was the type who did not share work stories with anyone, including my family, but I never buried them. This manifestation of keeping my experiences private, and then choosing to write them down for everyone, allows for a certain degree of irony. It's like staunchly refusing to give someone your phone number when it's scribbled on your forehead in large red numbers.

Perched on this limb of imminent retirement, I have a bird's-eye view of the past twenty-five years along with a glimpse of what's to come. I'm satisfied I chose the right career. Like being cast in a never-ending saga of tragedy, comedy, action, and intrigue, there is really nothing quite like it. Most of all, I will miss the brotherhood among officers—the glue that holds the profession together and keeps us laughing when we should be losing our minds. And while I will miss it, I know it will carry on.